The Art of
Eating In

The Art of Eating In

HOW I LEARNED TO STOP SPENDING AND LOVE THE STOVE

Cathy Erway

Foreword by Robert Sietsema
Illustrations by Evah Fan

GOTHAM BOOKS

GOTHAM BOOKS
Published by Penguin Group (USA) Inc.
375 Hudson Street, New York, New York 10014, U.S.A.

Penguin Group (Canada), 90 Eglinton Avenue East, Suite 700, Toronto, Ontario M4P 2Y3, Canada (a division of Pearson Penguin Canada Inc.); Penguin Books Ltd, 80 Strand, London WC2R 0RL, England; Penguin Ireland, 25 St Stephen's Green, Dublin 2, Ireland (a division of Penguin Books Ltd); Penguin Group (Australia), 250 Camberwell Road, Camberwell, Victoria 3124, Australia (a division of Pearson Australia Group Pty Ltd); Penguin Books India Pvt Ltd, 11 Community Centre, Panchsheel Park, New Delhi – 110 017, India; Penguin Group (NZ), 67 Apollo Drive, Rosedale, North Shore 0632, New Zealand (a division of Pearson New Zealand Ltd); Penguin Books (South Africa) (Pty) Ltd, 24 Sturdee Avenue, Rosebank, Johannesburg 2196, South Africa

Penguin Books Ltd, Registered Offices: 80 Strand, London WC2R 0RL, England

Published by Gotham Books, a member of Penguin Group (USA) Inc.

First printing, Feburary 2010
10 9 8 7 6 5 4 3 2 1

Copyright © 2010 by Cathy Erway
Grateful acknowledgment is made to the following for permission to reprint: Page ix. *An Alphabet for Gourmets* by M.F.K. Fisher, reprinted with permission of John Wiley & Sons, Inc. Page 43. Reprinted from *The Elements of Cooking* by Michael Ruhlman, Scribner © 2007. Page 135. *The Way to Cook* by Julia Child, Alfred A. Knopf © 1989.

Gotham Books and the skyscraper logo are trademarks of Penguin Group (USA) Inc.

LIBRARY OF CONGRESS CATALOGING-IN-PUBLICATION DATA
Erway, Cathy.
The art of eating in : how I learned to stop spending and love the stove / Cathy Erway.
p.   cm.
ISBN 978-1-592-40525-1 (hardcover)
1. Cookery, American. 2. Food habits—New York (State)—New York. 3. Erway, Cathy. I. Title
TX715.E7155   2010
641.5973—dc22   2009040836

Printed in the United States of America
Set in Celeste and Caecilia · Designed by Sabrina Bowers
Illustrations by Evah Fan

Penguin is committed to publishing works of quality and integrity.
In that spirit, we are proud to offer this book to our readers;
however, the story, the experiences, and the words
are the author's alone.

To my parents, for teaching me to cook.
And to my brother, Chris, for helping me do
literally everything else.

Contents

A great deal has been written about the amenities of dining, but few writers have seen fit to comment on the very important modern problem of eating in a public place.

—M.F.K. Fisher, *"D is for Dining Out,"* An Alphabet for Gourmets

Foreword

I first became aware of Cathy Erway two years ago. As I sat eating in a fancy midtown restaurant, a dining companion leaned over his foie gras torchon and asked confidentially, "Have you ever heard of Cathy Erway? She's decided to not eat out in restaurants for two whole years, and she's blogging about it."

I suppose he expected me to express contempt or outright derision, since my livelihood as a restaurant critic depends on everyone eating out as often as possible. I harrumphed something noncommittal but felt a rush of excitement. What a cool idea, I thought. As a fan of performance art—which this project surely was—I was instantly intrigued. As a blogger and gung-ho home cook, I couldn't wait to visit the site and see how she'd translated action into words.

Her blog—"Not Eating Out in New York"—became a favorite of mine, and over the next year I checked it often to see what she was up to. The site offered a fascinating potpourri of culinary punditry, practical cooking advice, social observation, and recipes that often featured a running commentary. Moreover, much of her cooking incorporated novel elements that owed nothing to any hidebound culinary school. She was an improvisatory cook, par excellence, and seemed to prefer freestyling with stumbled-on ingredients to simply reading and executing predictable recipes. She also backed up her recipes with details about how much ingredients cost, making her website consumer friendly.

A year later, Erway's two-year experiment was up, and I won-

dered whether I'd run into her at one of the culinary events that
kept herds of foodies wandering across the city like nomadic
tribesmen. I didn't have to wonder long—soon after her experiment ended, I met her for the first time at the loft of Winnie Yang,
a mutual friend from the Slow Food Movement, who frequently
hosted events in her Fort Greene loft.

Cathy was as skinny as a rail, and half Chinese, two things I
hadn't expected from her blog and her name, respectively. She
proved a keen conversationalist, and when she told me she was
working on a book about her experiences, I wanted to get my
hands on a copy. I convinced her that once the thing was finished,
she should send me the manuscript.

When it finally arrived in my e-mail inbox with a resounding
ping, I sat for several hours reading it. While I'd feared it would be
merely a collection of material cadged from the website, the book
turned out to be quite a different kettle of fish entirely, a narrative
for which the website was only a starting point. Not only had she
not eaten out, but she'd explored all avenues of not eating out, including forays into freeganism, urban foraging, bread baking, competitive cook-offs, agricultural sustainability, and amateur chefing
at the dining clubs that were currently popular all over Brooklyn.
And who but a virtuoso writer could make the act of cooking itself
seem as interesting as a car race or a shipwreck?

She began by pondering, "How can you date if you can't go out
to dinner?" From the answer to that fundamental question flowed
new friendships, and, eventually, romance. We see her moving
from apartment to apartment, sometimes lucky in love, sometimes
not so lucky. One boyfriend continues eating out, even as she cooks
delicious food at home. One kitchen is large and commodious,
while another is so small she can barely turn around in it. Gadgets
come her way; she keeps some and throws others out. We meet
her parents and musician brother, along with a cavalcade of other
memorable characters, some celebrities in the sphere of foodism,
some just extras.

In total, the book is really one woman's coming-of-age novel,
with recipes, a sort of *Portrait of the Artist as a Young Cook*. Cathy
has a real eye for pictorial detail and knows how to tell a story,
complete with dialogue and denouement. Moreover, the book is
a bird's-eye view of the youth culture—we might call it a "counter

culture," due to its kitchen orientation—during an era that will be gone in the blink of an eye. Cathy is a combination of Holden Caulfield and Henry David Thoreau, and if she gets her readers out of the restaurants and back into the kitchen—at least a few times a week—her experiment will have been a complete success.

Robert Sietsema, food critic,
The Village Voice

EATING OUT IN NEW YORK

A few years ago when my friend Ari was apartment hunting, she was shown a two-bedroom in Brooklyn with plenty of sunlight, a patio, a nicely sized bathroom, and a tall industrial sink in one corner of the living room.

"Where's the kitchen?" she asked her Realtor, looking around at the unfurnished space. A two-year-old was seated on her hip, and her belly bulged with another little-one-to-be.

The Realtor splayed his arms out wide as if to measure the preposterousness of her question.

"This is New York—everyone eats out!" he retorted.

She didn't take the place. But you could hardly blame it on his argument. It's not just in New York City; everyone *does* eat out—at roadside diners, upscale restaurants, drive-through fast-food pickup windows, and street-food carts. An estimated one-half of America's meals are prepared away from home. We spend far more money in restaurants than we do in grocery stores each year. And eating food that's prepared away from home is almost as prevalent among the impoverished as it is among the rich. We are halfway down the road to forgetting how to cook.

Across America we've experienced an eating-out revolution that's changed the way we perceive food. From Big Macs to "small plates," restaurant-prepared food is an everyday commodity and plays a part in popular culture more than ever. We talk (and often argue) with our peers at the office about the best places to eat. In restaurants, we conduct business, court one another, fill up on dinner alone. We go home to television shows such as *Top Chef* and *Hell's Kitchen* that feature the business of gastronomy, and we have our favorite celebrity chefs. Eating out has also become a fiercely competitive sport, in which dining in the hottest restaurants in town is akin to owning the latest fashion accessory, and food blogs feature up-to-the-minute reports of the lines outside these restaurants.

But perhaps nowhere in the United States do restaurants play such an important role in daily life as they do in New York City. Eating out is so intrinsically New York, so vital to the city's cosmopolitan and workaholic lifestyles, that it's also an immense source of pride. Fine dining is to New York what the opera is to Vienna. The brown-bag lunch is a social taboo, frowned upon in the same way that not knowing how to use chopsticks is. Many New Yorkers would view choosing not to eat out as foolish at the least, disrespectful at the worst, and overall, perfectly nonsensical.

So how did our restaurant infatuation begin, and when did this service industry come to feed us night and day? What *is* a restaurant, really? When did they first appear, and what are they doing in our world?

The notion of eating food being prepared by another probably dates back to the earliest hominids, or to Eve handing Adam that fateful apple. But the idea of a restaurant where a paying customer could choose his or her meal from any number of predetermined courses prepared by a chef became common only in modern times. Throughout the many centuries and civilizations in between, class-divided societies appointed servants for day-to-day chores, while the upper classes for the most part relinquished any hand in food preparation. Skilled trades such as meat curing and bread baking developed, as did shops where one could purchase these goods. There were cafés, teahouses, and taverns where patrons could sip a drink, and there were inns, guesthouses, and monasteries where communal meals were served with little or no options of food choice for each diner. None of these instances exactly qualified as a restaurant, though.

According to some sources, the earliest known restaurants emerged in the Middle East during the late tenth century. At roughly the same time, in Kaifeng, China, then its northern capital, a thriving arts culture led the way to theaters that served food, and soon after, stand-alone restaurants became a common place to eat. According to Marco Polo, restaurants specializing in many different types of food were abundant in 1260 in Hangchow, China. "There are noodle shops . . . fish houses, restaurants serving vegetarian 'temple' food prepared in the style of Buddhist temples, places specializing in iced foods," wrote James Trager of Polo's culinary discoveries in *The Food Chronology*. "The restaurants have menus, and waiters carry orders in their heads, repeating them when they get to the kitchen and remembering who ordered what with absolute precision (mistakes are severely punished)." As with the arts the popularity of restaurants may typically indicate a society's prosperity. But in some cases, restaurants may have sprung from postdisaster situations. When fire swept through Edo, Japan, in 1657, market stands and prepared-food shops that previously sold food under takeout conditions were rebuilt as shops where patrons could sit down to eat.

The restaurant emerged in the Western world sometime around 1766, in Paris. At this time, a *restaurant* was not a place to eat, but a nourishing consommé or broth served to those in poor health, or to those who wanted to boost their well-being (hence the root word *restore*). French law stated that these broths or tonics could be served only by businesses that specialized in them, following similar laws at the time that restricted bakers from selling anything other than breads and pastries, butchers from selling anything but meats—essentially, to each artisan his own trade.

Most credit the development of the restaurant in Europe to a restaurateur in Paris at this time named Boulanger, who, according to legend, was sued by a guild of cook-caterers for serving mutton with white sauce to customers instead of a traditional *restaurant*. The case is said to have gone to the French high court; some say that he won it, others that he lost. Either way, history was made in its course. However, according to Rebecca L. Spang in her book *The Invention of the Restaurant*, historical evidence of such a case is unfounded. Rather, the first restaurant was the brainchild of an intellectual and sometimes banker named Mathurin Roze de Chantoiseau.

The portrait of Roze de Chantoiseau that Spang paints is of a defiant, youthfully zealous, "lesser genius" of the eighteenth century. Driven by a desire shared by most intellectuals of his era to bolster Paris's economy and reputation, he tried and failed at several schemes to improve the city's banking infrastructure. But the two concepts that he did manage to establish were truly lasting. The first, in an effort to welcome and inform commercial travelers in Paris, was the earliest predecessor of what we might now call the *Michelin Guide*, which Roze de Chantoiseau published. His *Almanac Royale* listed the names and current addresses of all the most desirable wholesalers, merchants, bankers, courtiers, artists, and artisans in the country. (It was updated in numerous later editions.) The second was the restaurant as we know it.

When Roze de Chantoiseau opened his own *salle du restaurant* in 1766, he stretched the definition of the eponymous menu item by expanding his offerings to "exclusively those foods that either maintain or reestablish health." At a time when science, particularly that concerning the health of the body, was in vogue, his enterprise straddled two elite concerns: the pursuit of optimum physical health and a burgeoning fascination with cuisine. The idea behind his *salle du restaurant*, according to Roze de Chantoiseau, was to "improve Paris life by freeing the fastidious traveler of the need to depend on an unknown, and potentially unreliable, innkeeper or cook-caterer." In other words, the first restaurant served only medicinal foods to ward off sicknesses garnered from what we might refer to today as "sketchy" restaurants and hotels. (Now, why did we have to do away with this concept?)

Finally, to promote his ideas, Roze de Chantoiseau included the address and a short description of his own restaurant in *Almanac Royale*: "Fine and delicate meals for 3–6 livres per head, in addition to the items expected of a restaurateur." The first restaurateur was a natural self-promoter.

After the French Revolution, the code of laws requiring artisans to keep to one trade dissolved. From that point on restaurants flourished. Since then, the concept of the restaurant has branched out in myriad ways, from the advent of fast food in the last several decades to the development of niche food-service styles such as tapas, dim sum, *omakase*, and the all-you-can-eat buffet. In addition to informing our culinary culture, eating meals in restaurants has also led to various social customs. The "power lunch" is taken in restaurants, where the food is second to the meeting's purpose. The same can more or less be said for the restaurant date. Banquet-style dining, or "harmonious" meals in Chinese culture, is something of a learned art in regard to ordering courses for the table. And few public places are more favored for the modern sport of "people watching" than restaurants, especially among solo diners.

In the United States, restaurants evolved from family-style meals at innkeepers' tables to a smorgasbord of fascinating eats and dining-out traditions. No historian, though, can argue against the birthplace of restaurant culture being New York. The island of Manhattan and its surrounding boroughs make up a dense nugget of multifaceted food lore and the seedling for our appreciation of so many ethnic cuisines, owing to its numerous ethnic communities.

Restaurants existed before John Delmonico opened his first café and pastry shop on William Street in downtown Manhattan in 1827, but they had never truly solidified their place in the daily life of Americans the way they had begun to in Europe. The Swiss immigrant, born Giovanni Del-Monico, brought his brother Pietro to the States to bake at the café what were then the most impressive pastries in the city. Moreover, they were served in a comparatively clean, pleasant setting. Empowered by the success of this little shop, the Delmonicos took a gamble on purchasing the storefront next door, hiring a French chef, and serving full, hot meals at lunchtime. Their mission was to attract businessmen and other working people who could afford to eat finer meals midday and actually appreciate the novelty of the French delicacies they served.

The Delmonicos would send for more relatives and open three more restaurants, each one more refined than the last, over the next decade. They would set the mold for fine dining in New York City and America as a whole. Before this time, restaurants were mostly taverns that offered limited food options and often served only shared meals to which customers would help themselves. There was also an oyster trend, and New York had four oyster bars by 1805. In fact, the oldest restaurant still in operation in America is the Union Oyster Bar in Boston. Oysters were a beloved snack food in nineteenth-century America, but they were also incredibly cheap, sold by street hawkers and in cellar bars, some of them for an all-you-can-eat price. (Again, why did they have to do away with these?)

Yet these taverns and inns that served food were often raucous places, bound to have uncouth fellows lurking about (America was in a particularly boozy place in time then), not suitable for women, and shocking to European travelers. And the food they served was, by all accounts, extremely crude. New York was very far indeed from the foodie destination it has become. For the most part, the middle class still had yet to see food as something more than plain sustenance. The Delmonicos' restaurants paved the way for the sit-down restaurant culture that New York City would thrive on over the next century and beyond.

Taking this workday lunch concept further, William and Samuel Childs established their first restaurant in 1889, with just that middle-class lunch crowd in mind. In contrast to that of Delmonico's, their fare was more modest, down-home American cooking—pancakes and omelets, sandwiches, and oysters on toast. Their most famous dish was butter cakes, and the Childses showcased them with panache by setting the griddle by a window facing the street. The restaurant had a self-service buffet line, where diners could select their food and take it to a table. It was a more casual, less expensive affair than upscale restaurants and soon became something of a midtown cafeteria for the working class.

Many more restaurants would mimic the success of the Childses' "lunchrooms," as they were popularly called, while others would try to top the opulence of Delmonico's. Even today, the takeout or sit-in restaurants of New York's busiest commercial areas don't sound so far off from the buffet lines at Childs'. Taking this cue, many more cafés, soda shops, and bakeries would begin selling full meals instead of quick bites. Eating the foods from these places, instead of eating at home, became increasingly popular throughout the twentieth century.

This isn't a book about all that, as you know. Still, the world might be a very different place if it weren't for that loftily ambitious Parisian, the Swiss American dynasty, and all the other great restaurateurs through the ages who fanned the flames on the art of eating out.

In contrast, home cooking has seen better days than the last half century in the United States. The prevalence of eating out has risen quickly, gaining significant momentum with the development of the interstate highway in the 1960s. As Americans hit the road more, they relied on restaurant food more. As meticulously observed in Eric Schlosser's *Fast Food Nation*, fast-food moguls were there to capitalize on the trend (and subsequently claim a large chunk of our diet). Just thirty years ago, in 1980, Americans were still spending twice as much on groceries as they did in restaurants. Heavy restaurant advertising, car culture, relative prosperity, and many other factors have all contributed to the reversal of this stance today. If national trends continue at the same rate, eating out will soon eclipse the home-cooked meal altogether. Eating out is also a habit that gets passed on to subsequent generations, something of a dominant gene. If a person hasn't been raised in a household that cooks, how will she or he know how to cook for her- or himself? Many of my friends who claim they never eat in as adults say they rarely did while growing up.

The restaurant revolution has had graver effects on American society than our forgetting how to cook. Today, one in three Americans (one in two African Americans and Latinos) will be diagnosed with type 2 diabetes. This is due to the overindustrialized, overprocessed foods that have engulfed restaurants as well as supermarkets today. But leaving aside easy targets like fast food for the moment, most restaurants across the country do not typically serve very healthy food. Most households, on the other hand, typically cook food for their families that they believe is healthy. Waiters in restaurants don't tell you to eat your greens before you can be excused from the table. Instead, restaurants aim to pamper your taste buds, tell you it's okay to have that buttery pasta or bacon burger because it was created by a renowned chef or a trendy restaurant. This should come as no surprise—restaurants are profit-seeking businesses after all, founded on the idea of making something that tastes better than what you could cook at home. Therefore, chefs add much more fat, salt, and sugars to their dishes than one would likely reach for at home, hoping to gain repeat customers hungry for another taste. Several of the entrees at the nation's largest restaurant chains, such as Applebee's and Chili's, have close to twice the government's recommended daily sodium limit alone. Thanks to recent legislation in New York City, large chain restaurants must now be transparent about the number of calories in each food option with signs posted in their stores. But this law hasn't swept across the nation yet, nor does it affect independent businesses or small chains.

Many point to the advancement of women in the workplace as the reason for fewer family meals cooked by Mom. Indeed, the rise of women at work from the 1960s on neatly parallels the national trend in eating out. Even as early as the women's suffrage movement in the early twentieth century, cooking was looked down upon by feminists as a stifling relic of female subservience. As Charlotte Perkins Gilman put it, "Why should half the world be acting as amateur cooks for the other half?"

The feminist movement of the 1960s and 1970s and its relative achievements may have succeeded in bringing more women into the workforce, but the issue of equality when it comes to traditional roles is still up for debate. Regardless of equally busy schedules, it seems that, if not the actual cooking, at least the responsibility of feeding a household has largely remained in female hands. Enter the days of family buckets from KFC. Turn on primetime TV today and you're bound to see at least one commercial depicting a triumphant mom winking toward the camera as her family dives into a "just like homemade" takeout meal—or in other instances, calling for delivery pizza as she rushes out to make a meeting. Instead of acting as amateur cooks, today women and men alike turn to professionals to feed their families. Add to them the "food scientists," responsible for canned, instant, just-add-milk, or just-microwave foods.

Another reason for the wane in home cooking is that the profit margin for prepared foods is generally much higher than that for groceries. It's not because fewer people patronize grocery stores. Rather, grocery stores are just not a terribly profitable business. There is tremendous loss involved in keeping fresh products stocked on the shelves. Much is thrown out at the end of the day due to expiration dates or just to make room for new products. For stores without vertically integrated brand-name products or a prepared-foods section for which the extra labor can command higher prices, the lack of these items and the fierce competition among grocery stores for the lowest prices possible means paltry profits compared to those of restaurants. Throughout Brooklyn, Queens, and the Bronx, the number of supermarkets has continued to dwindle over the last few years. A 2008 study by the Department of City Planning estimated that as many as seventy-five thousand people in what were considered high-need neighborhoods lived more than five blocks from a grocery store or supermarket. These are areas typically rife with fast-food establishments. Even more frustrating is the proliferation of restaurants in close proximity to schools, opened with the intention of luring youngsters away from the cafeteria.

For young women today, it might seem almost perversely backward to embrace an activity that our feminist forebears fought so hard to distance themselves from. But so what if the success of the women's movements contributed to the demise of home cooking? Let's not kid ourselves; men are not all helpless individuals searching, sad-eyed, for a woman to feed them, any more than a woman is looking for a man to look after her. Cooking is an especially gender-bridging activity in this day and age, if my young peers are any indication. I have many male friends who cook. I have just as many female friends and acquaintances who've admitted to never cooking, or to not knowing how. In 2007, *The New York Times* published a delightful article about couples in which one member was the "alpha cook" and the other the feckless "beta." Most of the alpha cooks in the article were the husbands or boyfriends. In the media, there are just as many if not more male cookbook authors or celebrity chefs. There is a wealth of male-driven food writing today, and a somewhat macho infatuation with adventurous eating, meat eating, fatty cuts and offal eating, and regional food pride, seen in the many male-dominated barbecue brawls or chili cook-offs throughout the country. On the flip side, there is also a fervent vegan community that is very much mixed in gender. Whether it's for passion, status, politics, or budget purposes, preparing a meal is no longer strictly the territory of just one half of the world.

Cooking has become a tool of many persuasions in this country, and it has seeped its way into our culture far beyond the basic need to feed oneself. But how good are we at doing just that—cooking, simply to feed ourselves, on a daily basis? For no other aim or purpose? Less and less, it seems. So long as busy workdays and constant commutes dominate our schedules, and restaurants populate our neighborhoods more than grocery stores, so will the eating-out regime dominate cooking.

I recently attended a panel discussion at the 92nd Street Y on "food finds and trends." One of the notable food critics on the panel, Gael Greene, said at one point that she didn't think people actually cooked at home. "I think they get frozen meals or takeout," she said. I think she's right, for the most part. Then I almost fell out of my chair when another panelist, *Bon Appétit* editor Victoria von Biel, countered that statement by mentioning a food blog written by a young woman called "Not Eating Out in New York." (Thankfully, I had a friend sitting beside me to keep me from running up to the stage right then to shake her hand.) However, at another lecture given at the American Museum of Natural History a few months later, I listened to Michael Pollan observe that more Americans were getting back into the kitchen and rediscovering how to cook once again, and that this was "a healthy change."

In *America Eats Out*, John Mariani attested that restaurants particularly in this country always hinged upon a gimmick: "Lunch wagons, milk bars, diners, drive-ins, speakeasies, restaurants shaped like hot dogs, restaurants designed to look like a pirate's den, restaurants where the waiters sing opera, restaurants with wine lists as thick as family bibles—all are, in their own way, gimmicks to hook in the crowds." The gimmicks go on. It could be foods that restore the health, or fine meals in the middle of the day. It could be purely outstanding food, food being served all night, how about waitresses who wear tight T-shirts over their well-endowed chests? It could be ribs. Fifties nostalgia. Or chefs who serve the patrons themselves, like at *The New York Times* restaurant critic Frank Bruni's pick for best restaurant of 2008, Momofuku Ko.

Well, I decided to give home cooking a gimmick of my own. To eat for a prolonged period of time without the assistance of restaurants whatsoever. Was that something that a New York–born, New Jersey–bred, working, middle-class, twenty-six-year-old American such as myself could achieve?

It seemed only fitting to test this humble experiment in the eating-out capital of the world.

CHAPTER 1

The Start of My Restaurant Fast

It began as a lark.

"I think I'm going to swear off restaurant food for a while," I told my friends at a beer garden in Brooklyn. It was the middle of August, the dog days of summer 2006.

"Yeah? How come?"

I looked down at the wooden table separating myself from my friend and roommate, Erin, and her friend Sergio. It was covered with four or five grease-blotted paper plates, two of which had half-eaten hamburgers on them, three plastic cups surrounding a plastic pitcher of light golden beer, and a white paper boat that had previously held a hot dog.

"Well, I've been wanting to start a food blog," I began.

Erin perked up in her seat. I told them that my blog would be based on home cooking, a repository of sorts for all the recipes I had brimming in my head all the time. Just the other day, I had some leftover pesto, and when I started to make a potato salad to bring to a party, I decided to use the pesto instead of mayonnaise and added some sliced radishes and bits of red pepper to the mix, along with a splash of balsamic vinegar. My blog would be about easy-to-prepare, healthy, and hopefully unique home-cooked dishes like that, I explained. And as an added, extremist measure, I would quit eating out in any of the five boroughs of the city where we lived.

"Not eating out in New York?" Sergio said after I told them what I wanted to call the blog. "That sounds . . . perfect. I only eat out, but I would read it." He shrugged and took another chomp of his burger.

A cloud of smoke wafted to our table just then, and I couldn't make out Erin's exact expression. It was a muggy, severely hot day, and the ceiling of patio umbrellas in the cramped backyard created a virtual hotbox of stale, smoky city air. Sergio's normally olive-complected face had turned bright sunburn pink.

I suddenly wondered why the three of us couldn't be sitting at home, in the comfort of a room with an air conditioner or a fan, or in the shade of someone's backyard, drinking much better beer, and making ourselves better burgers. Why did we have to come here, forking over our hard-earned dollars in exchange for the basest of barbecue food and being squashed in this pebble-floored patio, waiting for service, and yelling over the din of our too-close neighbors? Pure habit, I guessed. I wondered whether this habit was something we could reverse.

"Yeah, do it!" Erin pressed.

I picked up my third or fourth burned slider from my plate. It had been baking in a slice of sunlight on the table for a while, and the cracked black patty looked and smelled like a charcoal briquette. I took a swig of flat, lukewarm beer to wash down the regrettable last bits of bun.

"Yeah, I think I will," I said.

Despite that underwhelming meal at the beer garden, it was a good time to be a gourmand in New York. "You are what you eat" might be the universal food motto of all time, but in today's metropolitan food meccas, the old adage might be better put, "What you don't eat will come to define your limitations in character." In the midst of a national foodie renaissance, especially in New York, *not* eating anything, by principle, was simply not cool. Even friends of mine who are vegetarians are routinely pooh-poohed by the cultured and elite. And vegans? They might as well wither and die. But not eating out in New York? That was like not seeing the sea lions at the Central Park Zoo, or not *not* drinking the tap water in Mexico.

Even as I described the plan to Erin and Sergio that day, I felt a creeping trepidation about how my blog would be received by those who were not my friends. I braced myself for severe backlash; the concept would seem sacrilege to many. *For shame*, people would shake their heads and say. In this town, you could eat a bagel or bialy with lox for breakfast, a stuffed dosa from that amazing street cart for lunch, bistro steak frites for dinner, and for late-night eats, a steaming bowl of ramen or a mean slice of real New York pizza, all within the radius of a few blocks. The world is our oyster bar, so let's start slurping it up.

So awesome and plentiful is restaurant, takeout, and street-stand food here that New Yorkers eat it for almost every meal. I certainly did, at first. For those first two years or so living in the city, my head was very much in the game; my budget, on the other hand, was not up to speed. Any financial expert will tell you that your twenties are the best years of your life . . . to save. I wasn't a fluid spender, at least compared to some people I knew, but I simply wasn't saving up, either. I was living pretty much from paycheck to paycheck, what with paying rent, utilities, transportation, weekday lunches, a lot of takeout and casual restaurant dinners, afternoon brunches on the weekends, and the occasional splurge at a nice, new restaurant. I was fond of seeing music gigs and movies, and grabbing happy hours, too. Saving was not the first of my priorities when I began working and living in New York City, obviously. It's no wonder that people of my generation have coined terms such as *quarterlife crisis* (dealing with insurmountable debt, among other things) or the *boomerang effect* (when college graduates move back in with their parents).

Something had to give, I resolved. But I was already living with two roommates at this time, in a cheap apartment in the outer borough of Brooklyn. How many other corners could I possibly cut? Set aside sustainable food and eating with a conscience for a moment: My eating-out lifestyle was not sustainable—with my income, that is. I was going to have to separate some of the needs from the wants. Buying food that's already prepared is a want, even if buying food itself is definitely a need, I reasoned. Since I was beginning to get bored and disillusioned with many of the restaurant meals I was eating (for example, the beer garden burgers), and because I felt a creative urge drawing me into the kitchen more and more often, I decided that the prepared food—or eating out—was the one habit I'd try to kick. But what was going to motivate me to rush through a frenetic grocery store, drag back ingredients to my apartment, and cook up enough food to feed myself, twenty-four/seven?

Doing it with panache, I eventually decided. And showcasing my recipes as well as my kitchen disasters in a food blog oxymoronically called "Not Eating Out in New York."

Granted, I am very grateful to be among the fortunate minority of the world's population to have had the pleasure of eating at a restaurant. I happen to hail from one of the richest, most developed countries in the world, the United States, whereas billions of people have never seen anything like the luxuries of restaurant dining. So I'm happy for that.

You could also say that I am a native New Yorker. I was born in Manhattan, at Cornell Medical Center on the Upper East Side. But just before I reached the tender age of two, my parents put a down payment on a house across the Hudson and whisked my older brother and me from the playgrounds and promenades of Brooklyn Heights to the clipped lawns and tree swings of Maplewood, New Jersey. Growing up in a middle- to upper-middle-class family, I was exposed to restaurants early on. My parents are very fond of food and love trying out new cuisines through both cooking and eating out. They are experts at finding the "good" Chinese restaurants of New Jersey, meaning the ones that serve truly authentic Chinese food that is good. When a "good" restaurant was discovered, there was a dramatic scramble to invite an uninitiated couple or family, or to round up the several Chinese families my family was friends with, and get to the place before the rush. (It should be noted that bringing friends was less socially than gastronomically motivated; with family-style Chinese dining, the more people you have at your table, the more dishes you can order, and the more varieties of deliciousness you can sample. According to my father, it's completely not worth it to have dim sum with two people.) I remember crawling underneath the white cloth–covered tables at endless Chinese banquet dinners with the children of my parents' friends. When a good restaurant closed without apparent reason or warning, it was bemoaned for months. My parents were willing to drive forty-five minutes each way to towns we had never heard of—or take the train to New York City—to get good dim sum. We would also walk to the local diner on the weekends every now and then for filling breakfast specials, or pick up a couple of pizzas for dinner at home. My brother and I never begged and squealed for our parents to buy us restaurant food, as I had seen my young friends do. I am a fortunate foodie for that.

As much as we enjoyed the occasional restaurant trip, my family had strong ties to the home kitchen. My parents cooked, much more often than not, and they demanded a certain ritual of communal eating every night. I remember the embarrassment I felt when I couldn't meet up with friends until after dinner. My parents insisted on eating together every night, and my brother and I would take turns washing the dishes after the meal was done. When it was dinnertime, my parents would sit at the table (usually hollering at us to come) and not start eating until both of us had joined them. Things were not so rigid in other households, I gathered through the years. Dinner at friends' homes often meant takeout pizza or boxed macaroni and cheese mix at the "kids' table" or in the playroom while the parents ate something else, somewhere else, at some other point, if they even ate at all. As late as high school I wasn't allowed to leave the house at night until I had sat down at the table with the rest of my family, or at least was made to feel very guilty about not doing so. I envied my friends, who, if they were hungry after seeing a movie in a theater, grabbed a slice of pizza next door. One high school friend of mine, Misha, lived with his father in Maplewood's modest downtown strip, and literally everything he ate came from the bagel place, the sushi place, the taco place, the Chinese place, and so on. He was particularly amused that I had to work my schedule around a family supper. Misha moved to town from New York City when we were in middle school.

In any case, I was deprived neither of eating out nor of eating in by the time I decided to draw the curtain on eating out in New York for a while. In fact, I was pretty spoiled when it came to food in general, and I am eternally grateful for it. But it was an episode during college that greatly inspired my decision to begin my not-eating-out experiment. When I was a junior at Emerson College in Boston, I took a class taught by a professor of media criticism and theory who saw a situation in the media similar to my food overload in New York. He thought, what a jungle out there—people are listening to music on their headphones while they shop in stores blaring music from loudspeakers; advertisements bark at drivers from billboards while they're stuck in traffic jams between buses and trucks with advertisements on their sides; television newscasts are played in elevators and taxicabs; the radio plays from waterproof speakers in our showers. Basically, almost every activity of modern urban life is inundated with the media in almost every place imaginable.

Professor Thomas Cooper then introduced our class to his "media fast." Crediting Thoreau's wilderness retreat from society in *Walden,* he made us pledge to avoid any books, newspapers, films, television, recorded music, or radio for a period of two weeks. Alternatively, we could choose to fashion ourselves a "media diet" of limited media intake. During this time, we would keep a journal to record our observations. Professor Cooper himself had engaged in a lengthy "media fast" in the 1970s. With a mission to explore his topic thoroughly and publish his findings, Cooper visited several communities whose cultures discouraged or altogether restricted modern media: the Amish and other plain peoples of North America, and tribes in South America's isolated mountainous regions. He lived with these people, ate with these people, and reflected on their cultures, taking pains to understand why people living in places where media was readily available, such as the Amish, chose to withdraw from it entirely. In the end, Professor Cooper came away with a greater understanding of not only these ways of life but also, oddly enough, the media.

At this time, in college, I was an avid film fanatic. I'd rent three or four movies a week from the library or local video store and would methodically watch all the films by my favorite auteurs. The media fast was a jarring bolt of abstinence from my film obsessions, but, like the rest of the class, I was fascinated by Professor Cooper's example. At the end of the experiment, I handed in my spiral notebook of scribbled reflections, a requirement of the project (so as to avoid any possible contact with media I might have been tempted with if I were using a computer). I've forgotten most of my notes, the specific thoughts and discoveries I suppose I made during those weeks. But I never forgot the novel strategy.

*   *   *

Fasting has always been tied to spiritual or otherwise deeply mental engagement, whether it be a fast from food entirely or from certain types of foods. Religious practitioners have been fasting from food for thousands of years in order to reach a place of mind desirable for certain meditations, or to observe certain traditions, like Lent. It's a trade-off your body and mind undergo: You sacrifice one thing to allow new things to set in.

Sometimes, fasting comes with a financial incentive, too. When I was eight years old, my brother, who was then ten, bet me $10 that I couldn't be a vegetarian for a month. We shook on it. Thinking it would be impossible for me to give up my normal eating routine, my brother thought he had made a solid investment that would pay out in a month's time. After the first few days, however, he'd begun to realize whom he was dealing with.

I was stalwart about my new diet. He heckled and hounded, ate drumsticks with gusto before my eyes, tried to trick me into eating meat a few times, and made me forgo dessert once by proving that Jell-O involved a certain animal by-product, but by the end of the month, he was forced to give up his lawn-mowing earnings for about that same length of time.

I was too young to cook for myself then, but I took a lot of interest in whatever my mother made for me. She knew about our shenanigan and made sure there was always something I could eat at family meals, which helped my end of the bargain considerably. But it also made me begin to think about food a lot more, in ways that I hadn't thought about it previously—where it came from, what it consisted of, and how to cook it.

Around suppertime, I was usually delegated menial kitchen tasks such as setting the table or unloading the dishwasher. But I liked to stick around, watching my mother slice flank steak into thin strips for a stir-fry with vegetables and douse the splattering pan with extra soy sauce, sometimes causing droplets to jump feet in the air. Other times, the aroma of sliced mushrooms simply sautéed in butter would envelop the kitchen as she prepared a spaghetti dinner, with the fresh vegetables added to a jar of tomato sauce. I'd watch, mesmerized, as the mushrooms' juices drooled over the bottom of the pan and slowly evaporated, noting the way the mushroom slices not only shrank but also turned from white to translucent brown.

"It all cooks down to nothing," I can hear my mother say as she stirred, wryly though not without fondness. Its bulk was mostly liquid, I understood then.

With a wooden spoon, she offered me a few slivers to taste. The hot morsels were coated in a viscous gray liquid. Now concentrated in flavor, the savory aroma I'd been smelling burst in my mouth, accented with butter and salt. I wanted to eat them all up on the spot instead of adding them to the sauce that was warming in another pot.

During that month of eating no meat, I was reading *The BFG* by Roald Dahl. In one scene, while devising a plan to wreak revenge on a clan of savage giants, the book's kid-hero, Sophie, says to the Big Friendly Giant:

> *"I think it's rotten that those foul giants should go off every night to eat humans. Humans have never done them any harm."*

The BFG responds:

> *"That is what the little piggy-wig is saying every day," the BFG answered. "He is saying, 'I has never done any harm to the human bean so why should he be eating me?'"*

Goodness, did that quote ever stir my eight-year-old sense of ethics. Under normal circumstances I might have skimmed past it just like with any other book about giants who ate children. But now that I had become a vegetarian for a month, it stuck with me in a way that kept me thinking.

I never did become a vegetarian again after that monthlong stint. (But I will say that I strongly believe in respecting and preserving the earth, and this weighs greatly into my eating habits today.) What I took away from the experience, $10 notwithstanding, was the small discovery that changing one's diet can have profound effects on a person.

That was the last time I engaged in any extended aberration to my eating habits. What eventually turned me on to not eating out and blogging about it, aside from financial incentives, was a series of frustrations and misplaced motivation, which I imagine is not so unusual for anyone who has ever started writing a blog. I moved to New York immediately after finishing college. I had spent the last semester of my senior year not in Boston, where my school was based, but at a university in Taipei through a scholarship program. I tutored English to college students twenty hours per week, while the rest of the time I finished up the few credits I needed to graduate and, for the most part, explored the city, especially its food. By the time I landed back in the States, took off my cap and gown, and began looking for jobs in New York, I was more than a little disoriented, and perhaps disillusioned. But I knew that this was where I wanted to live. New York City was only a short train ride from my hometown, and during college I'd spent every summer living in apartment sublets there, working in book-publishing internships and as a barista at coffee shops. It felt like home already. Thanks to those internships, I quickly found a job as an editorial assistant at a publishing house. I cobbled together some furniture, found roommates on Craigslist, and bought a fresh wardrobe to begin my adult life.

For my first year on my own, I was earning a salary of $27,500 a year and living in a cramped, three-bedroom apartment in Park Slope, Brooklyn. These conditions didn't offer much leeway in terms of leisure spending. They were hardly amenable to eating in restaurants all the time. Still, I was eating out—and so, it seemed, was everyone else I knew. I bought my lunch from nearby delis, soup shops, cheap sushi places, and the occasional street vendor and would scour midtown for the best-tasting bang for my buck. Pretty soon, I realized that trying to find a reasonable and satisfying meal in midtown Manhattan was like searching for fool's gold. No matter how hard I tried, it was a barren wasteland, food-wise. The type of food and the prices at local lunch spots that I'd go to—that everyone went to—on a daily basis were almost like branches of the same fast-food chain. And to fill up for the rest of the afternoon, I found it nearly impossible to spend less than $7. It wasn't just the expense that irked me, though. Picking at the bright orange salmon roe that clung to my wooden chopsticks from sushi rolls, I'd wonder how on earth it had gotten there, to that deli a few doors down, in so many stacks of identical plastic cartons. Summoning my best inner William Blake, I'd ask the morsel at the end of my fork, "Little lamb meatball, who made thee?" I was tired of mindlessly forcing down food when I had no idea where it came from or how it was made.

At night, I went out with friends for live music, art exhibits, and movies, and tried to seek out the city's best-kept-secret restaurants and bars. I began to feel more and more like all this culture I was so anxious to soak in was where my real passions lay, and that it had little to do with my workday. I was horrible at organizing my two bosses' schedules and paperwork, too, which was unfortunately the brunt of my job. I could never seem to photocopy an entire important document without missing pages. And I didn't have much in common with the four coworkers in my department who were my age, and whose names, strangely (or not strangely) enough, were either Sarah or Megan.

I began dating a graphic designer who worked two floors below me. I lost pretty much any other interest in my job, and it showed. I'd take long breaks, arrive late every morning, and dream about how I could best take advantage of my paid vacation days. I took a weeklong trip to Thailand that winter, and when it was over, I came back to the same desk and the same cluelessness about what I was doing there.

In 2005, just after I had been at the publishing house for one year, I was called into my boss's office and told that I wasn't "a good fit." I was given two weeks' severance pay and asked to pack up my desk that day. Once I gathered all my stuff and said my awkward good-byes, I walked out of the office building for the last time—stunned, speechless, and dizzy. My stomach felt foul. I looked at my watch; it was one in the afternoon. I hadn't yet had the chance to eat.

Over the next couple of months, I worked odd jobs or spent my time looking for less-odd ones. I eventually found full-time employment as an executive assistant at a head-hunting firm, a field I had little experience and less interest in, creating PowerPoint presentations and trafficking phone calls. In my free time, I poured my energy into an independent film festival. But after a successful and exhausting season, the volunteer-run organization decided to call it quits. I found myself back at my desk, twiddling my thumbs.

I tried to pitch stories to food magazines, and I wrote for small publications on the side. I loved cooking and began doing so fervently at home, more often than going out to eat. Oh, and I managed to keep the graphic-designer boyfriend, Ben. Which brings me back to the summer of 2006 and that balmy day in the beer garden, with Erin and Sergio.

So began my two years of not eating out. While the explanation I gave my friends the day I decided to move forward with the idea had been my enthusiasm for cooking, and desire to spend less, I was harboring a deep distaste for the restaurant routine that so dominated our diet. Most people, when confronted with the term "eating out," conjure vibrant images of three beautifully plated courses brought in succession to a two-person table, in a pleasant atmosphere. To be clear, I didn't want to start writing a blog for the sole reason of criticizing this type of experience. Most Americans do not eat like this very often. Today, 77 percent of all restaurant meals are purchased from fast-food restaurants. Much of the time they are taken from there and eaten on the road, at home, in the office, or at another public place. Enjoying a leisurely meal inside a restaurant is generally reserved for the more fortunate. But however it's done, "eating out" has become a habit almost as natural as breathing. It's a sandwich wrapped in cellophane. A cardboard box with a pizza, hamburger, or pieces of fried chicken inside. I wanted to start a blog about no longer relying on profit-seeking enterprises (backboned, of course, by low-wage kitchen staff) to feed me every meal. In short, I wanted to figure out how to undo the trend that has engulfed our eating habits.

To be sure that I'd stick with the project, I came up with a mental framework of rules. Essentially, I would not eat out in any of the five boroughs that made up New York City. Technically anywhere outside of the city proper, it was okay to eat out. So if I was going to be out of town for a week, then I would of course eat out there. I wasn't traveling too often around this time, so in general, the occasional restaurant meal would mean that I was celebrating special occasions in New Jersey with my family, and everyone wanted to go out for a nice meal.

I would, however, pay respect to occasional mandatory meals associated with my work environment. I had no reason to conduct business lunches, but my employer occasionally ordered the catered staff lunch or threw holiday parties. If I was asked to join a group headed to a restaurant for a coworker's birthday, I'd tag along only to those celebrations that were for higher-ups—such as bosses. I wanted to keep my job; I wasn't trying to play games with my livelihood here. Likewise, if I were truly in danger of going very hungry—if I was stuck at the bus terminal and there was absolutely no other option—then I would eat restaurant food. Fortunately, this was never the case, since there are at least as many convenience stores as there are restaurants in New York City, many of them open all night.

Next, I determined that this wasn't a project about trying to make everything that I ate using the basest of raw ingredients. I wasn't setting forth to cure my own salami, or churn goat's milk into chevre, as much as I'd like to. I basically took *not eating out* to mean not eating anything purchased from a restaurant, whether it be a sit-down establishment or a takeout window. There are many businesses that blur the line between restaurant and grocery store. Many high-end groceries, such as Whole Foods, have extensive prepared-food sections, and you can order a deli sandwich at any bodega. These types of meals would be off-limits, too, I decided. Food from bakeries and bagel shops could also be borderline cases, as they were generally ready to eat. I'd use my best judgment here—if I could simply go home, slice the bagel that I'd purchased, and top it with whatever I wanted, then I would.

Also, this wasn't about trying to convert the people around me into not eating out. So if my friends were all starving and wanted to stop at a restaurant while I was hanging out with them, then I'd either have to go along and just order coffee, or else not go. Drinking—anything—from a restaurant, café, or bar would be perfectly fine. After all, I wasn't going to start making my own gin in the tub.

I couldn't decide on an exact length of time that I would limit myself to eating in; one year sounded too much like a stint, or an impractical joke of some sort. I was eager to start blogging about it, and I didn't want to put a cap on the blog's duration. So I left that question unanswered.

After I set these guidelines and thought about how I would write my blog, I realized that something was missing. I knew that there are plenty of people who don't eat out, even in New York. So, like Professor Cooper did with his media fast, I decided I should seek out other examples of not eating out within city limits. I would find as many avenues and lifestyles that qualified as not eating out in New York as possible. I also wanted to meet more home-cooking aficionados and put our minds and resources together on a number of fun projects and community events. After all, mealtimes are not just about filling one's belly until it's no longer hungry; mealtimes are a social activity, too.

Did I ever "cheat" during the course of these two years, and eat out in a New York City restaurant? There are a few memorable experiences when I did, which come up in later chapters. As for allowed dining-out occasions, such as work parties, I can count the number I attended on both hands. Many people have asked me whether I cheated with occasional takeout meals while at home, alone, when nobody was looking. I can say in good conscience that I didn't, because the strangest thing that happened—far stranger than any of the weird groups and events I would encounter while not eating out, and far weirder than the schemes and dates that I would fashion in order to fit my restaurant-free lifestyle—is the fact that I grew so comfortable with eating in that I simply didn't want to cheat. If I was craving something amazing or unusual, I would set out to make something amazing or unusual. The thought of buying something premade at any of the mediocre delis near my office, or dialing up for takeout from any of the restaurants that had slid their menus underneath my apartment door, rarely entered my mind. It was unappealing if it did. It was *unusual*.

I should point out that I may have been better prepared than the average New Yorker of my age when I began this journey, because I had become by then so enthralled with cooking. I loved food, of course, but there was something doubly satisfying about enjoying a really good meal that I made myself. In the months and weeks leading up to the start of the blog, I cooked dinner two or three nights a week, as my passion for learning about new dishes and techniques increased. I had never taken cooking classes. I had only one cookbook at home, and I didn't subscribe to any food magazines. I preferred to make up dishes as I went along, adding this and that, whatever was left over in the fridge, whatever was on hand.

The frequency of my dabblings in the kitchen left me well prepared for cooking and eating in nonstop. I understood how to use
up leftovers and shop for groceries wisely. I also learned that a dish
does not have to come out perfectly to be edible, either.

Throughout the entire time I was not eating out and blogging
about it, there were of course innumerable homemade meals that I
made and never bothered to share with readers. I tried to leave the
simple, dull, everyday recipes out of the blog and this book, so as not
to bore readers. But just as I experienced, I guarantee that if you just
get into the habit of cooking at home more often, you will figure out
ways to make the process more efficient, and the things you cook
more satisfactory. Practice can't be learned from books. Plus, with
practice, you will figure out how to cook in a way that suits your
taste and lifestyle, and not mine—I'm not sure everyone wants to
eat fried rice with scrambled eggs any given night of the week.

Six years after taking Professor Cooper's course and two years of
not eating out later, I think I finally get what his media fast was
aiming at. He was trying to get us to make more mindful choices
when it came to media, art, maybe even ourselves. He was also
asking us to consider, what are we losing, as a culture, in exchange
for the conveniences of modern life? What might we have already
lost? In return, what can we gain from doing away with it for a
while?

I was at a dinner party one night, and my neighbor in the next
seat told me about how, during a phone conversation with his
mother, he'd expressed a little frustration with paying for restaurant food. She followed up by mailing him a stack of recipes written by his Dominican grandmother. Not only were they greatly
helpful in allowing him to re-create some of the dishes he'd always
loved, but he said it was almost like receiving a diary from his
grandmother.

Had my friend never taken up cooking, he might not have gotten to know his grandmother as well as he did through her cooking
advice and recipes. And had I never done so myself, then I would
have never discovered a whole lot of unique things about myself,
and the people around me, through food. And that's been by far
the best part about the journey.

CHAPTER 2

Breaking into Bread

"A loaf of bread," the Walrus said,
"Is chiefly what we need:
Pepper and vinegar besides
Are very good indeed."

—*Lewis Carroll*, Through the Looking-Glass

Squash rolls: Put 1 cup milk, ⅓ cup sugar, ⅓ cup butter or margarine, and 1 tsp salt in a glass dish and heat in microwave until scalded. Add 1 pkg cooked squash thawed, but cold, to the milk mixture to cool that off (if the squash has a lot of water that separates when you thaw it, drain most of it off).

In a small cup or bowl, put ½ cup very warm water and 1 pkg (about 2½ tsp) yeast and a pinch of sugar. Add 2 cups flour to the milk mixture and stir well. Add the yeast/water and mix very well. Keep adding flour (about 3 cups or so depending on how much moisture is in the squash). I add about 2 cups, still mixing it with a spoon, and then turn it onto a floured surface and knead the rest of the flour in until it isn't so sticky—it probably takes about 10 minutes or so.

Put the dough into a generously greased glass or metal bowl and turn dough over so that some of the grease gets on the top. Cover with a dish towel and put into a warm place and let rise

until double its size (about 1 hour). Punch down dough and form into
small balls.

I leaned back from my computer screen. The recipe went on, but
I wasn't ready to scroll down farther. I was about a month into
my not-eating-out habit, and for motivation I'd asked my friends
to send me some of their favorite recipes. I didn't think I'd have
enough ideas of my own to keep the mission afloat. But were these
really the directions for the simple squash rolls that DJ had talked
about a few nights ago? It sounded like an elaborate science project,
with things bubbling over in beakers or creeping off the counters.
Punch down the dough? Was this really necessary? Couldn't it just
be pressed? What was yeast anyway, and where did you get it?

I reread the beginning of DJ's e-mail:

Here's my mom's recipe for squash rolls. We always have them
with our Thanksgiving meal, so I figured they'd be a nice fall-time
food. Note that you may want to halve this recipe, as it will produce
much more than you would want to eat yourself. Also, the preparation time is kind of long, but it's completely worth it. Oh, and they
don't really end up tasting anything like squash (which is a major
plus because they're made from freezer squash, which is a cheap
replacement for syrup of ipecac if you don't have any handy).

I typed out an e-mail response.

Thanks so much for spilling your mom's secret recipe! I think I'm
going to try it out tonight.

I paused.

One question, though: where can I find yeast? Is this something you
can only get at a special baking supplies store?

While I waited for his response, I took a quick mental stock
check of my kitchen supplies. I'd need to buy butter and the squash.
There was only one mixing bowl in the apartment, which belonged
to my roommate, Erin, and I doubted it would suffice for all that

flour. Then, I didn't think we had any flour either. There was a dusty box of biscuit mix on top of the refrigerator, which Erin used every time she couldn't resist a craving for chicken and biscuits, and which I'd used instead of flour once or twice, to dredge some meat in before splashing it into an oily pan.

Wait, weren't biscuits essentially the same thing as rolls? How come I didn't see Erin punching down any dough or kneading for ten minutes? What did yeast even look like? Just then my boss walked by my desk, and I closed the window for my e-mail.

I began wondering whether it would have been better to pick a weekend to make DJ's recipe instead of beginning the recipe once I got home from work on a weeknight. But my mind had already been made up; I was determined to make the squash rolls. The sooner, the better, to learn how to knead, and let dough rise with yeast.

DJ's response came back a couple of hours later.

You can find yeast packets in pretty much any grocery store. Or that's where my mom always found them. I think they should say on the label, "dry active yeast."

As I walked down the baking supplies aisle of my local grocery store that evening, I realized I had no idea what I was searching for. I should have tried to look up an image online while I still had the chance at the office. I didn't think I'd ever seen one of these packages of yeast before, and I had no concept of its shape or size—was it inside another box, bag, or canister? How big was it? I stared at boxes of sugar and baking soda for a moment. How did a twenty-eight-year-old bachelor like DJ, who barely ever cooked for himself, know more about baking than I did?

At times like these, I was reminded of the little differences between my mom and what I had gathered about most American moms, from friends or the television. My mom didn't bake. I'd never watched her take a tray of cookies out of the oven, or helped her ice a birthday cake. Even cake mixes or tubs of frosting were curious objects to me from the crowded grocery-store shelf. I should back up by explaining that my mom is Chinese. Her home cooking is done on the stovetop, in pots and wide saucepans (she didn't have a wok, as she didn't feel they were very different from regular sauté pans), and is typically completed in twenty minutes or less. Of course, she made long-simmered stews and soups from time to time. She also cooked plenty of American dishes, like spaghetti with meatballs. But she simply didn't bake. When moms were called on to bring in food for a potluck or bake sale at elementary school, she brought Chinese pot stickers (and they were always a hit). At a family get-together at our house once when I was young, one of my aunts turned on the oven to preheat it. She ended up scorching a bunch of cutting boards and cookware that were stored inside it. My mom stopped using the oven for storage not too long after that, but she never used it much for anything else—least of all for baking bread.

My dad was different. He'd use the oven four or five times a year, maybe, to roast an enormous piece of meat or to fill its racks with various homemade pies. When he wanted to cook, it was a production; he would tie on the kitchen's sole tartan apron and take up its entire space with open cookbooks, their pages pocked with crusty splatters, tools like flour sifters and garlic presses, bowls and measuring cups, cracked eggshells, and his general, kitchen gadget-wielding self, which moved slowly and deliberately as if he were a surgeon bending over an operating table rather than a stove. He would spend an entire leisurely Saturday on whatever he was making. When my mother would come home, her heart would stop at the sight of every smear on the refrigerator handle and onion paper on the floor.

So loyal, though, was my dad's passion for pies that he never bothered to bake any other types of dessert. Nor did he bake bread.

My eyes ran across a crumpled deck of three small envelopes on the baking aisle shelf. *Fleischmann's Active Dry Yeast*, they each read, in jumping-bright yellow and pink print. I picked one up and tossed it into my basket.

Back outside along the busy street in Brooklyn's quaint Park Slope neighborhood, restaurants were just beginning to fill up with customers. As I made my way home from the grocery store, I passed several couples and groups hesitating in front of restaurant windows, or gazing at menus on their doors. I walked past a restaurant I had loved going to just a month before. It was a small, unassuming place that specialized in pressed sandwiches—with any combination of the works. It was a little pricey, though, for what it was. Maybe I should invest in a panini press, I mused. In front of another restaurant, a new one I'd never been to, a tall young man opened the door for his female friend.

I quickly reminded myself of why I had taken on this mission. Currently, my total spending for the day was $18.13. That accounted for the yeast packets, frozen squash, bag of flour, quart of butter, and the makings of dinner for at least three people, with leftovers. The flour, yeast, and butter would make it into many more meals, too. For dinner, I'd gotten some chicken leg quarters, which I was thinking of simply braising or else roasting on trays like I'd seen Erin do for her chicken-and-biscuit nights, and a bunch of Swiss chard. I knew my boyfriend, Ben, would be showing up at some point that night also, so with the rolls, there would be plenty for all of us.

I turned the corner to my block, leaving the quieter parts of the neighborhood to the noisy street with four lanes of traffic that I lived on, Fourth Avenue. This was totally going to be worth it, this whole not-eating-out thing.

Once home, I cleared aside all the piles of CDs from the kitchen counter and wiped it down with a fresh sponge. This was it: I was making bread for the first time. Just think of it: I might never need to buy bread for sandwiches and let the rest go moldy again! I ripped open one of the foil paper yeast packets and let loose a spray of grayish, millet-sized pebbles all over the counter.

Nearly since the dawning of agriculture, bread has been the quintessential food of the Western world. But before my blog, I'd never thought of it as something people actually made themselves. The puffy, spongelike textures and uniform shapes of store-bought bread and dinner rolls resembled no food I'd ever seen produced in a home kitchen. This wasn't counting banana bread, or muffins and other cakelike breads, which I later learned are quick breads, as opposed to yeast-based breads. Even those I didn't have much experience making. I'd heard of bread machines that you could buy and bake loaves inside of, but these sounded unwieldy and complicated.

In *Near a Thousand Tables: A History of Food,* Felipe Fernández-Armesto proposed that it was bread—and not beer, another common usage for wheat—that propelled the grain's popularity in the Neolithic period: "Wheat has no obvious advantage over other edible grasses for the farmers who first favored it or for the peoples subsequently seduced by it, except that it has a secret ingredient—gluten. . . . This makes it a peculiarly good source of bread, because gluten is the substance which combines with water to make dough malleable."

Indeed, people have been subsequently seduced by bread, in all ways, shapes, and forms: flat or leavened; sweet or sourdough; sliced or crumbled into coarse crumbs; whole grain or refined; topped with sauce and mozzarella cheese or cradling a ground-beef patty and ketchup. The prominent American food critic Jeffrey Steingarten asserted that "bread is the only food that satisfies completely, by itself" in his book *The Man Who Ate Everything.* That's a big compliment for plain old bread (though, in all fairness to supporters of the beer theory, this wasn't coming from the man who *drank* everything).

Let alone its deliciousness, bread became so significant throughout the course of history that the word frequently stands in for food or basic needs: "breadwinner," "dough," and in the Lord's Prayer, "Give us today our daily bread," to name a few examples.

Basic, primal sustenance—this is what bread means to us as a culture. But when you look at all the steps involved in making it, it seems anything but simple. I couldn't fathom how someone had first come up with it. First, whole wheat needed to be dried, cracked, and milled to a fine dust. Then you had to mix it with some leavening agent, like yeast, or probably back in the old days, just rotting ale. Then you had to pump gluten into it by kneading—for at least eight minutes, until you had worked up a sweat, all the while remembering to flour each and every surface of your workstation unless you wanted bits and pieces of white goop all over your counter and your hands. Then you had to bake it. Then it was fresh and usable in its current state for only one day—maybe two. Afterward, you had to come up with innovative ways to sneak it into other foods, like grinding it up to thicken soups, or to stretch meatballs, or making French toast or stuffing when it was stale.

Whoever came up with this system anyway?

*   *   *

It was alive!

I stared down at the bowl of dry active yeast, which I'd just mixed with warm water and sugar. It was bubbling and fizzy, but not in a familiar, Alka-Seltzer kind of way. More like a murky-gray-and-smelling-more-than-slightly-fetid sort of way. Active, I surmised.

I followed the next two instructions in DJ's e-mail, swapping out a large saucepan in lieu of a mixing bowl big enough to fit everything in. After stirring the thawed package of squash together with the flour, milk, and yeast, I had a big pile of what looked like bright orange Play-Doh.

Turn it onto a floured surface and knead the rest of the flour in.

I dusted a cutting board with some flour and scraped up the orange putty with my hands. I played with the dough for a few minutes, rolling it into a ball and smushing it back onto the cutting board with the flat of my palm. The dough was so sticky that it stuck to my palm and spurted through the slats of my fingers as I worked. Stubbornly, the bits and pieces that coated my hands would never quite integrate back with the rest of the ball.

Form into a ball and place inside a greased bowl. Cover with a towel and let rise until double, about 2 hours.

That should be easy enough. I slicked butter inside Erin's mixing bowl and plopped the dough ball into it.

The lock of the apartment door clicked and Erin walked through. A shuffle of plastic immediately followed her steps as she plopped her groceries on the floor to coddle the cat that was waiting for her.

"Want to make dinner?" she said as she came through the hallway.

"Yeah, let's do it," I said. "I've got stuff on the way, but it might take a while."

"Good. I picked up some snacks," Erin said.

By then it was about eight o'clock, and I was famished. I considered cooking the rest of the ingredients I'd bought for dinner and leaving the rolls for later, as a dessert. That was what I would have to do.

Erin shoved a bag on the kitchen counter. She took out a couple of avocados, a bag of tortilla chips, and a six-pack of beer. We spent the next couple of hours talking, listening to music, talking about the music, talking about our latest projects—my new blog-writing ventures and Erin's songwriting ventures—and scraping chips against the sides of a bowl of guacamole. We cooked, too, roasting the chicken with simple seasonings in the oven and giving the Swiss chard a quick sauté with garlic. Ben made his way over just in time for dinner. We had been dating for about a year, and we'd gotten into the habit of staying at one or the other's apartment on most nights. Hence, I usually cooked dinner for at least two people—often three when I was at home and Erin was, too. But unlike Ben, Erin actually cooked fairly often, and she always shared whatever she was making if I was around.

Once we were full from dinner, and the beer bottles were all emptied and piled up in the heaping recycling bin, I remembered to check on the dough. I glanced at my watch—it was a little after ten o'clock. The towel was now draped across a round, protruding mass coming from the inside of the bowl. I lifted off the towel and stared at the balloon of bright orange before me. It was more alive! Now for that punching part . . . I balled my hands into fists and gave the dough a gentle whack. The air trapped inside it escaped with a *poof*, and it slowly fell back to half its size. I had to admit, that was pretty satisfying, though I still wasn't convinced there was any reason for blunt force, or the use of the word *punch* in this and so many other recipes I'd seen for bread when describing the same step. Was this some relic of a particular baker's angst? Or a hand-me-down from generations upon generations of women in the kitchen, not socially allowed to express their true feelings toward their husbands in an open or direct manner?

Now that I was no longer hungry, I preheated the oven and patted the dough into balls. Twenty minutes or so later, I took the baked rolls out of the oven. They gave off a deliciously familiar odor, reminding me of all the times I'd walked down the street at night and suddenly caught a whiff of an industrial bakery doing its business. It was toasty and slightly pungent. And these rolls certainly looked like the real thing. The balls I had formed had expanded to soft, foamy mounds in the oven. They were still very orange inside but had a darker cast on their crusts as if they'd been bronzed in the sun.

Once they were cool enough to taste, I couldn't tell the difference between these and countless other warm dinner rolls I'd had before. True to DJ's word, they didn't taste at all like squash, which held a mystery for me in itself. (Was the squash just a way of squashing more nutrition into your average dinner roll? Or was the intent to lend flavor, however ill-envisioned? Or was it for color?) All in all, this recipe was a success for me. I had created a breadlike substance at home, on the first shot. And the results were satisfying.

"Yummy!" Erin concurred.

I ate squash rolls for breakfast and snacks throughout the next week. I also wrote a post in my blog about DJ's mom's recipe, and moved on to other recipes and cooking experiments not involving bread for a couple of weeks.

Then an article in *The New York Times* caught my attention—along with that of the rest of the food-obsessed world. It was describing a "revolutionary" method of bread making developed by Jim Lahey, proprietor of New York's Sullivan Street Bakery. It had been dubbed "No-Knead Bread," and the key lay in two simple maneuvers: letting the dough rest for twelve hours or more before baking it, and heating up a heavy cast-iron pot as the vessel to bake the bread in. Lucky for me, I had recently acquired a bright red Le Creuset Dutch oven, which I had been drooling over for months. I had to put it to this fascinating new use.

Many, many other articles and food bloggers' tales cropped up based on the intoxicating prospect of not kneading before I had the chance to blog about it. In general, they were giddy with raves about the process—how easy it was and what terrific bread it produced. I gazed at so many photos of loaves forged from this uber-clever method that I almost didn't want to give it a go—how could anything I made ever compete with these perfect, crackly-topped, fancy bakery–looking loaves of bread?

The impetus finally came in an announcement. The Brooklyn Kitchen, a recently opened kitchen store whose husband-and-wife owners I had become chummy with, was holding a "No-Knead

Bread-Off." "Come bring your finest loaves using the recipe that has changed the way we think of bread," the invitation from co-owner Taylor read. All right, I thought. It was time.

The thing I liked about Jim Lahey's recipe, as published in *The New York Times*, was that it suggested a little more malleability than most published recipes. It wasn't so much a recipe as a new theory on making bread. Therefore, when it said to let the flour, water, yeast, and salt rest covered for "at least 12 hours, but preferably around 18," I decided to go the extra mile and begin my bread two days before the bake-off. I let it sit there, literally, for around forty-eight hours. I also used an alien ingredient: potato water. While boiling potatoes one day, I thought to myself, why pour all this starchy, potato-flavored water down the drain? I covered it and saved it for a day in the fridge. When I began mixing together my dough for the bake-off, the idea of using this instead of regular water popped into my head.

Thinking black pepper was a good accompaniment to potato, I decided to add some cracked peppercorns to the dough, too. I poured about a half-cup of whole black peppercorns into a Ziploc bag and pressed the air out before sealing it shut. I rolled over the bag with a wooden rolling pin several times, making indentations in the pin while crushing the peppercorns into coarse, cracked pieces. I stirred this into the flour, salt, and yeast in my Dutch oven and added as much potato water as the recipe instructed for regular water. I covered the pot and left it alone until the next day.

When I checked on the pot after coming home from work, I was immediately greeted with a funky, beery odor, about ten times stronger than that of the grayish fizz I had noted when mixing up the yeast for the squash rolls. It was powerful. The dough had spread to an even layer across the bottom half of the pot and was marked with tiny air bubbles on its surface. Studded with the cracked black pepper, it resembled a gooey, bubbling broth of some sort, only the bubbles were stationary, as if frozen in time. It wasn't like anything I had seen or smelled before. I placed the cover back on the pot and left it there for another entire day.

The next night, I uncovered the pot again. The surface of the dough had dried slightly, but there were still air bubbles there. But this time, the stench was almost overbearing. A devastating thought hit me: The potato water had completely rotted. I had a fetid, rotting, decomposing pile of potatoes, flour, and peppercorns. Plus, the dough around each little piece of peppercorn was beginning to take on an unsightly brownish color.

But the bake-off was that night! What was I going to do? There was definitely no time to follow the recipe all over again.

Panicked, I wrote a desperate e-mail to Taylor from the Brooklyn Kitchen.

Um, I was just wondering: my bread smells really bad. I mean, really bad. I left it out for two entire days, instead of just twelve or eighteen hours. Do you think it went bad? Am I going to make people sick? Is there live bacteria in it that can harm someone? Should I not come to the bake-off at all, lest I impart some sort of contagion from myself even without bringing the gross bread?

Taylor wrote back a short while later.

I think it's probably just the normal fermenting process. Yeast is a living thing, you know. Plus, I think a 450-degree oven should definitely kill anything harmful.

Somewhat appeased, I went on with the recipe. Taylor's words made a lot of sense, when I thought about it from a scientific point of view. I'd realized by then that bread making, or good bread making at least, had a lot more to do with actual science than with thinking about flavor combinations or other sensory details. I was never much good at science.

I arrived at the Brooklyn Kitchen later that night toting a large, round loaf of cracked peppercorn potato no-knead bread. The top had mushroomed to a beautifully browned crust, and a deep crack ran across the top. It was fascinating to look closely at this crust and see how the dough had stretched and baked solid just inside that crater. The small, tidy store was located on a quiet block in Brooklyn's Williamsburg neighborhood, which, for better or worse, is known for its youthful hipster scene. I'd met owners Harry and Taylor while writing a piece on the store's opening for a local magazine. They had spoken of plans to hold regular events, cooking demos, classes, and contests like this bread-off, and so far I had gone to almost every one of them.

A group of ten or twelve was clustered around the large counter, where six or seven different-looking loaves of bread were lined up on cutting boards. I was running a little late. I took my loaf out of the bag and handed it over to Taylor, who was slicing the others.

"Wow, looks great!" she said. Then she smelled it for a moment. "Ooh, I see what you mean!" She shrugged and placed it on a cutting board at the end of the table.

My bread, even baked, did indeed give off that fermented, beery smell, but somehow, it was a lot more appealing now that it had been baked. It smelled more or less like . . . bread. Like that smell when you're walking past an industrial bakery. Only now, it was tinged with a peppery spiciness.

Taylor began slicing up pieces of my loaf to put out for everyone.

"What's that?" a few people approached me to ask. When I told them it was just black pepper, their eyes widened, and they eagerly reached for slices.

"This is awesome. Whoo—that pepper is spicy!" said a tall, older man, who had for his part baked a delicious semolina loaf with golden raisins embedded in the dough. I liked my bread, too, which was pleasantly savory and had an airy texture inside and a crackly crust; each bite seemed to have a different-sized explosion of black pepper. I also chatted up my friend Bob, who had baked a rosemary-crusted loaf with olive oil brushed on top before it went into the oven. Taylor had baked a dark, crusty pumpernickel loaf using the no-knead recipe, which tasted earthy and spicy at the same time. I also enjoyed a whole-wheat loaf with cracked grains visible throughout its surface. I ate slice after slice of bread as I mingled with the other contestants and attendees. I'd seen a few of them around at previous events, but most were strangers. Taylor put out an assortment of flavored olive oils to dip the breads in, and a couple of bottles of wine.

"What was in your bread again?" a girl with blond hair and a pink sweater asked me. I told her the ingredients in mine, including the day-old water left from boiling potatoes. She took it down clearly in a notebook, beside a page's worth of notes on all the other breads in the bake-off.

"Are you writing about this for something? A magazine?" I asked her.

"Yes, for *Vogue*," she replied.

"Oh, cool," I said.

"I'm Jeffrey Steingarten's assistant," she added.

I stopped chewing.

"He really wanted to come out to this, but he couldn't make it. So he sent me to check it out," she went on.

"Cool," I repeated, looking at her as if I were looking at a fairy messenger from God.

She introduced herself as Marisa and told me that her boss was writing a piece on Jim Lahey and his no-knead bread for the magazine. She pulled out a business card of Jeffrey's and wrote her e-mail address on the back before handing it to me. I told her I'd look out for the article and wrote down the name of my blog and my contact info on a spare piece of paper (for lack of a business card), telling her that I'd be happy to help answer any questions. Marisa had to leave before the contest winners were announced that night, but she took off with small slices of every loaf of bread in the competition.

"I think we can declare a winner for the 'best overall bready ap-pearance' category," Taylor said, after counting all the folded-up pa-pers spread before her on the counter. "It's the peppercorn one."

A round of applause erupted in the small store, and smiles and nods were shot at me from everyone at the bake-off. Hooray!

"Next, the award for best texture is . . ." Taylor double-checked a couple of scattered papers. "Mine."

We all cheered again. The next award, for best flavor, was handed over to the contestant with the semolina and golden raisin–studded loaf.

"Now we have to take a final vote for the best overall loaf in the contest!" Taylor announced. I managed to dip another two or three slices of bread into olive oil before casting my ballot in the mason jar on the counter. I couldn't get enough of that golden raisin–studded bread; that one got my vote in the best-overall category.

Taylor shook up the jar and then poured all the papers out of it.

"Let's see!" she cried. "Oh, one for the peppercorn bread! Peppercorn again! Whole wheat! Another for the whole wheat! Ooh, semolina raisin!"

Taylor continued to unfold the ballots and put them into stacks, though less verbosely as she went on.

"I think we have a tie!" she finally cried. "So best overall goes to the whole wheat by James, and Cathy's peppercorn bread!"

After another round of applause, and a high-five with James, we were each given a new serrated bread knife with a decoratively etched handle still in its packaging, along with Brooklyn Kitchen refrigerator magnets.

I left the Brooklyn Kitchen that night with a bellyful of starch and an enormously satisfied ego. Who knew that my first attempt at baking a whole loaf of bread—not rolls this time, but a real, bready-looking loaf of bread—would make me a champion bread baker? I was the breadwinner. Or at least one of them that night.

But the real moment of triumph came a few months later. In that time, I had baked so many loaves of no-knead bread, it was hard to put a number on my variations to the recipe. There was always another use for two-day-old or three-day-old bread, too: to make fresh breadcrumbs, or to slice and layer in a casserole dish with sauce, cheese, and other ingredients much like sheets of lasagna. I had made cinnamon-raisin bread once, using Lahey's no-knead recipe, and then I made French toast out of its slices when it had gone stale a couple days later. I made bread with a sprinkle of sea salt baked on its top crust, which Ben liked the most. In fact, every night that I pulled a fresh loaf of bread out of the oven, about half of it was gone by the morning, since Ben couldn't stop eating the oven-hot slices slathered with butter.

I'd use the rest of these loaves for sandwiches throughout the week, or just pop them in the toaster for a quickie breakfast before heading off to work. After the first few tries, I stopped measuring quantities and just began stirring in enough water as the flour, yeast, and salt I'd sprinkled haphazardly into the bowl would allow to make it sticky. It didn't matter—it might taste or rise a little differently each time, but it was still *bread*.

In any case, three months after the bread bake-off at the Brooklyn Kitchen, I walked down the street to my closest newsstand and bought a copy of *Vogue*. The fat issue contained one three-page story that I had spared the $3.99 for. It was written by Jeffrey Steingarten and titled "Easy Riser." The day before, my friend Karol had tipped me off to the fact that it was out on the shelves. "Nice shout-out in the *Vogue* story," she'd written me.

My heart was pounding as I opened the magazine, turned the glossy pages, and finally located the story, one of the last in the perfume-smelling issue. I read all about the food writer's own trials with baking the recipe devised by Lahey. Steingarten came up with a few modifications to the no-knead bread recipe that Lahey had originally published in *The New York Times*. Then I came to the first mention of the Brooklyn Kitchen's contest, stating simply that it had taken place. A few paragraphs down was another mention, and finally, in the author's notes, was this one:

> According to Marisa, most contestants at the bake-off at the Brooklyn Kitchen flavored their breads heavily; I'll admit to enjoying one made with potato water and cracked black pepper and another made with semolina, golden raisins, and fennel seeds, an apparent homage to Amy's Breads best-known loaf, though it had an excessively flat shape.

I put down the magazine and pumped my fist in the air. Someone in a car driving by right then whooped in response. I was seated on the front stoop of my apartment building, having not yet made it inside. I read the sentence again: *I'll admit to enjoying one . . .*

Gosh, he sounded reluctant. But at least he enjoyed mine! I skimmed the rest of the article and came across another slight jab: "Judging from half the entries at the Brooklyn Kitchen bake-off—which were flatter than they should have been—it seemed obvious that some home bakers need more instruction in how to form a loaf."

He was right; most of the loaves were pretty flat at the bake-off. Except for mine! I scuttled my feet on the concrete stair below me.

So, bread: check. I'd baked a loaf that had not only won a kitchen store's contest but had earned the favor of the most respected food critic alive. No more soliciting recipes from friends, readers, friends' moms, cousins, and brothers, I decided right then. If I could bake bread from scratch, kneading or not, I now had the confidence to cook any food in the known world, and even some that weren't yet.

~~~~~~

Peppercorn, Potato, and Parmesan No-Knead Bread

This is a slightly updated version of my winning peppercorn no-knead bread, with a small addition. Who can resist a sprinkle of Parmigiano-Reggiano on top of anything? You won't see an ungolden crust with this trick.   (MAKES 1 1½-POUND LOAF)

> 3 cups all-purpose flour, plus more for dusting
> ¼ teaspoon active dry yeast
> 1½ teaspoons salt
> About 3 tablespoons black peppercorns, cracked (I placed mine inside a Ziploc bag and rolled over it with a rolling pin several times)
> 1⅝ cups water that was used to boil a potato, slightly cooled
> Parmesan

In a large bowl, combine flour, yeast, salt, and pepper. Add water, and stir until blended; dough will be shaggy and sticky. Cover bowl with plastic wrap. Let dough rest at least 12 hours, preferably about 18 (or two days), at warm room temperature, about 70 degrees.

Dough is ready when its surface is dotted with bubbles. Lightly flour a work surface and place dough on it; sprinkle it with a little more flour and fold it over on itself once or twice. Cover loosely with plastic wrap and let rest about 15 minutes.

Using just enough flour to keep dough from sticking to work surface or your fingers, gently and quickly shape dough into a ball, tucking folded parts underneath. Sprinkle and gently pat the grated Parmesan across the top of the loaf. Generously coat a cotton towel (not terry cloth) with flour, semolina, or cornmeal, and place loaf seam-side down on it. Coat another cotton towel with flour and let rise for about 2 hours. When it is ready, dough will be more than double in size and will not readily spring back when poked with a finger.

At least a half hour before dough is ready, preheat oven to 450 degrees. Put a 6–8-quart heavy covered pot (cast iron, enamel, Pyrex, or ceramic) in oven as it heats. When dough is ready, carefully remove pot from oven. Slide your hand under the towel and place dough Parmesan side up in the pot. Cover with lid and bake 20 minutes; then remove lid and bake another 15 minutes, until loaf is beautifully browned. Cool on a rack.

~~~~~~

Sun-Dried Tomato and Zucchini Breadsticks

These breadsticks make a tasty appetizer at dinner parties and are great for bringing to work for snacks. I like using some of the oil that the jarred sun-dried tomatoes are packed with to brush on top of the breadsticks before baking; also, chopped olives would make a nice addition or alternative to the sun-dried tomatoes.

(MAKES ABOUT 9 8-INCH BREADSTICKS)

3½ cups all-purpose flour, plus more for dusting
1 package active dry yeast
2 teaspoons salt
1 tablespoon rosemary
3¾ cups water
4 tablespoons extra-virgin olive oil (or a combination with some of the oil from the jar of sun-dried tomatoes)
1 medium-large (or 2 small) zucchinis, halved lengthwise and thinly sliced
¼ cup sun-dried tomatoes, finely chopped
Sprinkle of sea salt (optional)

In a large bowl, combine flour, yeast, salt, and rosemary. Add water, and stir until blended; dough will be shaggy and sticky. Cover bowl with plastic wrap. Let dough rest at least 12 hours, preferably about 18, at warm room temperature, about 70 degrees.

Heat a sauté pan with about 1 tablespoon of the olive oil over medium heat. Add zucchini and a sprinkle of salt and pepper, and toss and stir until just wilted, about 2–3 minutes. Remove from heat and let cool. Combine with the chopped sun-dried tomatoes in a bowl.

Knead the dough a few times on a lightly floured surface, then divide into roughly nine even pieces. Roll each one out into a thin log about 10 inches long and 2 inches wide. Distribute the zucchini and sun-dried tomato evenly along the length of each breadstick and fold in half lengthwise to close (dough does not have to be fully sealed around the fillings). Carefully twist the breadstick lengthwise a few times. Place them three inches apart on floured cutting boards or cotton towels. Cover with floured cotton towels and let rise for about 2 hours, in a relatively warm place.

Preheat oven to 400 degrees. Lightly oil the bottom of cookie sheets and transfer breadsticks to sheets, placed about 2 inches apart. Brush tops of breadsticks with remaining olive oil and sprinkle with sea salt if desired. Bake for about 20 minutes, or until golden.

CHAPTER 3

Mise en Place

Excellent mise represents the ultimate state of preparedness, whether the physical mise en place of food and tools or the mental mise en place of having thought a task through to the end and being ready for each step of it.

—*Michael Ruhlman*, The Elements of Cooking

Despite all this talk about baking, I've failed to describe the physical surroundings where my not-eating-out mission took place. The kitchen in the small two-bedroom I shared with Erin was more of a hallway between the living room and the bathroom. On one side were a refrigerator and a stove, pushed precariously close to each other. The other side held a sink and a small counter space that fit one person standing before it; it was usually one of us cooking and one of us talking just outside, maybe, but never could we both be actively using the kitchen at the same time. For lack of many drawers or space to put cooking tools, we'd hung a ruffled, red-and-white-striped apron against the wall just below the cabinets. Its front pocket was where we tucked all our wooden spoons, ladles, whisks, and spatulas. The weight from the utensils drew the pocket outward, so that the handles protruded into the counter space, ready to poke me with any move too flagrant.

The air was getting cool by the end of September, reminding me of how soothing it felt to cook when it was cold outside. Prompted by countless nights of staying in and cooking with Erin, I was becoming quite confident in my kitchen skills. I decided it was a good time to bring others into the fold by having guests over—if only because of the fact that there were so many different dishes I wanted to make and not enough mouths to feed them to.

One Friday night when Erin was out at band practice, I invited my friends Richard and Sam over for dinner, along with Ben. Richard and Sam had gone to art school with Ben, and the three of them were longtime friends. Richard was a Web designer, to Ben's print graphic design. His girlfriend, Sam, who often wore her long, curly black hair in braids, was a jewelry designer and freelance painter and sculptor. The couple's true calling, however, might have been hosting barbecues. Over the summer, they'd held more backyard feasts than I could remember, or at least remember in full. Their barbecues generally consisted of the basics: hamburgers, hot dogs, a pit bull trying to steal bites of your hot dog, kabobs, grilled corn on the cob, a table crowded with condiments baking to warm sludge in the hot late-afternoon sun. And plenty of beer. These were the makings of a classic Richard-and-Sam barbecue.

But that fall, I wanted to treat these friends of mine to something altogether new: a quaint four-person dinner at my apartment.

The main course, I'd decided, would be the Taiwanese dish *san bei gi*, paired with some simple sautéed green beans. Translated as "three cup chicken," the dish is a savory braise of chicken with one cup of rice wine, one cup of sesame oil, and one cup of soy sauce, hence the name "three cup." The intense flavor of the dish really came from the smothering portion of fresh Thai basil leaves, whole garlic cloves, and thick strips of ginger that were cooked into the sauce. It seemed like a nice, yet easy dish to kick off the fall with, and since it was so similar to a lot of the stir-fries I learned how to cook from my mother, I figured it would be pretty intuitive to prepare. I secretly hoped my friends wouldn't know this, though, and would be as blown away as I'd been when I experienced the real stuff in Taiwan.

Ben came early with the beer and wine. He began to clear the living room table of the stacks of CDs and mail, something I had neglected to notice in the midst of getting the food prepared.

"Thanks!" I yelled to Ben. Next I put him to work at finding enough chairs from around the apartment to make sure everyone would have a seat. I stared at the stack of stuff I'd piled on the kitchen counter. This was a quick dish to prepare, so I didn't want to start it too early. But I supposed I could get some of the ingredients lined up, ready to toss into the pan. I began slicing the ginger into hearty slabs. The chicken was already portioned out in pieces, a whole cut-up fryer. The authentic version of *san bei gi* was made with small, roughly thumb-sized chunks of chicken legs, which were hacked straight through the bone by a skilled chef or butcher. Once they were cooked, the tender meat surrounding the bone easily fell away with a poke from one's chopsticks or a bite.

I looked at the chicken-leg pieces and looked at my dull, five-year-old knife. It didn't have to be served that way, I decided.

My doorbell rang at eight o'clock on the dot. At the moment, I had raw chicken tenaciously clasped with tongs in one hand and in the other a bottle of beer that I was trying to set down. The sesame oil was splattering away in a large pan on the stove.

"Ben!" I squealed. "You get the door!"

He went downstairs to let them in. A minute later, Richard and Sam were standing in my tight living room, with orangish painted walls and a large square coffee table that took up almost all of its traffic space.

"Should I take my shoes off?" Richard asked.

Just behind him, I noticed the cat rearing its body into a tight, spiky ball.

"Mreeeowww!"

The cat lunged at Richard's ankles, clawing at his laces in three lightning-fast jabs, then quickly scampered into the hallway, stopped, and stared back, as if admiring his work.

I'd been roommates with Erin in many different housing situations, at separate times, beginning with our sophomore year of college. But before we shared this apartment, I'd never lived with her cat, Dracula. She had adopted him as a kitten just a year before, and in the first few days he'd been with her, he'd shown the combative streak that inspired his name. Of course he had been only a cute, cuddly kitten then. Now he was a full-sized, slithering, tiger-coated devil.

"Is there something wrong with your cat?" Sam asked.

I looked at Dracula. His marbled brown-and-black coat shone under the harsh overhead light in the narrow hallway. He had inquisitive eyes, and they were now looking into mine as if to ask whose side I was on—his or theirs. He lowered his hind legs into a clenched position once again and looked ready to spring at any moment.

"Uh, just ignore Dracula," I said. "He's better with new people if you just ignore him."

"His name is Dracula?" Sam asked.

"I was ignoring him. I didn't even know he was there," Richard said.

I muttered an apology, and then remembered the stove. Back in the kitchen, the pan with the chicken quarters I'd dropped in moments earlier was popping with sesame oil going off like firecrackers. I felt a hot, stinging fleck on my wrist as I reached for the tongs.

While Ben got drinks for Richard and Sam and comforted them with stories of how Dracula had also tried to kill him, I went back to work in the kitchen.

San bei gi is a decidedly simple dish, reflected in the way its name sounds almost like a bare-bones recipe itself. One cup of this, one cup of that . . . Like most Chinese stir-fries, it takes a short time to make, although longer in my case since I didn't hack the chicken to small pieces. But with the three even portions of liquids, it comes out looking more like a stew than a stir-fry, and the deep hue of the soy sauce stains everything reddish brown. Once the dish was cooked, it was almost impossible to tell a whole, softened garlic clove from a chunk of chicken that had fallen off the bone.

My first encounter with the dish was at a hole-in-the-wall Taiwanese restaurant in Boston, at the beginning of college. Little did I know at that time that I'd go on to spend several months in Taiwan a couple of years later, for my last semester. I had already taken one semester abroad, in the Netherlands, and from there I traveled throughout Europe. During my time in Taiwan, I traveled to China for a while, too, but mostly took the opportunity to explore the country where my mother grew up. The university I attended was in Taipei, the island's capital, and it was my mother's native city. I'd been there once before, to visit relatives when I was six. I can't remember much of that trip, but by the end of my semester in Taipei, I felt much more connected with the culture—especially the food—of my mother's side of the family.

There are many signatures of Taiwanese cuisine, but *san bei gi* just might be the most famous. I didn't know quite how to describe to Ben what I was making that night, except that it was "really good." (He seemed satisfied with that.) Unlike some of my favorite Taiwanese foods, it wasn't spicy, either, and since I wasn't sure how Sam and Richard felt about spiciness, I figured it was a safe bet. Richard had a passion for grilling the perfect burger; Sam was gifted at making delicious salsas (which she claimed had no secret to them); my forte would be this complex balance of assertive Eastern flavors.

Glancing at the clock, I hoped that this might make up for a bit of wait time. I realized then I hadn't thought to prepare any appetizers.

I lowered the heat on the stove. The chicken pieces had seared and were now impenetrably bound to the bottom of the pan. Pushing them around would only mean ripping the half-cooked flesh from the bones. So I decided to add the garlic, the ginger, and the liquids, and let those kick around for a while, loosening the pan's grip on the chicken. Over the pan I upended a bowl of thick, unpeeled ginger slices and whole garlic cloves that I'd prepared. Guesstimating, I poured in what seemed like equal portions of soy sauce and rice wine.

The oil sputtered, protesting. Then, the pungent, slightly spicy smell of the aromatics softly dissolving in hot oil began to waft throughout the kitchen. I stirred as I waited for the liquid to reach a boil.

I reached into the freezer for one of the beer bottles I'd put on quick-cool. I needed some cooling down myself. Using the hem of my sweater, I twisted off the cap. It clattered onto the floor, and when I reached down to grab it, I noticed Dracula a few feet away, lifting his tail in alert.

Under normal circumstances, I'd have put on a pair of tall boots. These at least protected my lower shins from his claws. I had grown so accustomed to cooking while wearing my tall cowboy boots that Erin had even picked out a floor mat for the kitchen emblazoned with an image of a sultry cartoon cowgirl tipping her hat. Even so, Dracula's claws had a way of striking straight through whatever cloth I happened to be wearing on my upper shins, above the boots—corduroys, jeans, or the short-lived pair of tights. On most nights I was at home, Dracula would prick several little thumbtack-sized holes into my legs before the night was over.

But tonight I had no patience for this cat. I had enough on my hands already with dinner for guests.

"Go!" I whispered, bulging my eyes at his serpentine irises. As if conceding, Dracula sauntered into the living room.

I poked my head into the room. Richard and Sam were sitting on the threadbare love seat, swathed in dim orange light. Ben was seated in a wicker armchair, and the three were engaged in a conversation I couldn't quite make out above the splattering oil. But I didn't see Dracula anywhere.

"Can I help with anything?" Sam asked me.

"Nope, everything's under control." I smiled. I lowered the stove's heat to a simmer and partially covered the pan to cook off some of the liquid.

"Smells good, whatever it is," said Richard.

It did smell good. I wondered whether they were all hungry. I wanted to kick myself for not coming up with something to serve as an appetizer. It had all seemed so simple: Cook up a big pot of something, spread it on the table, and eat. That at least was the way Erin and I had enjoyed our dinners before. When you're cooking, you often get to taste as you go along, having scraps and other little "chef's treats." This time, only I had that privilege.

I suddenly remembered that I needed to get the rice started. I pulled out my old rinky-dink rice steamer from a cabinet; it made a cacophony of clangs as it hit every other pot on its way. I quickly filled it with my approximation for four servings of rice, topped it with some water, and flicked on the COOK switch. A few moments later, I thought it better to play it safe and prepare at least enough rice for six. The steamer coughed up a faint cloud of vapor when I lifted the lid. Holding the bag of rice in one hand, I quickly poured another stream of grains into the bowl, filled the upturned lid of the steamer with some water from the faucet, and clanged it down shut.

Thunk! Thunk! Thunk!

An all-too-familiar pinching sensation warmed three spots on my shin and ankle. I looked down just in time to see Dracula slink away, having sunk his claws into me three times in the mere blink of an eye. I was wearing jeans, but still, without those boots, I could feel my skin welling up with little droplets of blood. The cat was now looking quite cozy, sprawled out on the living room floor as if expecting a nuzzle in return.

"How do you live with that thing?" Richard asked. "I should have brought Amazing over tonight." Amazing, a pit bull terrier, was Richard and Sam's dog.

I scratched my leg.

"Why don't you come over here and stop cooking for a moment," said Ben.

"All right." I glanced at the partially covered pan on the stove; the brown sauce was gently bubbling, and the pan emitted a steady puff of steam from one side.

"So how's your blog going?" Sam asked.

"Oh, it's going. Right now, I'm just trying to get a handle on all the technical stuff," I told them, truthfully.

"Your brother helps with all that, doesn't he?"

"Yep. So it's just a matter of tracking him down on the phone and asking him to fix stuff." I saw that everyone in the room had a drink in their hands but me. I got up to get another beer from the kitchen. Dracula took that as his cue to reenter the living room.

"Don't come any closer," Richard warned. He was waving the cat away with one baggy-panted leg.

"Good kitty," said Ben. No one was convinced.

Dracula slinked into one corner, eyeing each of us dartingly. His predator instinct settled on Sam, and he began to move in on his next target.

"Okay, you can come closer . . . if you want to be nice . . ." Sam offered her hand to the cat, who immediately struck at it.

"Ow!" She frowned at her finger, with its newly acquired claw streaks.

"Maybe it's time he lost his privileges?" Ben suggested.

I nodded in agreement. We'd have to shut him up in Erin's room. I went into the bathroom to search for the Band-Aids. When I came back to the living room, the cat was nowhere to be found.

"He went under the couch," Sam said gloomily.

"Let's wait for him to come out from there, then chase him into Erin's room," Ben finally said after a pause.

"Can I use this broom?" I went into the kitchen and pulled the broom out of the corner. "Maybe it'll help get him out."

"Mm, I don't know about that," said Ben. "You don't want to provoke him any more."

I put it down. We all stood there for a moment, dumbfounded. I could smell the *san bei gi* simmering away. "Why don't we just have dinner first?" I suggested. There were nods all around the room.

I went back to the kitchen and removed the lid from the pan. The chicken was clearly cooked, the drumsticks looked ready to fall off the bone, and the ginger and garlic were soft and red-brown. The rice cooker hadn't yet clicked off to indicate that the rice was fully cooked. In another pan, I heated some oil and a coarsely chopped clove of garlic. I spread some trimmed green beans onto the pan once the oil had begun to pop, added a pinch of salt and pepper, and tossed in some water to quickly braise them.

Sam scooted in to help me. I set her to work getting the plates together and bringing them to the table. Once all the plates were on the table and the drinks renewed, it was time to set out the courses. I took out a large serving bowl from the cupboard, the only one big enough for the main course. Part of a set that Erin and I had bought on the cheap, it had orchard fruits brusquely hand painted around its muddy beige border. I almost laughed at how wrong it looked once the *san bei gi* was poured inside. I'd never before given a second's thought to my tableware when I planned on having people for dinner. To me it was all about the food, but carrying the main course to the table, I realized my first rule of hostessing for the night: how much presentation should play a role.

For lack of another serving bowl, I simply took the rice steamer over to the table and placed a large spoon on top of it for serving. We could just barely fit all of our plates onto the square coffee table with the bowl of *san bei gi* and regular dinner plate that I'd plopped the finished green beans on. So I ended up moving the rice steamer to the floor. Dinner was served.

"Shall we toast?" Ben suggested.

We clinked beer bottles. Everyone looked around the table and at their empty plates, and made a move toward the rice.

"Ouch! This thing is hot," Ben said, brushing his hand against the metal of the rice cooker while piling white tufts onto his plate. My guests awkwardly passed the steamer around the table, being careful not to touch its sides. It didn't make things easier that the rice was filled to the brim, and a bit on the dry side. It looked like I had cooked enough rice to serve at least ten.

This wasn't a very quaint or elegant dinner at all, I thought. Richard and Sam probably weren't expecting a family-style Chinese meal, with communal courses placed in the center of the table, instead of individually plated dishes, either. Why did I think this style would impress my first dinner guests?

But then it happened: People actually looked happy while eating my messy, slurpy, Taiwanese meal.

In between bites, Sam managed to get out, "This is really good," as she scooped up the *san bei gi* and rice with a fork. Richard and Ben echoed her compliments. I was enjoying the food, too, but a creeping sense of failure was still festering inside.

I suddenly cursed under my breath. The basil. I'd forgotten to add it to the chicken. Fresh Thai basil is practically one-third of the dish's seasonings. Without it, it isn't *san bei gi*. I opened the refrigerator door and immediately saw the full container of basil inside. I cursed again.

"What is it?" Ben asked, looking up from his plate.

I heaved a long sigh. "Never mind." No one knew, and it was time to learn another important rule of hostessing: What your guests don't know won't hurt them. Especially if they've already complimented the dish.

As soon as I'd convinced myself my guests would be okay without the basil, I noticed that everyone was pushing their chicken bones to the side of the plate. I wondered whether I should place a bone plate in the middle of the table. Too barbaric?

"I forgot that Ben hates chicken with bones," I remembered aloud, watching him twist his fork into the flesh of a chicken leg as if it were a bowl of spaghetti. I went back to the kitchen and grabbed knives for everyone.

"The bones are supposed to be good for flavor, though, right?" asked Sam.

"Yep. That's why they're kept in. But you can just sort of put a whole piece in your mouth and spit out the bones onto your plate if you want," I suggested, describing the common Chinese way of removing mouthfuls of meat from the bones. Immediately I regretted saying it. I'd apparently crossed some unspoken cultural line; there was complete silence in the room for about a minute, and I didn't get the sense that anyone would be taking me up on this suggestion.

I was piling a second helping of green beans on my plate when I heard the first moan. It was a deep, guttural sound, its tone undulating and sorrow stricken. It didn't sound like a cat at all, really. More like a dolphin. A dolphin in distress.

"Um, Cathy, the cat is crying," Ben said.

"Yeah . . ."

"And it's making hissing noises," Sam added. She was sitting on the love seat, right above where the sharp hissing noise was now coming from.

My first instinct was to bend down and peek underneath the couch. I quickly realized that I shouldn't if I wanted to keep my eyes.

"*Glarrrggg . . . glarrrggg . . . glarrrggg,*" the cat went on, doing his warbly dolphin-moan thing again, this time even louder.

"Is he okay?" asked Ben, his eyebrows furrowed in concern. In all the months I'd known Dracula, I'd never heard him make such noises, either.

"I have no idea. We should really try to get him out of here. He's just afraid of new people." I picked up the broom again. I couldn't wait to get him inside Erin's room and shut the door.

"Uh, what are you going to do with that?" asked Richard suspiciously.

"You know, just sort of nudge him out from underneath there." I placed the bristle end of the broom underneath the couch and gave it a gentle wave. An angry hiss erupted from below.

"It sounds like the devil!" cried Sam.

A marbled paw shot out from beneath the couch and beat three times on the back of Richard's sneaker.

"Holy—!" Richard swung his legs in the air as if he were on a carnival ride.

"*Hissssss!*"

The paw shot out again, this time swatting furiously at the air. Everyone had gotten up from their seats and retreated to the far end of the room. We witnessed three other strikes from the paw against thin air. The furry arm made no appearance for another few moments while everyone watched, breathlessly. I began to move the bristle end of the broom toward the couch. Holding it from the end of its handle, I dipped its bristles underneath the couch again. I felt it just brush against something, the cat, probably.

"*Glaaarrr! Glaaarrr!*" He was wailing loudly now. The dolphin in his throat had been harpooned.

"No, stop. He's freaking out," said Sam.

"He's going to kill us all," said Richard.

"Well." I put the broom aside. "What now?"

"Here, the only way to make him go into Erin's room is to not stand here, waiting for him to get out," said Richard. "Right now he doesn't want to see us when he comes out."

"Okay. So let's wait in the hallway?" suggested Sam.

"Yes, but then he'll have to walk by us on his way to Erin's room," I said.

"Or we could wait in your room?" Richard suggested.

"It only fits a bed," Ben cut in. My room was only a few square feet larger than a double bed.

"Okay . . ."

"We could wait in the nook," I offered.

"What nook?" asked Sam.

"But, Cathy, Dracula's still going to have to walk by us if we wait there," Ben said. The nook was a small alcove at the end of the hallway, just before the door to Erin's room.

"Yeah, but he won't see us in the nook until he's at the end of the hallway, and by then he'll probably just run into Erin's room," I said.

"Or he might turn around and run back here," said Sam.

"Yeah, that's a possibility."

We looked around at one another for a moment.

"Let's do it," I said.

We decided to turn off the lights in the living room and hallway, thinking it might encourage a calmer mood. Taking our beers along with us, we headed for the nook. It was imperative to stay silent so that the cat wouldn't know our whereabouts. We quietly moved aside some boxes and a chair that were crowding the nook and got settled in.

We sat there for five minutes, tuning in for any sound of the cat coming near. I took a slow sip from my beer. The only sounds in the whole apartment were from little waves of beer every time a bottle was tilted to someone's mouth. This was ridiculous, I thought. My first dinner party had turned into some strange urban safari with *very* dangerous wildlife prowling around. I tried hard not to laugh. Then Richard's eyes widened. Sitting across from me, he had the clearest view of the hallway.

"He's coming," he mouthed. A minute or two passed. I narrowed my eyes at Richard's, as if to ask, "Are you sure?"

Very softly, the cat stepped into view. He stopped. I was afraid he might pounce. We turned our gazes to each other, the ceiling, anywhere but at Dracula. Out of my peripheral vision, I saw the cat slowly lift a paw and take a hesitant step. Again he stopped. He turned to face the four of us for a moment, as if trying to place who we were. This is it, I thought. We were like sitting ducks in that nook. I thought of all the scratches and puncture wounds on my shins and tried to imagine how they would look on arms, neck, and face. Finally, he took another few steps and sauntered casually into Erin's bedroom.

Everyone looked at me with bulging eyes. I could read their expressions instantly: *Shut the door behind him now!*

I tiptoed toward the door. I had to reach into Erin's room to grab the knob, then swing it back toward me to close the door. A swish of air hit my face as it swung shut, trapping the cat inside.

We all erupted with a cheer.

"Oh, my God . . . finally!" Sam sighed, lifting herself from the floor wearily. Ben's face looked completely drained, as if he'd been holding his breath for the last five minutes. Maybe he had been.

I flipped the lights back on. We put on some music. I cleared the finished plates from the coffee table.

"Thanks a lot for dinner; it was really good," Richard said.

I shrugged. It would have been better with the basil, I thought.

Whoops, and maybe dessert. For some reason, the notion of dessert had completely slipped my mind in planning the dinner. And with that, I made a mental note of hostessing rule number three: Guests might appreciate more than a piece of chocolate or a leftover cookie for dessert after a dinner party. For the time being, though, I took another beer out of the fridge.

Standing around the cat-free living room, we all shared another toast.

"To many happy not-eating-out nights. Hopefully none of them like this one," Ben offered.

"To Erin, for taking care of Dracula," said Richard.

"And me, for living with him," I added.

"And you said that he never attacks Erin?" Sam said.

I nodded. I'll never understand cats.

As the empty beer bottles piled up in the bin, metal caps crowded the tabletop, and we continued to chat, our conversations the rest of the night somehow never ventured far from Dracula.

"I'm going to have to get Amazing to come over here and show up Dracula," said Richard.

"Stop, you've already said that three times," Sam said, rolling her eyes.

When they were finally ready to start their long walk home, Ben and I accompanied Sam and Richard to the door.

"So . . . should we do this again?" I asked jokingly.

"Only if I bring Amazing," said Richard.

"No, definitely, though. The dinner was awesome." Sam smiled.

We said good night. I looked on sadly after the door was closed.

"So they had the night of the cat," I mused.

"Yep," Ben said. Noticing that I hadn't been smiling, he added, "But dinner was very good."

I frowned, knowing that it hadn't been all that I'd hoped. Ben gave me a little hug.

Later, as I thought about all the things I could have done better, I had to hand it to restaurants for creating not only great food but distinctive atmospheres that heightened the food's sense of importance—and the diners' sense of self-importance. We couldn't have lowered ourselves that evening any more than by using our animal instincts to dodge a predator.

When dining at home, there is no room for illusions. I'd have to get used to that, no matter how much I managed to improve my entertaining know-how in the future. Entertaining at home will always throw wild cards at you—a noisy neighbor, forgotten ingredients, or a killer cat. But it also allows you to loosen up and put your elbows on the table—or coffee table—if you like, and fight back against that killer cat. So I had a little room to grow at entertaining guests. Unlike a rejected restaurant, though, I knew that my friends would come back again.

I didn't see any reason to keep Dracula cooped up in Erin's room once Sam and Richard had left, so I opened the door. I saw Dracula for a glimpse once more that night, while heading to my room to shuck off to sleep. He, too, was sleepy-looking and serene, curled up on the couch just as innocently as a kitten.

Late that night when Erin came home, I could hear her cooing and snuggling with him through the closed door of my room. A thought crossed my mind somewhere in between sleep and consciousness. It had something to do with reports I'd read in newspapers about cheap restaurants cooking up stray cats instead of chicken. For a moment, I could almost understand why.

Hearts of Palm Crostini

Since the dinner party in this chapter, I've come to rely on a few simple appetizers that keep guests from starving while I'm cooking. This one needs little preparation other than slicing the hearts of palm and scooping them onto the bread slices. Yet it's always been a hit. (MAKES ABOUT 24 PIECES)

> 1 French baguette, sliced into ½-inch rounds
> 1 15-ounce can hearts of palm, thinly sliced crosswise
> ¼ cup Italian flat-leaf parsley, finely chopped
> 1 teaspoon fresh lemon juice
> 1 tablespoon extra-virgin olive oil
> Sprinkle of salt and freshly ground black pepper

Preheat oven to 400 degrees. Place the baguette rounds in a single layer on baking sheets and bake for about 5 minutes, or until lightly toasted. Remove and let cool completely before topping.

Combine all the rest of the ingredients in a bowl (can be made a day ahead). Top each toasted baguette slice with a spoonful of the hearts-of-palm mixture. Serve immediately.

Red-Curry-Glazed Roasted Eggplant

Another great party snack with a bold flavor. These eggplant bites can be served with toothpicks or placed on top of crostini or seeded crackers for a bit of crunch.

(MAKES ABOUT 4 APPETIZER-SIZED SERVINGS)

2 medium shallots, chopped
1 large garlic clove, minced
2 teaspoons grated fresh ginger
2 teaspoons red curry paste
1 teaspoon fish sauce
2 teaspoons sugar
1 teaspoon soy sauce
¼ cup vegetable oil
4 long Asian eggplants, halved lengthwise and chopped
    into about 2-inch pieces

Combine all the ingredients except the eggplant in a food processor or blender. Transfer to a container with a lid and enough room to fit the eggplant pieces. Toss the eggplant in the sauce until fully coated by covering container and shaking. Let marinate for about 15 minutes before roasting.

Preheat oven to 400 degrees. Spread eggplant pieces across an oiled baking sheet. Bake for about 8 minutes or until crisp on the edges. Remove carefully with a spatula and let cool a few minutes before serving.

Boneless *San Bei Gi* with Green Beans

I recommend trying the classic version of this Taiwanese dish, but this bastardization using boneless strips of chicken and the addition of green beans for a complete meal has been a popular and tasty variation that many have found easier to digest. (SERVES 4)

3 pounds boneless chicken breasts and/or thighs, sliced
    against the grain to ¼-inch-thick pieces
1 tablespoon cornstarch
⅓ cup soy sauce
⅓ cup plus 2 teaspoons sesame oil
20 cloves of garlic, smashed or coarsely chopped
20 slices of fresh ginger
⅓ cup rice wine
3 tablespoons sugar
1 pound green beans, ends trimmed and snapped in half
    to roughly 2–3-inch pieces
2 scallions, chopped
2–3 dried whole red chilies (optional)
1 large bunch Thai basil leaves
Rice for serving

Mix chicken pieces in cornstarch and 2 teaspoons of soy sauce in a bowl. Cover and chill to marinate at least 30 minutes, or up to overnight.

In a large nonstick pan, heat sesame oil with the chilies, garlic and ginger until oil just begins to bubble. Add chicken and stir to brown pieces on all sides a little bit. Add rice wine, remaining soy sauce, and sugar. Stir until boiling, then cover. Let simmer on medium-low 8 minutes or slightly longer if using chicken with bones. Add the green beans and basil and stir the pan to evenly distribute them. Cover partially and continue cooking for 5 minutes. Add scallions and toss once more. Serve with white rice.

CHAPTER 4

Chilaquiles and Meringues

COOKING QUIRKS AND CHARACTERISTICS

The way a man cuts his meat reflects his life.

—*Chinese proverb*

A blotted canvas tarp was heaped in the center of the room. On top of it stood a paint-speckled three-step ladder with a can of white paint and a toolbox at its feet. The rest of the hardwood living room floor was bare, and so was the front of the cupboard in the bathroom. It smelled of fresh paint in the apartment, and I got the feeling that someone had just been inside it a short time ago.

Our new landlord had assured us that the apartment Ben and I were moving into would be ready by November first. About a week before the move-in date, he called me to see if we could move on the fifteenth instead. Actually, we didn't have a choice—his contractors hadn't finished the renovation. This sent off a wave of complications involving subletters, tricky math regarding our rent payments, and inconvenient timing—the fifteenth fell in the middle of the week. And now, at eleven o'clock on a Wednesday night, we stood in our new one-bedroom apartment, a van full of our stuff and three friends waiting outside.

A short month and a half ago, Ben and I had made the decision to move in together. Neither of us had really thought about leaving behind our old living situations before; I couldn't have asked for a better roommate than Erin, and Ben loved his old neighborhood and apartment, which he also shared with just one roommate. But with the way we had been living for the past few months—together, essentially—a dramatic change seemed inevitable. Wary that we were burdening our roommates with a part-time third roommate, and prompted by the fact that our leases were due for renewal at the same time, we began looking for our own place.

Neither Ben nor I had ever lived with a significant other before. It had been somewhat nerve-wracking to think about at first, but once Ben and I started finding apartments that we liked and envisioning the new situation, it all seemed like it was meant to be. I'd started a new job that month, too. Finally I'd no longer be manning the office of a busy executive, taking phone calls and pushing papers around; instead I was working as a copywriter for a clothing company, where I had the chance to flex some creativity. It was a step in the right direction for me, and of course, I was still cooking and blogging away in the meantime. Ben helped me refresh my website with new graphics that he'd designed. There were plenty of changes that fall.

When we went to see the one-bedroom that we eventually rented, we immediately loved its old-fashioned details and the historic block of mansions the building was situated on. We also loved the neighborhood, Fort Greene, Brooklyn. It had a farmers' market, a beautiful park, and a diverse community, yet the influx of trendy restaurants that were beginning to dot its main street told of its recent gentrification. We began imagining how we'd decorate our place, and collecting household odds and ends while checking off a list of items that we'd now have two of so we could discern which was better. But as we stood there, stunned at the scene when we opened the apartment door as tenants for the first time, our elation hit the floor.

After many harried trips up and down the block with our friends helping, we managed to move all our stuff into the center of the living room, and called it a night. The next morning, I discovered a new problem with the apartment. When I called the gas company to register for service, the rep was confused.

There was no record of our particular unit in the building in their
files. But it had been occupied for the past twenty-five years, by
the same tenant right until we moved in. How could this be, we
asked?

It turned out the previous tenant had had the gas turned off
for some twenty years. Before it had been renovated, the kitchen
hadn't even had a working stove. We'd seen how spare and de-
crepit the old kitchen in the apartment had been on our first walk-
through of the space, before the contractors gutted it and installed
new appliances. Unless he was remarkably handy with a microwave, it was pretty clear that the previous tenant had never really
cooked at home. So there I was on my first day in the new place,
flicking the round knobs of the stove fruitlessly.

"Maybe you should give yourself a break. Let's order a pizza or
something," Ben suggested.

We were unpacking. The tarp and tools that were on the floor
the night before had been removed mysteriously sometime during
the day, while we were at work. Here and there little tasks had been
hastily finished off, like the addition of the mirror on the bathroom
cupboard. We had a huge chore on our hands between unloading
our stuff and arranging the place, and I had to admit, the takeout
option sounded pretty tempting. But I shot Ben an annoyed glare
instead. He shrugged and went back to ripping boxes open.

I'd picked up a package of frozen gyoza dumplings and
edamame beans from a Korean grocery on my way to the subway
after work. Heating them up had been my idea of a quickie, short-
cut meal. Now they sat stiffly on the counter, impossibly frozen
through. We didn't own a microwave—neither Erin nor I could
find much reason to get one at our old place, and the microwave at
Ben's old apartment had belonged to his roommate. I looked at the
polished, never-before-used stove. How was I going to cook these
things? I'd never felt so eerily out of my element before. How did
humans accomplish anything without fire?

I watched Ben unloading a cardboard box of kitchen tools. He
lifted one of my towel-wrapped knives out of a box, then pulled out
my shoddy plastic coffeemaker. Then it hit me: the rice cooker. It
had a steaming tray inside, and it ran purely on electricity.

After that first night of steamed dumplings and edamame, we
had to wait an excruciating week and a half before the gas com-

pany could properly install a connection to our unit. I survived the week by eating a lot of salad, bread, cold cheeses, fruits, and cured meats. I'd bring sandwiches or chopped salads to work. But every now and then, I had a hankering for something hot.

One of my favorite comfort foods growing up, and also one of the first foods I can remember eating, was a bowl of foamy steamed eggs. Its custardlike texture and bubbly, yellow froth that clung to the sides of the bowl it was cooked in was unlike anything else in the world. It was essentially half eggs, half water, gently seasoned with salt and white pepper, and every spoonful of egg came with a hot slurp of water. My mom said it was a common Chinese baby food, since it was so soft. Because I had only the steamer to cook with that week, I remembered the comfort food and began steaming scrambled eggs, sometimes with bits of chopped vegetables and cold cuts like ham scrambled in. I made steamed omelettes, deliciously soupy and hot—perfect for the early fall.

I shared some of my first batch with Ben. He decided he preferred traditional scrambled eggs cooked on a pan but ate it anyway. When we were living apart, I never imposed my eating-in-only diet on Ben, and I didn't plan to now that we were living together. But it was clear now that whenever I was cooking at home, there would always be another mouth to feed. And that mouth had a different palate from mine.

My life changed profoundly when I bought an ice-cream maker that fall. Beforehand, Ben and I would walk down to the corner convenience store for snacks at night. Usually, it was ice cream. We'd lean over the slide-top freezer chest, arguing over what flavor to choose from the many pint-sized cartons of Häagen-Dazs and Ben and Jerry's, and how much fat it should have, to the amusement of our neighbor, a Korean couple who owned the small store. Then we'd compromise—sort of—and bring home our icy treat. These pints cost $4.25 each. Now, thanks to the $50 ice-cream maker, I was making vanilla-bean-speckled premium ice cream with a splash of Bourbon, coffee ice cream, green tea and honey ice cream, or fresh peach or mango frozen yogurt by the quart. After I'd learned how to make an ice-cream base, the sky was the limit. We always had at least two quart containers of homemade ice cream in the freezer after that purchase.

I also bought a food processor, which I used a lot at first to make chickpea hummus. Finding that chickpeas didn't need to be the only type of bean dip in the world, I began creating other spreads, dips, sauces, and pestos using the food processor. With these tools, I had lots of treats in storage at any given time, either in the freezer or in the refrigerator. Thawing a bit of pesto or fresh tomato sauce to mix with pasta, I found, made for an easy route to dinner, as did slathering some hummus on bread with veggies for lunch.

I learned how to pickle in mason jars from my friend Bob, who had recently launched his own pickling business, McClure's Pickles, with his brother. Soon I had reserves in my fridge of homemade pickled radishes, Brussels sprouts, and any vegetable I could see fit to brine. Other DIY kitchen experiments of mine were less successful. One friend gave me her yogurt cultures after she decided she didn't have the patience to tend to them daily anymore. After dutifully adding milk and straining the curds from the whey each night for a while, I found that I didn't have the patience, either. Neither did I particularly enjoy the runny, excessively sour character of homemade yogurt.

My mother came to visit our apartment one day and was awed to find, stacked on top of the kitchen cupboards, the food processor and ice-cream maker. I suppose our extra coffeemaker had added to the scene, because she cried, "You have so many gadgets!"

What a transformation, I thought, that this apartment, once occupied by an old man who for decades never even boiled water on his stove, was now inhabited by a young couple who had kitchen gadgetry on display and a dire need for that kitchen to work properly.

We had an upstairs neighbor who was quite a character. His name was Harvey, and he was the first person I met in the building and the most visible one on a regular basis. Harvey lived alone and worked on his paintings at home during the day. When he wasn't at work, he was undoubtedly chatting beside someone at a coffee shop down the street, or on another neighbor's front stoop. He was a thin man, probably in his seventies, with feathery white hair and thick glasses. He had an unpredictable temper, which I'd learned about after a couple of skirmishes between him and our landlord.

But the rest of the time, he had an affecting kindness to his voice, like that of a kindergarten teacher. And if you allowed him to, he could keep you talking for hours.

I'd often run into Harvey on the front steps of our building, as he was coming indoors with a pair of weighted-down plastic grocery bags at his sides. I could tell from the frequency of these grocery excursions that Harvey cooked, unlike his friend who had lived in the apartment that Ben and I now occupied. I often wondered what kind of groceries Harvey was carrying. Eggs? Milk? Bread? Things that went bad quickly, or had to be replenished regularly? Maybe he liked shopping for groceries so often just to see what items were marked down that day, a habit of my late paternal grandfather's, who was legendary for his frugality. At the coffee shop, Harvey would nurse a single cup of coffee for hours, holding court at a table as friends, acquaintances, and new conversation partners came and went. Though they served pastries and sandwiches at the café, for all the hours he spent there, I'd never seen Harvey eat a single bite.

"I always see you coming in and out with groceries," Harvey said to me one night, as we ran into each other at the stoop. I'd smiled and said yes, not knowing what else to say.

Other times we'd linger and talk longer. Harvey once told me, with alternating fury and pride, the story of how he and the five other tenants who'd lived in the building for several decades had triumphed over their landlord's attempt to raise their rent. The building had been rent-controlled ever since our current landlord's parents lived in it. This couple had raised their children in the building, and according to Harvey, had "just wanted to have nice neighbors." That was it. They weren't greedy. But after they passed away, their son, now our landlord, wanted to adjust all the tenants' rents drastically to bring it up to modern real estate standards. They went to court, and after many months, the tenants won, leaving the two parties bitter. They would be forever bickering about management issues large and small, I'd learn through my months of living there, either from passive-aggressive announcements issued from our landlord or further rants from Harvey. "I've been living here for my entire adult life," Harvey had said once. He'd gone to Pratt, the art school a few blocks away, to study painting. "We were the people who made this neighborhood interesting," Harvey said.

"Well, I've got to get going," I told Harvey one night, holding up my tote bag filled with groceries to indicate that they needed to get cooked. He smiled and nodded.

"You have a good night, Cathy," he said, allowing me to pass through the doorway. "Tell Ben I said hello, too."

Ben and I joked that Harvey was like the king of the block. His presence on stoops and sidewalks, in hallways and at coffee-shop tables, was nearly constant, and confirmed his popularity in the neighborhood. I worried about who would help Harvey cook and buy groceries once he became too old to do it on his own. Once, he'd asked Ben to help him take down some huge ceiling plants in an apartment belonging to Harvey's friend down the street, which he was house sitting. I hoped that many friends would be ready to spring to his aid when that time came. For now, though, he was defiant and independent, doing his laundry, cooking his meals, living his life very much his own way within his five-block radius.

Ben and I were invited over for brunch at Sam and Richard's one Sunday. To repay us for the dinner at my old apartment, they planned to make us one of our favorite foods that morning, *chilaquiles*. Ben had been going through a lot of restaurant withdrawal lately, and one of his favorite places for brunch was a Mexican restaurant that specialized in *chilaquiles con huevos*. We'd eaten it there probably more than a dozen times. The brunch entree came in a steaming individual casserole. Underneath two soft poached eggs were crisp corn tortilla strips steeped in a bubbling green tomatillo sauce and connected by stringy, melted cheese.

Despite how exotic and enticing this dish seemed to Ben and me, *chilaquiles* were, according to Sam, one of the simplest of leftover dishes in her native Mexico—a peasant food, really. It was just another way of using up any scraps left over from previous dishes (bits of shredded meat were often thrown in, if one should be so lucky as to have any), and day-old tortillas really were the best for soaking in all these juices and flavors while retaining some measure of density. Whatever it was, we were eager to try Sam's homemade version.

Also due for a dining-in date with us were our friends Sean and Meredith. They had recently moved just a few blocks away, and coincidentally invited us over for dinner the evening of our Sunday brunch at Sam and Richard's. It would be a back-to-back day of being served homemade food by our friends, hence, no cooking on my part for an entire day. I couldn't remember when I'd last had that leisure.

When we got to Richard and Sam's apartment, the entire kitchen was steaming. It was autumn, but the kitchen smelled like a taco joint in the middle of a Mexican heat wave. Sam's normally wavy black hair was matted to her forehead in frizzy curls as she stood by the sink, rinsing her hands.

"Whatever you do, don't fry in the morning," she said as she greeted me.

I looked at the counter and saw piles of crisped tortilla strips lying on paper towels. Evidently she meant business when she said she was making *chilaquiles* the authentic way—the corn tortillas were freshly fried at home. We sat down and brought out the orange juice and seltzer water we'd bought at the corner store on the way over. As we talked, I watched Sam layer a large casserole with the chips and ladle a green tomatillo sauce on top. I got up to take a closer look and offered to help, but she insisted there was little else to do.

"What kind of cheese is that?" I asked as I saw her slicing up rounds from a soft white brick.

"It's just mozzarella. The real cheese they would use is *queso blanco*, but since it's not in most grocery stores, this is the closest thing. It's pretty much the same thing." She shrugged.

With my limited experience in Mexican cooking—real Mexican, mind you, not Tex-Mex, not nachos supreme—I wouldn't have thought to opt for the familiar Italian American pizza cheese. I admired her anything-goes nature.

She next retrieved a Tupperware container filled with shreds of pink-colored meat and began to place chunks throughout the casserole.

"I made roast pork the other night, so this is just some leftovers," she explained nonchalantly. She left a small portion in the plastic container. "I'll save some to top this with once it's out of the oven."

I helped clear some dishes off the counter and put them into the sink as Sam popped the casserole into the oven. Meanwhile, a pot was still heating over a low flame on the stove.

"What's that?" I asked.

"Black beans," said Sam, lifting the top to reveal a mass of shiny, purple-black beads bubbling in a viscous broth. "You serve them with pretty much everything. These ones were actually half leftovers, half new ones, after I realized I had some from the other night. So some of them are going to be more cooked than the others. Oh, well."

Fifteen minutes later, she declared it was time to eat.

"God, I'm so hungry," Sam said as she plopped herself down at the table. A plate of *chilaquiles* and black beans was set before each of us. The assembly had been simple: a scoop from the casserole of *chilaquiles* on one side, and a scoop of the black beans flush against it. On top of the *chilaquiles* Sam had placed a few thinly sliced rings of onion, the warmed extra shredded pork from the leftovers, and a dusting of *cotija* cheese.

I took my first taste of the beans, which were salty and hearty. I could be happy just eating a plate full of those. But I quickly moved on to the *chilaquiles*. Sam's homemade tortillas crackled in my mouth, and the small explosion was followed by the sharp tang of the tomatillo sauce.

"Oh, wow," said Ben, wiping his mouth.

"Like it?" Richard asked.

We both nodded ecstatically. Sam, being modest, just shrugged and shoveled the food into her mouth. There was plenty of food for seconds, which we all helped ourselves to. From watching her layer the casserole to observing her garnishing it once it was baked, I was keeping tabs on every step of the process, thinking of how I might make it myself. But there was one key element I'd missed out on observing: the tomatillo sauce.

"How come you always see green sauce with *chilaquiles*?" I asked Sam.

"You don't have to; you can make it with red chili sauce if you want. Doesn't matter," she said. "Just whatever you have on hand."

I appreciated this flexibility, but there was no way I'd have either tomatillo or red chili sauce left on hand very often.

Ben and I went back home an hour or so later, patting our tummies and thanking our friends profusely for an excellent meal. It was already midafternoon by the time we left, after lingering and talking at the table awhile. We'd have to regain our appetites for Sean and Meredith's dinner by not eating for the rest of the day.

Sean and Meredith were late eaters. On typical weeknights, they both worked until at least eight or so, we'd learned of their late patterns over the month or so of becoming neighbors. Sometimes the phone would ring at eleven o'clock, Sean asking us if we wanted to come for a round of cocktails, or to try some cake he had just pulled out of the oven. So when Sean called to apologize that he and Meredith were running a little behind for our scheduled eight o'clock dinner that Sunday, Ben and I weren't surprised. After another call to push back the start time, we finally arrived at their apartment around nine thirty. When we stepped in, Sean was standing in the kitchen with his hands in his pockets and Meredith was holding an unopened bag of carrots. They were both dressed impeccably, even though it was the weekend, Sean in his typical suspenders, bowtie, and dress shirt beneath an apron and Meredith in a ruffled blouse and buttoned cardigan.

"Those just need to be cut up," Sean told her, nodding toward the carrots.

"Like how? In strips? Discs?" she asked.

"Discs," he said.

I asked if I could help with anything, but Sean assured us they had everything under control. I handed him a bottle of white wine that we'd picked up on our way over.

"Oh, thanks. I'll pop that in the fridge," he said, and swung open the refrigerator to squeeze it against two other white wine bottles on the door.

Sean and Meredith had moved into their place only a few weeks before, and the spacious living room had the appearance of a hobby shop filled with antique clothing and horse-riding memorabilia. An old jockey helmet was placed here, on the wall, a Gatsbyesque straw hat there on a stack of books. Boxes of more books lay in the center of the living room floor, a few thick ones with marble-painted sides placed on top and opened to ecru-colored pages. Cooking magazines littered the single wicker-framed couch, many of them opened to a page with a recipe. The walls had been decorated with old photographs and paintings with antique frames, while other framed art leaned against the walls, yet to be hung. And taking up one large card table just outside the kitchen was Sean's liquor collection. He picked up a bottle of red wine and showed it to us.

"I just picked this out the other day. It looked amazing. It's from this tiny little vineyard in Austria that you couldn't get anywhere else in the States before. So I got two bottles of it," he said, pointing to an identical bottle on the floor. They both were unopened, as were most of the other dusty bottles underneath the square side table. Some were cut-glass flasks with different-colored liquors, and the whole collection of bottles spilled out to the living room floor, well beyond the margins of the table. He pointed to a bottle of liquor with a warm golden hue.

"I also got corn whiskey," Sean said, picking it up and bringing it to his eye level as if holding a newborn baby. "I just love the color of it."

He put the bottle down, then clapped his hands and looked at us expectantly. "Can I fix you a drink?"

Ben and I eagerly accepted. As Sean set about fixing us old-fashioneds, first reaching for a vintage ice crusher with a manual hand crank, we seated ourselves at a drawing table in the living room.

"Oh—yeah, I guess we can use that for dinner. We don't really have a dining table, but that should do," Sean said.

Meredith came over to clear a few books off the table and went back to chopping carrots on a cutting board she placed on her lap, while sitting in a chair. The counter was covered with bags of produce and kitchen tools that Sean was using. At the stove, a wide pan was bubbling with a fragrant sauté.

Sean presented us with two cocktails expertly filled to the rims of the glasses, which were frosted on the outsides, having been chilled in the freezer.

"I made them a little strong, so watch out," he warned.

"So what are you cooking tonight?" I asked him.

"It's a recipe that I tried once; it was in *Gourmet*. It's called tarragon chicken. Really nice, because you can really taste the tarragon, which is something I never really tried much of with anything else before," Sean explained.

He scooped crème fraîche from its container into a measuring cup.

"It smells wonderful," Ben added.

"Oh, yeah, and sorry it's taking so long. I just realized that it needs to be served with rice, and I forgot to make it until about two minutes ago."

We waved our hands, signaling that it was all okay. But by this time, I was starting to feel my stomach churn with hunger. It was funny; in all the time I was cooking for myself—or for myself and others—I'd forgotten what it felt like to not be in control of when exactly I ate. It suddenly came back to me: the anticipatory minutes of sitting in a restaurant, waiting for your meal, hoping that the waiter who just emerged from the kitchen was coming over to your table.

We sat and chatted for a while about our day, telling Sean and Meredith about our brunch with Sam and Richard.

"I guess we can start with some cheese," Meredith said. She swished around in the kitchen for a bit and came back with a platter of crackers and three different wedges of cheese.

"Oh, and is that Brie still in the oven?" Sean suddenly said.

"Yes," said Meredith. "Oops."

The two of them scrambled around to find hot pads and finally pulled a large, uncovered casserole tray out of the oven. On it was a bubbling wedge of Brie surrounded by a thick orange sauce.

"What is this?" Ben asked.

"I just love this. We've made it before a couple of times. It's just baked Brie with mango sauce. It's a little overcooked right now, but it's the best thing ever on crackers," Meredith explained.

"How do you make the mango sauce?" I asked.

"Oh, you can just buy it in a jar. It's just two things, really, cooked together." She took a spreader and spread a mixture of the melted Brie and some of the mango sauce on a seeded flatbread cracker. Ben and I followed her lead and dug in. The hot mango sauce mingled with the mild cheese in my mouth as it went down with the crunch of the cracker.

"It's delicious," I said.

Our dinner was served about twenty minutes later. On my plate was a helping of white rice topped with boneless chicken in a creamy, fresh tarragon–flecked sauce. A heap of soft carrot slices spiced lightly with grated cinnamon lay on the other side. The portion was generous, and I ate heartily.

"This is the kind of food you just want to keep spooning up,"

Meredith commented, after we had all congratulated the chef. "It's just so soothing, and mushes together really well." We agreed.

After our plates were cleared, Sean came back to the table bearing what looked at first to be a tall, iced wedding cake. When he put it down I noticed that the icing on it was stiff, like a gingerbread house's.

"Viennese meringue pie," he declared. It looked like a fairy had made it appear with a swish of her wand. On top, the meringue had been dolloped in spokes toward the center, finished with a piped tube around the rim. Once cut into, the crisp, yet light surface gave way to a cognac-spiced whipped cream with fresh blueberries and blackberries embedded inside.

We left dinner that night completely filled up, boozed up, and saturated with anecdotes on European culinary history, as well as everything from men's fashion to 1980s British comedy TV. Sean was a men's neckwear designer by day, and we had also gone to the same college together. Over dinner, we shared a few stories about characters from those days as well. Meredith worked in public relations, and she hadn't attended school with any of us at the dinner. Often when I was with Ben and Richard and Sam, I felt as if talk about their old college days dominated conversations. It was a refreshing change of pace to experience the opposite this time.

As we walked home, I thought about how different the two hosting methods had been that day. There was no mistaking that both meals were terrific—delicious, made with care, and sprinkled with personal touches. But Sam's laissez-faire attitude about exactitudes couldn't be more different from Sean's recipe-following cooking style. Over dinner, he'd shown me the recipes for each of the dishes he'd cooked, pointing out exactly what steps he'd found the most interesting or had fumbled on. Details were everything when it came to Sean. They defined how the pattern of one near-identical tie differed from that of another—patterns the normal, non-tie-designer eye wouldn't be able to tell apart. I thought about Sam for a moment, and her artwork. All the sculptures and jewelry she made looked fluid, loosely connected, and organic somehow. She wove metal mesh by hand into naturally lopsided rings, or irregular icicle-shaped necklaces, or earring pendants that hung from a chain.

"Cooking can say a lot about a person's character," I said to Ben later on that night.

I began wondering what my cooking might reveal about me, or vice versa. What was my cooking style? Aside from the fact that I didn't eat in restaurants, was there any type of food that defined me?

At this point in my experiment, I had grown accustomed to cooking every day. I looked forward to it—I'd dream up recipes during the day, or browse recipes or food stories on the Internet. Then I'd buy some ingredients and spend the rest of the night enjoying the new process, the ingredients, or the flavors. If I was too busy, or simply wasn't up to a night of serious recipe making, I'd throw together something light and easy—like pasta with a few chopped-up vegetables and grated cheese, or a stir-fry of one meat and one veggie over rice. I found the simplicity of these dishes satisfying, too, and knowing I could always whip up one or another of these gave me the strength to bluster on.

Ben offered little more than a shrug in response. He wasn't a hobbyist cook himself, so the rare times he did make a spaghetti dinner with jarred pasta sauce, or a bowl of cereal, said very little about his character. But Ben wasn't completely undomestic, either. He had an eye for design, while I had none. So he took it upon himself to do all the careful arranging and decorating of our apartment. Within a week of moving in, he'd painted one wall off-white with thick, beige vertical stripes. He projected an old photograph of cross-country bicyclists on another wall and painted over the projection to create a mural. The rest of the walls were filled with framed art, and he'd picked out furniture to mesh with the setting. The way I would have furnished an apartment on my own would have been to dump a chair I found on the sidewalk here, a table I found on the sidewalk there, until the place just barely resembled a room. I guess that doesn't say very much for my taste or character except that I'm lazy and very thrifty.

During the next few months, I found myself wanting to cook with more meaning somehow. Currently, the recipes on my blog were of all different types of food, usually ones that I had never made before and was trying out for the first time, to varying levels of success. I wanted to find more of a niche, to hone in on some sort of focus in my cooking. Was it budget friendly? Time saving? Earth friendly, perhaps? Maybe I'd try to think about all those things a little more from now on, and see where that went. I also wanted to discover more about the idea of cooking, or not eating out, from other voices, like my friends, but also people whom I didn't know. I wanted to see what they expressed through what they were cooking, meet them, get to know them through food. There had to be plenty of people out there who were cooking at home often, and might be doing so for purposes beyond just eating. These were the types of people I wanted to meet soon.

~~~~~~

Smoky Black Bean and Spinach *Chilaquiles*

This is a savory vegetarian version of chilaquiles with black beans (which Sam served on the side with hers), and a deep red ancho chili sauce. Swap in cooked (or leftover) shredded chicken, pork, or any other meat in place of the beans if you like.

(MAKES 3–4 SERVINGS)

1 15-ounce can black beans, rinsed
About 3 medium-sized dried ancho chilies
3 cups water
1 tablespoon vegetable oil
1 large shallot, finely chopped
1 jalapeño pepper, cored, seeded, and chopped
3 garlic cloves, finely chopped
1 teaspoon salt (or more to taste)
½ teaspoon oregano
2 teaspoons brown sugar
2 teaspoons cider vinegar
¼ cup chopped onion
About 5 ounces fried salted corn tortilla strips; can be stale (or substitute with tortilla chips—these will get mushy anyway)
2 cups packed fresh spinach, chopped
12 ounces smoked Monterey Jack cheese, shredded (or substitute with regular Monterey Jack or Pepper Jack)
Small handful of grape tomatoes, halved
Sprinkle of finely sliced red onion (for garnish)

Place beans in a medium pot and fill with just enough water to cover.

Tear off the stems of the ancho chilies and pour out the seeds. Break each one into a few pieces. Place into a covered pot with 3 cups of water and bring to a boil. Turn off heat, and let sit, covered, for 15 minutes.

In a large pan, heat up the vegetable oil and sauté the shallot, jalapeño, and ⅔ of the garlic on medium heat for about 5 minutes, until softened. Add the ancho chilies with their soaking water and bring to a low simmer. Add salt, oregano, brown sugar, and vinegar. Turn off heat and let cool for at least 15 minutes. Transfer chili mixture to a food processor. Add onion and remaining ⅓ of the chopped garlic. Pulse until liquefied into a smooth sauce. Taste for seasoning. Sauce may taste very bitter at this point, which is fine.

Preheat oven to 375 degrees. In a 9 × 9 baking dish at least 2 inches deep, begin layering the *chilaquiles*. Scatter a somewhat even layer of half of the tortilla strips on the bottom. Add about ⅓ of the sauce evenly on top. Add a layer of half the spinach. Add about ⅓ of the shredded cheese, then about half of the black beans. Add another layer of tortillas, more sauce, the rest of the spinach, more cheese, and the rest of the beans. Top with the rest of the sauce, then the rest of the cheese. Scatter the halved grape tomatoes on top. Bake for 30 minutes. Remove from the oven, and scatter sliced onion on top. Let cool a moment before serving.

Baked Brie with Cranberry Sauce and Crackers

A variation of the appetizer served by Sean and Meredith with tangy, homemade cranberry sauce instead of mango sauce. Cranberries are best bought fresh in the fall, when they're in season, but keeping them in the freezer year-round and thawing before using them works just as well here.

(MAKES ABOUT 6 APPETIZER-SIZED SERVINGS)

1 orange
1 lemon
½ cup sugar
12 ounces fresh cranberries (or substitute frozen and
    thawed)
½ cup water
1 8-ounce wedge of Brie

Zest the orange and lemon with a fine grater or citrus zester and reserve. Juice each fruit, removing the seeds, and reserve. In a medium saucepan, combine the sugar, cranberries, water, zest, and fruit juice, and heat at medium-high. Cook for about 20 minutes, stirring occasionally. Cranberries should be very soft but still just intact. Taste for seasoning, adding more sugar if desired. Let cool for 10–15 minutes.

Preheat oven to 375 degrees. In a 9-inch-deep pie pan, place the Brie in the center and pour the cranberry sauce around its edges just until it fills the pan (leaving a little more than ½ inch from the top, or else it may bubble over the edges). Bake for about 15 minutes, until the mixture is bubbly and the cheese just begins to ooze into the sauce. Let cool 5 minutes. Serve with crackers.

CHAPTER 5

Getting Dirty

TRASH DIVING, FREEGANS, AND FRUGALISTAS

Be industrious and frugal, and you will be rich.

—*Benjamin Franklin*

"No, no, no. That's just gross."

"I really can't think about doing that."

"That's wrong."

I honestly couldn't understand what all my friends had against eating garbage. Some people instantly shut off when they hear *eating* and *Dumpster* used in the same sentence. Others seemed interested in trash diving, or even appreciative of the cause, but weren't ready to get down and dirty themselves. A few others were less turned off by actual trash diving than they were by the ruffian attitudes of the trash divers they'd encountered personally. Then there was the look on Ben's face when I told him I wanted to give it a try. Actually, I think I might have asked him if he wanted to come along with me. Either way, it was completely still, devoid of any humor.

"Seriously, that's just not for me. You can do it, though."

All this fuss over looking for usable objects in the trash, I thought. That was essentially what trash diving meant. It's also a practice that's done in the name of social critique along with reclaiming goods for personal use. For many, it's less about actually needing the goods for pure survival than about the ideology of reusing and repurposing instead of buying. And I was very intrigued by it that winter of 2007. I can't remember when I'd first heard murmurs of the terms *trash diving* or *freegans*, people who consumed thrown-out or otherwise free goods. But I had friends and friends of friends who were involved to some extent in this lifestyle, as well as in related ideas like communal habitats, bike repair, and basically salvaging whatever refuse they could from what they felt was an overly materialistic culture to make art, clothes, food, or shelter or to fulfill other needs.

Freeganism popped up sometime in the mid-1990s, the coinage a play on *free* and *vegan*. Yet even though vegan culture has close ties to freeganism, the two are not mutually exclusive, and freegans are not always vegans. The first waves rose within radical activist groups such as Food Not Bombs, which served free vegetarian food, often dug up from the trash, to those in need. The anarchist street theater group of the 1960s Haight-Ashbury scene called the Diggers also touched on what would become freegan ideals by giving away salvaged food. I had little knowledge of all the history and tenets of freeganism at first, but I was intrigued by tales of large feasts cooked and shared by these friends-of-friends freegans, which were supposedly all made from food found in the Dumpsters behind supermarkets. A gold mine in disguise? I wondered. Was creating a banquet based around thrown-out produce and packaged goods sort of like the food version of making art only from found materials?

For some reason, I wasn't averse to the thought of foraging through trash bins for food. I couldn't put my finger on why this was. My parents had raised me to eat bread no matter if it was stale, and to drink milk a few days past the store's sell-by date so long as it didn't reek. As long as the food found in the trash wasn't creeping with mold and rot, so what? I reasoned. I imagined lifting a Dumpster bin and uncovering a cache of things like unopened packages of cookies. It seemed a heck of a lot more appetizing than the crumbly, half-stale things on the top of my fridge. It wasn't until I received such strong reactions against it from my friends that I decided I might actually be meant for this habit—or at the very least, that I should check out a trash tour and see for myself what this whole freegan thing was.

I went to the website freegan.info and signed up for the New York City–based events and discussion e-mail lists. Immediately, I began receiving a daily string of e-mails as the group organized meetings and shared news; their messages ranged from the chatty to the philosophical. One day it might be a call for volunteers to sit at a table at an activist convention. A typical e-mail might provide a link to a news article somehow related to trash diving.

The website freegan.info was founded in 1998 by Adam Weissman, a New York City–based freegan. Begun as the offshoot of a grassroots activist collective called the Wetlands Preserve, the site now serves as a network for freegans around the world, posting activities and news for each city's local chapter. On the site one can also read manifestos, press clippings, and histories on the movement. Despite all this literature and activity, or maybe in part because of it, there isn't really any clearly defined code to freeganism; there are many varying thoughts and beliefs among individual practitioners as well as varying levels of commitment to these ideals. In one of Adam Weissman's statements, he attests that becoming a vegan came before his freeganism and further inspired his political beliefs. But the main emphases of the movement are clearly focused on minimum consumption of resources by reducing, reusing, and sharing, and on environmentalism. Weissman and other group members publicly acknowledge that it's impossible to follow these beliefs to their fullest in this day and age, subsisting solely on the waste, their own urban gardens, and so forth. But still, they try to live as best they can in accordance with their anticonsumerist beliefs.

I had met Adam that fall at a joint lecture and film screening in Williamsburg, Brooklyn, that he was giving alongside Heather Rogers, author of *Gone Tomorrow: The Hidden Life of Garbage* and director of a short documentary of the same name. The lecture was held at a small gallery space, and after the presentations, I briefly introduced myself over the buffet of freeganed refreshments. I explained that my blog was based on not eating out in restaurants, and he nodded appreciatively.

"Yeah, people ask me all the time, 'What do you do when you want to go on a date? How do you take someone out?'" he said.

I laughed. I tried to imagine Adam in a restaurant, waving down a waiter. In baggy corduroys and a couple of layers of chewed-up T-shirts, Weissman cuts something of an effortless and completely unintentional re-envisioning of Chaplin's famous "tramp" persona. The idea of him sacrificing his beliefs for the sake of dating just seemed preposterous.

A few weeks after signing up for the e-mail list, I opened an e-mail about a trash tour taking place that night. It was a mild spring day, and I couldn't think of anything else I needed to do that night. I wrote down the meeting address, grabbed a couple of plastic bags that were around my apartment, hoped it wouldn't rain, and headed out to meet them.

The moment Janet untangled the sturdy black plastic bag's double knot, a pleasant, oniony aroma greeted us, as if we had just entered a bagel store in the morning. Yet it was ten o'clock on a busy weeknight in Murray Hill, and we were gathered around a pile of trash bags on the sidewalk. Inside the bag Janet held open was a cornucopia of multicolored bagels that had been baked that morning. It must have weighed ten pounds. Beside it were two more giant black garbage bags filled with more bagels. All had come from the bagel store that we were standing in front of on Second Avenue, which now had a metal grate over its facade.

With frizzy gray hair and dressed in comfortable slacks, a fanny pack, and sneakers, Janet Kalish looked to be in her midforties. She and Madeline Nelson, who was middle-aged and sporting similar, no-nonsense clothes, seemed to be leading this night's tour. For some reason, I hadn't expected I'd be meeting two middle-aged women this evening when I headed out the door, but then here I was, listening in attentively to their observations gleaned from much trash-going experience.

Bread, Janet explained, was by far the most commonly wasted type of food in this city. Every bakery that takes any pride in its baked goods must throw out any unsold products at the end of the day. All the hundreds of bakeries, selling crusty baguettes or rich brioches, Jewish challah or Italian foccacia—these all went into the trash. No matter the type of bakery, almost every one in the city practiced this tenet of the business: Never stock day-old bread. Hence, bread is the bread and butter of the city's food waste.

Still holding open the garbage bag of bagels, Janet gestured to a French reporter who was standing near me: "I'm sure you know that in Paris, if you go to a bakery toward the end of the night, you're picking through the last crumbs left on the shelf, maybe a croissant here, one last roll there." The reporter nodded and scribbled. "But here the attitude is to always have fully stocked shelves."

I looked at the bagels practically spilling over onto the sidewalk: There were cinnamon-raisin, poppy, plain, egg, everything, whole wheat, oat, onion, and garlic (which accounted for that strong and still-fresh aroma)—every kind, in fact, was represented. Janet went on to stress that so often, food was purposely produced by restaurants in extreme excess simply for appearance's sake. A bakery knew it wouldn't sell out of every loaf each day, but the look of a nicely stocked shelf was a lot more attractive to potential customers than a near-empty one. Who wants to grab dessert and coffee at a place that has one cookie left? That was the American sensibility. Maybe we ought to do what the Japanese do, and place rubber models of food in the windows of our restaurants and bakeries instead of the real thing, I thought.

I thought about my bread-baking experiments of earlier that year, and how much pride the city's best bakeries and critics like Jeffrey Steingarten took in making the perfect loaf. I also recalled a passage about bread in Arthur Schwartz's book New York City Food: "If, as food philosophers say, the gastronomy of a place can be measured by its interest in bread, then by that criteria alone New York City must be judged the world's greatest gastronomic capital," he wrote. He goes on to explain how heavily bread—of every stripe—weighs into our culinary landscape. I wasn't sure if it was hypocrisy or pure clumsiness that so much of our favorite food was being left untouched, on these curbs, on a daily basis.

Arms dove into the trash bag as the group fished out their favorite bagels. I dug in and scooped out an oniony, poppy-flecked everything bagel (or was it only now "everything" because it had been rubbed against so many other bagels?). I resisted the urge to grab more only because I had just baked a loaf of no-knead bread that night. I always manage to end up with way too many carbs in my kitchen all at once.

"Did everyone bring plastic bags?" Janet asked the group. Most of the people around me indeed had. Only the reporter and her photographer shook their heads.

"No problem; I've got bags here for anyone who needs them. I just found this roll outside of a store, perfectly good," she said, holding up a tube of perforated plastic bags, the kind you'd find in a grocery store produce aisle. "And thrown out, for no reason, I guess."

When everyone had finished taking their bagel picks, Janet carefully reknotted the bag. It was important to leave everything as tidy as you had found it, she said. From the looks of it, we'd hardly made a dent in that hulking bagel bag. Beside it, those other two trash bags hadn't even been opened.

"We'll leave the rest for the homeless. Sometimes they like to pick through these, too," Janet said, giving the bags a last glance.

For our next stop on the tour, we walked a few blocks south to a small upscale grocery store. The store was closed, its dim lights exposing the aisles of gourmet food inside. At the curb in front lay our target—a disheveled heap of black garbage bags.

The group began tearing into the bags with a careful, yet determined dexterity that must have come from much experience. They would feel around the outsides first, then untie the top and take a peek in. I helped open one bag, which was filled with a variety of produce. Hands reached in from all directions around me, and one by one, fruits and vegetables were removed. Finally, I stepped back and surveyed what had come out of the group of bags so far. Along the sidewalk, the group had lined up a cluster of several decent-looking apples, some with bruises here and there. Many more spotted bananas were recovered, some good-looking pears, and several tomatoes, which looked wet on their surfaces, probably from condensation and being squashed beside something else, but otherwise fine. I was amazed to see bag after bag of prewashed mixed salad greens emerge from the garbage as well. The bags were sealed shut, and through the clear plastic, the greens still looked perfectly crisp. But the telltale expiration dates on their packages were one or two days past. Chatter floated around about what to set aside for the freegan group dinner the next evening. It sounded like the group was keeping all the salad bags for the dinner, and created a small pile of them in one corner. These were relatively expensive grocery items, I thought, and here were at least half a dozen of them going for free. I never bought these mixes myself, since I think it's easy enough to wash and chop heads of lettuce, which are cheaper. How ironic, I thought, that the freegans would be feasting on these. I spotted Madeline looking on and asked her whether the salad mixes were a common trash find.

"Yes, we see lots of these," she said. "They perish so quickly." They also worked out great for group dinners, since there were so many vegetarians. A big bowl of green salad was a staple at nearly every meal.

We opened another garbage bag and removed a smattering of various foods: a package of corn muffins, a quart of yogurt (expired), sour cream (unexpired), a package of chocolate-chip cookies (my daydream was realized!), and some deli sandwiches in plastic containers, to name a few of the finds.

"Any meat-eating freegans here?" somebody called out. The packaged sandwiches, which had most likely been made fresh that morning at the store, had cold cuts such as salami and ham stuffed inside kaiser rolls. A couple of guys in the group eagerly scooped them up.

"It's less common, but some of us do eat meat, or will at least eat it if we see it being wasted," Janet was telling the reporter. Since many freegans are vegan, though, they have little use for the meat and dairy products they find, even if they are still fresh. I looked at the sour cream container. The plastic was squashed in a little bit on one side, but its expiration date read that it wasn't due to go to waste for another two weeks. Probably it was there because the container had gotten smashed.

It sounded like a no-brainer to me at first that the majority of dairy and meat found in a Dumpster was there for a reason—because it had gone bad. But I'd sure have no qualms about eating those leftover deli sandwiches. And when another apparently meat-eating freegan scored a package of sliced prosciutto, I had to admit that it looked pretty tempting. Was it still good? I guess that would be left for him to find out.

Janet held up the quart of sour cream. She began talking about the terrible conditions on confined dairy farms where the animals who produced the milk for it were kept, how they were separated from their mothers practically at birth, and the trauma that this caused for both mother and calf. She went on to describe the conventional milk cow's unhealthy diet of cheap grains, when cows are meant to be pastured on grass.

"And in the end, after all that, this cup of sour cream is here, in the trash," Janet concluded. She plopped the carton disdainfully back with the stash of food finds.

A few people still picked through the last bag. The strained looks on their faces led me to believe it didn't hold much that was good. Janet stood back and surveyed the row of produce on the sidewalk, frowning. She announced to the group: "So this happens to be a rare, slow night for Dumpster diving. Usually we come away with a lot more food than what we've seen here tonight," she said.

The reporter's photographer was snapping away, taking shots of people holding their favorite food finds. A girl with an apple proudly posed before him. I eyed the food on the curb, wondering whether there was anything I wanted. My eyes were suddenly drawn to a familiar shape: a small head of garlic. I picked it up. It felt firm and fresh, though a few of its outer cloves were missing.

"Take it!" Madeline urged when she caught sight of me inspecting it. "We've got plenty of them."

I slipped it into my tote bag.

Moving along, we stopped next at a Dunkin' Donuts just a few doors down. I wasn't particularly thrilled about this stop. Fried dough coated with sticky syrup is not really my kind of food, free or not. Then again, I was starting to feel a little hungry right then. Does eating freeganed food from a place like Dunkin' Donuts count as eating out? I wondered. Nah, I immediately decided. And certainly not on the sidewalk at ten o'clock at night.

The bright neon storefront was still open. Late-night customers streamed in and out with coffee cups and crumpled white bags bearing the chain's pink-and-orange logo. Just outside, a small cluster of black garbage bags had already been laid on the curb. I was amazed at how invisible we seemed to passersby just then. The whole time we had been scavenging the trash at the gourmet grocery, I'd notice passersby glance our way every now and then. It was nearing ten o'clock, and many people looked like they were dressed up to go out for drinks or dinner. (By comparison, we looked more like bums, toting around a granny cart filled with trash, getting twisted in our plastic bags.) I didn't see a single person stop to look at us for longer than a second before walking on by, their culture barely brushing against that of the freegans.

The first bag we opened was filled with doughnuts and muffins. Most were sticking together in an unsightly fashion—a lot of the doughnuts were frosted—but the plentiful munchkins inside the bag looked just as intact as they would have on the store's racks. Two of the girls on the tour began collecting these. They'd be good as dessert for tomorrow's dinner, someone suggested. I thought about taking a few to pop in my lunch bag for tomorrow. Sure, the glazed ones wouldn't have quite the same chewiness as they had today, and the cake doughnuts would dry out to hardened nuggets. I watched the girls handpick the munchkins and drop them one by one into clear plastic bags. I declined taking one for the moment, lost suddenly in a sharp memory.

The summer between my junior and senior years in high school, my three best girlfriends and I made three remarkable discoveries. The first was that we could pull back and crawl underneath the wire mesh fence of the town swimming pool for a clandestine midnight dip. Second, we possessed a feminine attraction that could turn older guys into our minions for almost anything—giving us rides, getting us beer, and other shenanigans. My best friend, for instance, was five and a half feet of Indian American diva, with extra-long wavy hair that framed her curvy features. Our nights were filled with adventure. In something of an antecedent to number two, our third discovery that summer was that the Dunkin' Donuts in downtown South Orange gave away free doughnuts just before closing at eleven P.M.

I remember the first night we walked into the Dunkin' Donuts store a minute before eleven o'clock. We had gone in only to use the pay phone, which the lone store attendant had kindly let us use even after he explained he was about to close the shop, taking the cash drawers out of the registers. After one of us had finished the call, we turned to face the glowing, fluorescent racks of doughnuts. Collectively, we seemed to be wondering, "Are you going to eat that?" as we stared longingly at the treats. The store attendant in the white paper Dunkin' Donuts hat followed our stare for a moment and smiled.

"Lemon filled, blueberry cake, chocolate frosted," we began calling out.

"Boston cream, a French cruller, apple streudel." We didn't really want all that many doughnuts, I guessed, but the idea that he was giving them to us completely free was somewhat thrilling.

The attendant snapped open one small white paper bag after another, filling them with our picks. We pointed and deliberated behind the counter. By the time we were finished choosing, he'd given us at least one of every single type of doughnut left on the shelf. We'd cleared the racks down to the last dozen pastries. The attendant seemed to have somewhat limited English skills, but we left that night carrying several bags filled to the brim with doughnuts, and it wouldn't be the last time. He waved and smiled as we walked out as if we'd done him a favor instead, still holding the frosting-smeared waxed-paper sheet in one hand.

Yet as I smacked through those sticky, sugary, sludge-covered morsels of dough on those triumphant binges, something was nagging at me. Surely the rest of the world's Dunkin' Donuts didn't have a few hungry teenagers attempting to consume their day's surplus. Nor did the rest of the world's bazillions of eating establishments, like the other bakery that was probably closing up shop, too, next door to our gold mine of a Dunkin' Donuts.

"Anyone want some munchkins?" one of the girls called out to our tour. "I think I've got too many."

She shook her clear plastic bag briefly, sending its contents into a flurry of powdered sugar. Oh, for good times' sake. I reached forward, and she placed a munchkin in my hand.

I looked down at the bite-sized powdered thing in my palm. Cinnamon. Instead of eating it, I was suddenly filled with an acute and irrational sense of hatred for this nostalgic binge treat. It barely weighed an ounce. Really, it was no more than a millisecond's worth of cake dough, burped out of some machine, deep-fried in processed oils (then trans fats, before the chain's decision to move to non–trans fat oil in September 2007), and rolled around in powdered sugars. Maybe it was filled with a nanosecond's worth of drop-dead-red high-fructose corn-syrup goop dimly related to jelly. Or maybe it had food color and artificial cocoa flavor in the dough to make it "chocolate." And now it was landfill padding. I found myself hating the cutesy way in which it was advertised as a doughnut hole: presumably a leftover scrap created from the process of making regular ring-shaped doughnuts. Because it wasn't. Unlike the way I might have seen it as a teenager, none of this was kitschy or cute to me anymore. I gave my doughnut hole away to someone else in the group and wiped my fingers on my jeans.

As people were finishing up choosing munchkins, I wandered over to another trash bag. It had been opened and picked through a bit already. Inside was an endless-seeming concave pile of Dunkin' Donuts muffins, croissants, and more doughnuts. Streaks of glossy red syrup were visible on nearly all of them, as if a jelly-filled doughnut had spontaneously combusted inside. I picked up what looked to be a chocolate-chip muffin lying near the top. It didn't look so bad. I had suddenly lost my appetite, but I figured I could find some use for it later on.

At the end of the cluster of Dunkin' Donuts trash, a final bag lay unopened. Now, with the experience under my belt of feeling bags that were suspiciously full of bread, I put my hand against it and felt a firm, round orb of bread inside.

"Bagels," Madeline declared, summing up the packed plastic bag's contents. "But," she said, with knowing wryness, "we all know that Dunkin' Donuts bagels aren't that good."

So we left those behind.

With that final stop at Dunkin' Donuts, I called it a night and rode the subway back to Brooklyn. Unfortunately, I wasn't able to make it to the group dinner at one of the members' apartments the following night, a Friday. I wouldn't go on another trash tour for a long time after that, at least not with an organized group. But all the ideas that were brought up over the course of that night's tour were on my mind vividly in the weeks and months that followed.

The first thing I did when I got home was make dessert. The chocolate-chip muffin I'd brought back was crumbly after having ridden with me in my purse. After peeling the paper liner from the bottom, I placed the muffin in a bowl and broke it up some more, to coarse crumbles no larger than . . . wait a minute, "a pea." That was one of the frequent descriptors you'd read in pastry recipes, in the instructions on how to cut butter into dry ingredients. The muffin was so greasy that it clearly had plenty of butter or some sort of fat in it already. Normally, with a basic pie-pastry dough, one would roll it out and then line it against the sides of a baking dish. I took out my oven-safe ramekins. Instead of rolling out the muffin crumbles, I pressed them against the inside of two of the ramekins. Most of it stuck. Some fell off, a little. But with a little more pressing, I was able to form a somewhat uniform crust all around the sides and the bottoms. Now, what to fill them with?

I quickly got started on making a basic vanilla custard. In the meantime, I turned the oven to 350 degrees and stuck the ramekins inside to crisp up the "pastry" a little. By the time I was done whisking together my basic, milk-and-egg-yolk vanilla custard, or pudding, the crusts had been taken out of the oven and had cooled down a little. The custard would take several hours, however, to cool. Getting sleepy, I filled the ramekins with custard up to the rims of the crust, covered them with plastic wrap, and let them chill in the refrigerator the rest of the night.

The next day, I came home with some fresh berries. I topped my vanilla-custard, chocolate-chip-muffin-crusted dessert with a few raspberries and spooned it up. It was divine.

Could I become a freegan convert? I agreed with almost everything people were saying on the trash tour and was astonished to find that it did seem more than viable to live off of grocery store rubbish, and fairly well at that. Freeganed food isn't always stale or low quality, I'd learned. That head of garlic I took from the trash outside the upscale grocery? I used it to the last clove. Nothing was amiss about it—actually, it was a lot fresher than many bulbs I've purchased. But for me, there were a few problems with the freegan lifestyle. I loved to cook new things. And when I had an idea for something to run home and make, I wouldn't want to be limited by what options were in the trash that day.

Reliance on availability, I realized, was something that freegans by nature had to fully accept. Instead of the changing harvests of the year (pre–global economy), their food choices were determined by sell-by dates and happenstance. Yet through my encounters with freegans, both on the tour and at the lecture, it didn't seem as if anyone was too bothered by the types of food they found or didn't find. This would be my biggest challenge if I were to become a freegan—not being able to choose what I cooked and ate. Plus, I was already giving up restaurant food, let's not forget.

Overall, I got the sense that few of these freegans were "foodies," like myself. I'm sure there are plenty of creative freegan chefs out there, eager to take a skillful shot at cooking the "secret ingredient" found in the Dumpster that day in some imaginative way. But still, he or she would have to have a substantial amount of will or tolerance. And what if you couldn't find salt or pepper?

"I know—I never cook on the stove anymore. I use the toaster oven to cook everything these days," I'd overheard Janet confide to another person on the tour, smirking secretively.

To be sure, I had gone trash diving in only one city, New York. There are active freegan communities all over the globe, in Europe especially. I once received an e-mail from a reader of my blog who described a trash tour he went on with freegans in New Orleans. They'd shared a giant feast the night after the tour, and he'd been fascinated, and eager to share the discovery.

My friend Matt had been less impressed with a group of freegans he met in Cleveland. They'd identified themselves as vegans, even though Matt had witnessed them eating both meat and dairy products that were found in the trash. Matt found this hypocrisy intolerable, arguing that some of the most important tenets of veganism had to do with nutrition, and a rigorous belief in the more healthful diet of plants-only eating. Indeed, to many vegans, it is important to abstain from meat for more than waste-conscious reasons. Plus, when it came to actually cooking the meat, my friend said these freegans had been clueless. They'd botched cooking a whole, frozen turkey, and had haplessly boiled the sack of gizzards they found inside its cavity while it was still in its plastic bag.

Because of this run-in, Matt tends to see freegans as lazy people, freeloaders of the more responsible, paying society, who are all too willing to compromise their values to subsidize their personal needs. I don't agree with the generalization; however, as I found with the Dunkin' Donuts munchkins, there are some things that I simply do not want to put in my body, rescued or not. And with any activist or political group, there are bound to be tagalongs who might care more about their self-image than the movement's true missions.

Then there are people like Sam Gerlach. Sam plays the cymbals in a riot marching band called the What Cheer? Brigade, based in Providence, Rhode Island. My brother is also in the band, and I'd seen her several times when they came to play in New York. My first impression of her was, Wow, there's a really stunningly pretty new cymbalist in the band. During shows, like most of the band members, Sam wore face paint in warrior-like streaks or glitter around her almond-shaped eyes, and her clothes looked like they'd been hand stitched from various pieces of fabric to create form-fitting, raucous ensembles. Several months later, I was chatting with Chris and another bandmate, Mindy, who happened to be Sam's roommate. Mindy mentioned that Sam basically subsisted off of the Dumpster behind a major supermarket in their Providence hometown, and the middle rack of their refrigerator was constantly filled with food that she'd freeganed and was communal for the rest of the roommates. There was always Brie for some reason, according to Mindy, and lots of nice cheeses in general. Hence, the middle shelf was handy for snack food, or for entertaining guests. She offhandedly referred to Sam as a "frugalista," a word that had previously been unknown to me. I looked it up immediately and chanced upon a recent William Safire article from *The New York Times Magazine*. "A person who lives a frugal lifestyle but stays fashionable and healthy by swapping clothes, buying secondhand, growing own produce, etc.," *frugalista* was defined in the dictionary. Sam apparently also freeganed all her clothes, and if they didn't fit, she sewed them to fit both her size and her sense of style.

I wrote an e-mail to Sam the same day, asking whether I could pick her brain on freeganism. An hour later, she wrote back:

I must mention ahead of time, though, the importance to not "blow up the spots" is really high. That's one huge beef people have with the NYC trash-picking tour (which I've gone on with friends and enjoyed): they name spots and post photos online, and it leads to stores getting so annoyed or worried that they make throwaways inedible before they throw them out, and then no one can rescue/ eat them. But otherwise, a chance to talk about myself and my self-righteous beliefs? I'm in!

Then she added a link to a recent post she put on Instructables .com about how to fix a specific problem with Dell laptops that had previously not been covered online, obviously proud of her handiwork.

Frugalista is the word that William Safire, longtime columnist on etymology, wished had been named the Word of the Year for 2008. It was inducted into the *New Oxford American Dictionary* that year, and he painstakingly dissected its genesis in his column. He traced its origins to a 2005 article in the *Palm Beach Post*, and it was picked up by a *Miami Herald* blog written by Natalie Mc-Neal called "The Frugalista Files." The blog is still in existence, frequently updated with posts on lifestyles and topics that could be deemed "frugalista."

Getting back to Sam, though: She told me that she began trash diving as early as high school. Growing up in Rhode Island, many of her peers were into it, too.

"These days," Sam wrote, "I go trash diving less for political outspokenness than to just get a few nice, extra things in my fridge to share with my friends and roommates. It's a bit like going shopping—except, of course, I'm not spending any money."

When I asked her if she had run into any trouble with the law, since trash diving is, after all, illegal, she said no. In all these years, she hadn't ever felt as if she was in danger of being arrested.

"I don't go too often with big, bawdy groups like I used to when I was younger. I think this is inviting trouble, and attention—from the store owners, the police. But that's their aim, to make their mission heard, and I still respect that," she wrote.

I asked Sam a few other questions in my next e-mail, wanting to get a better sense of how she started trash diving, and what she thought of it as a whole. I received in return a generous, thoughtful response.

Sam's trash diving days had begun in the high school cafeteria. When friends kept throwing out half the food they'd purchased for lunch, Sam, who always brought her lunch from home instead of buying, was disconcerted by the waste. She began asking her friends if they were going to finish their lunches, and eventually they started giving her their uneaten portions of food instead of throwing them out. Pretty soon, she was ending up with far more food at lunch than she needed.

In Providence, where she grew up and still lives, Sam says it's pretty common for people to display unwanted items on the sidewalk for others to take. Recycling goods throughout the community is seen by a lot of people as positive, or at least more "normal" than in other parts of the country. Sam also hasn't purchased a new piece of clothing since she was in eleventh grade, and she is going on twenty-six. Much of her clothing comes from swaps with friends; some of it is found in the trash; and occasionally she'll buy a secondhand item, which she then alters to fit. "It's a mix of avoiding waste and not liking the way clothes are sold," Sam wrote. "Most seem designed to have limited 'shelf life' by responding to trends, plus they all fit awkwardly and cost too much."

I also asked her what kind of obstacles she encountered with trash diving as a lifestyle, aside from the chances of getting arrested (which were slim, according to her, as people were usually glad to see things thrown out going to use). She confided that some people are all too quick to insult her: "I've been treated like the food I have is harmful or disgusting, that going through the trash is somehow offensive, or that I'm doing this to develop a cool image. When people are afraid of not fitting in, they can quickly decide why the risk isn't worth taking, or immediately become critical. But if I'm confident without being preachy or insistent, people realize there's nothing to get excited about."

On the plus side, the unforeseen advantages of trash diving far outweighed the disadvantages, to Sam. Aside from just food or clothes, Sam felt like she had gained something a lot greater.

"Making a list and buying what's on it makes me feel bored and dead, like I'm wasting my time. When I find things by chance and improvise, I feel natural and alive. Not knowing what the groceries will be this time around is fun because I learn about new ingredients and recipes," Sam wrote. "I'm proud to look down and see that I've made or found everything I'm wearing, or to invite people over for a feast that didn't cost anything (including the dishes, dish soap, filtered water, furniture, lightbulbs, and in the past, booze!)," she concluded.

I couldn't have thought of a more justified finale for our e-mail correspondence on the subject than that last sentence. Needless to say, I was extremely humbled and impressed by Sam's will and creativity.

Being a frugalista, a freegan, or just a hobbyist trash diver might not be for everyone. But obviously, there *are* unique and great advantages to it for many. I could relate. I'm always one to use up leftovers to plan my dinners around, thinking first about what needs to be used up in the kitchen before deciding what to cook. That didn't seem so far off from what Sam did with the grocery store Dumpster (plus, it sounded like she lived nearby a particularly fruitful one). People in less prosperous times and places have been innovating with leftover and just-about-to-expire foods since the beginning of time, and traditional leftover dishes have a way of being some of my very favorites, too. These include cured meats, soups, fried rice, breakfast congee, *panzanella*, *chilaquiles*, or even nachos. What did it matter if it was left over from your own kitchen or the city's stores? I also never bought greeting cards or wrapping paper; I much preferred to make these things out of scrap paper or fabric. With a little skill and style, this is essentially what the frugalista lifestyle is all about. I'm not sure how cool any of my little DIY projects actually look, but perhaps that's not the most important part.

All told, I guess I could imagine myself being a freegan or frugalista like Sam. If only it were a little more ingrained in my repertoire, my community, my experience (especially the clothing part—I barely know how to sew). If these circumstances had been different, and if my foodie obsessions could be kept a little more at bay, then I wonder if I would have started writing a blog called "Not Buying Food in New York."

Savory Bread Pudding with Salvaged Vegetables

This comforting casserole is a great way to use up extra scraps of not-so-fresh-looking vegetables, like partially squashed tomatoes or bruised zucchini and mushrooms. It's also great for using up stale bread. In this version, I added some crisp bacon for flavor, though this is optional. (MAKES ABOUT 6 SERVINGS)

4 eggs
2 cups milk
1 tablespoon fresh thyme
1 teaspoon salt
¼ teaspoon cayenne pepper (optional)
Freshly ground black pepper to taste
4–5 cups stale bread (any kind), cut into 1-inch cubes
¾ cup shredded Gruyère or Swiss cheese
3 strips bacon, cooked crispy and crumbled
2 scallions, both white and green parts, chopped fine
4–5 cups washed and trimmed vegetables, such as broccoli florets, halved button mushrooms, chopped tomatoes, chopped asparagus, and chopped zucchini and summer squash

Preheat oven to 350 degrees. In a large bowl, whisk together the eggs with the milk, and add the thyme, salt, cayenne pepper, black pepper, and bread pieces. Let soak for 15 minutes. Combine the rest of the ingredients in the bowl. Transfer to a greased 9-inch × 12-inch casserole and bake for 45–50 minutes, until top is lightly browned and a fork inserted into the center of the casserole comes out relatively clean. Let cool 5–10 minutes before serving.

Almond Custard Tarts with Leftover Muffin Crust

I used the leftover chocolate-chip muffin that I freeganed from Dunkin' Donuts to create a rich tart shell. Any leftover muffin should do the trick. Add a little melted butter to the crumbled muffin mixture if your crumbs are very dry and stale.

(MAKES 4 TARTS)

> 1–2 leftover muffins, crumbled
> 1 tablespoon cold water
> ½ cup sugar
> 2 cups whole milk
> 4 egg yolks
> 1 teaspoon almond extract
> Fresh berries (optional)

Preheat oven to 375 degrees. In a bowl, break down the muffin into crumbs. Add the water and combine evenly with your hands or a spatula. Mixture should be moist but not stick together in one ball. Press the mixture with your hands or a spatula firmly against the sides of four ramekins. Place the ramekins on a baking tray and bake for 10–15 minutes. Let cool completely.

Whisk sugar, milk, and almond extract together in a saucepan. Scald mixture by bringing it to a boil. Turn off heat. In a bowl, lightly beat together egg yolks. While beating, add a small spoonful of the hot milk mixture. Gradually add a few more spoonfuls to the eggs while stirring. Mixture should be smooth and not lumpy. When about ½ cup of the milk mixture has been incorporated into the eggs, pour the egg mixture into the saucepan with the milk. Cook over medium heat, stirring occasionally, until the custard has thickened to a point where it coats the back of a spoon when dipped in. Pour custard into the cooled tart shells. Refrigerate about 3–4 hours until set. Optional: Top with (foraged!) fresh berries for serving. And don't forget to save the egg whites for an omelet.

From the Land

URBAN FORAGING 101

All good things are wild, and free.

—Henry David Thoreau

After my trash dive with the freegans I kept abreast of their activities around the city—actually, I couldn't help it, as my in-box was flooded daily with announcements and updates. I didn't take another trash dive that spring of 2007, or at least not a full-scale trash dive with a group of freegans. But I did begin to notice the garbage bins outside one small bakery that had recently opened up down the street from me. I wondered what could be found inside them. That place had the best baguettes in the neighborhood. It was tempting. But I felt a little bit awkward about doing a solo trash dive there, as my neighborhood was always bustling with people, often young families with kids and baby strollers. I didn't want to be too conspicuous going through the trash in front of my neighbors.

I settled instead for the next best option: a bagel shop in my neighborhood regularly sold large bags of day-old bagels and other baked goods, a steal at $1 for half a dozen. I'd buy these bags and often freeze the bagels immediately (slicing them in half first so that they'd reheat in a toaster nicely), saving one or two of them for more immediate eating. I felt like I was doing the local business a small favor by paying them for their surplus goods. I also appreciated the fact that they sold them at all and wanted to support that. Plus, there are a million and one uses for leftover bread—it can become bread crumbs used to stuff or coat things in a thousand different ways. I discovered a lot of them that spring.

It was late spring when I received an e-mail from the freegan event list that caught my attention. It was announcing a foraging walk in Prospect Park led by an expert in wild edibles, Tim Keating. It sounded right up my alley—and the park was close to my home. Eating stuff plucked from the wild was something I knew relatively little about, though of course I'd heard of it being done before—wild raspberry bushes in the countryside, a honeysuckle blossom that could be sucked on, that kind of thing. I hadn't heard of anything edible in the natural environs of New York City before, though. I read the rest of the event's description:

"As a longtime urban forager, Tim will show how foraging common wild plants in the city parks can not only provide fresh and healthful greens but can play an essential part of a freegan lifestyle. Rather than focusing on edibles that are uncommon and hard to find, the plants highlighted on Tim's walk are those that are very common and readily available in large enough quantities to supplement one's diet. During the walk, Tim will also discuss the mythology of the forager in relation to the dominant cultural paradigm," it summarized.

I rode my bike into Grand Army Plaza that Saturday morning and pressed my brakes when I spotted a small cluster of mostly young folks standing around as if waiting for something. I recognized Madeline Nelson standing cross-armed among them, in cargo shorts and sneakers. She gave me a smile as I pulled up with my bike. Aside from her, I knew no one else of the ten or twelve others in the group, who looked around my age.

A few people began to question why our guide was running so late. It was already ten minutes past the scheduled meeting time.

"We run on anarchist time frames," Madeline said to no one in particular, checking her watch. "It's always a little bit late."

Another minute or so later, Tim Keating arrived and began the tour. He apologized for running late and led us onto the paved path to the park. No sooner had we followed him for five paces than he stopped to introduce us to a plant.

"Here's a plant called common plantain," Tim said, pointing to a cluster of tall weeds.

He went on to say that the plant, which had thick, light-green stems and large, floppy leaves like an elephant's ears, was a good detoxifier and source of vitamin K. No relation to the larger relative of the banana, though. He passed around a branch and explained as we took a leaf to sample that it was best blanched before eaten, because it could be a little tough by late spring.

A longtime environmentalist, Tim directed the nonprofit organization Rainforest Relief when not promoting urban foraging. He'd spend months in the Amazon each year for work and research. Tim was a compact, densely built man who looked to be in his mid- to late thirties, with close-cropped grayish hair and pale eyes that could be intense when he spoke. Dressed casually in jeans and a muscle T, he looked like the kind of guy whom you could trust if he were strapped to your back while you were jumping out of a plane.

"I hope you like bitter greens," he warned us after we had each tried a taste of the common plantain, "because that's what we're going to be finding a lot of now."

Bitter greens, however, seemed to be just fine with everyone in the group. Maybe a generation ago this would have been different. But the national palate has softened in recent years to bitter greens. Arugula is strikingly bitter, and it's a favorite for fresh salads among gourmets. Broccoli rabe has become a darling in Italian restaurants and recipes. Many of my friends and foodie acquaintances agree that it's the vegetable's strong bitterness that makes it special and places it above its mild cousin, plain broccoli, in the taste lexicon. Another thing that distinguishes these two vegetables, broccoli rabe and arugula, is their steep price tags.

"The important thing about a lot of these greens, especially if you live in the city, is that they're detoxifiers. They have a lot of chemicals that help your body fight against all the smog and city air," Tim went on.

Next, he identified a patch of dandelion. I remembered helping my father pick them from the lawn as a child. Their long, sharply serrated leaves grow in petal-like clusters around the yellow dandelion flowers, which appear for a few weeks each year in early spring. They're easy to spot, these familiar-looking weeds that grow in the cracks of sidewalks from here to Sydney. Like arugula, they were also enjoying the embrace of haute cuisine as a salad green. Just as they were popping up in nature, dandelion greens were appearing on more and more menus that spring. These are biologically identical plants to the wild version that we were now picking in the park.

"It's really the same thing they have at the Union Square Green-market?" someone in our tour group asked. "I just saw them there going for three-fifty a bunch."

Tim nodded. The woman shook her head and began collecting more.

It's funny how leaves, when you don't know what you're look-ing at, seem to blend as one on the ground. Once my eyes were reacquainted with the dandelion's shape, I could pinpoint them immediately, tucked amid the grass and other weeds. I began fill-ing my plastic bag with them.

"Poor man's pepper," Tim said, pointing to another plant in the same patch just outside Grand Army Plaza. "It tastes really pep-pery, which is why it got its name. Kind of like arugula," he said.

An appropriate name in more ways than one, I thought. I took a leaf that the person standing beside me passed to me from a bunch that Tim had plucked for the group. The leaves had sharp, spiky teeth and very faint hairs on their surface. Most leaves of any plant have fuzz if you look close enough, Tim explained. I would find this was true throughout the tour, though I suspect that the more promi-nent fuzz on the poor man's pepper is one reason why this plant didn't become an overnight sensation in the culinary world. Once my front teeth bit down on the leaf, I detected a grasslike sweet-ness at the tip of my tongue. The leaf felt silky in my mouth, very thin and delicate. As I chewed some more, I could see what Tim meant—it was pleasantly spicy, like a kick of black peppercorn.

"Yum," I said, and passed the plant to the next person.

"These should get a lot more bitter as the season goes on; same with most of the plants we'll be finding here today. So they're best to eat now. Otherwise you can cook them," Tim added.

While people busied themselves picking sprigs of the plants they'd just learned about, I found a moment to ask Tim a question.

"How do you usually cook these plants?" I asked.

"You probably can cook them a lot of ways. Like, you could just cook them with some garlic, like broccoli rabe or something," he said. He shrugged. "But with ones like this, the common plantain, or other big leaves, I usually just cook them into tomato sauce, eat them just like that. I'm sure you can do a lot more with them, but that's just how I usually do it. Maybe you could make a stuffing with some of them. I'm not sure."

Clearly, Tim wasn't claiming to be a culinary expert. I thanked him, and as I gathered more of the three plants we'd tried so far, I began imagining what other uses I could put them to.

"Someone just asked a good question," Tim said, addressing the group. "How do you cook these? Well, you can just eat them without cooking, like the really young, tender greens, which we'll hopefully find lots of today, or you can boil them or sauté them on their own, or with garlic. If anyone else has any other suggestions on how to cook them or serve them, please feel free to share."

The rest of the group looked around at one another and gave a few shrugs before going back to collecting greens. We were a bit of a quiet group that day, considering the fact that most looked like young and opinionated activists. When he began the tour and introduced himself, Tim had taken a hand count of how many people had done wild foraging before, and only three or four hands were raised. Perhaps everyone else was as content as I was to just soak in all the new knowledge.

"Also, on how to store them," Tim continued. "These greens usually keep for a couple of weeks or more in your crisper. I still have a big bag of them at home. The reason for that is because what you're taking home has just been picked today, instead of the chard, or whatever you get at the grocery store, that was picked who knows when and traveled however far before."

I grabbed a bunch of poor man's pepper leaves and added them to my plastic bag before the tour moved on. We followed the path farther into the park and eventually made a stop at a tall plant with long green leaves that seemed to resemble the plants people might hang from the ceiling in their homes. But it was not the leaves that Tim had stopped for. This was a very common plant called burdock, but the edible prize jewel was underneath the dirt, its root. The burdock root is also known as *gobo* in Japanese cuisine, where it's a popular delicacy, and it has a mild, woody flavor and a texture like that of a potato. Once again, another haute-cuisine food find, free and plentiful.

Tim explained that the burdock is a biennial plant, so it takes two years to complete its full life cycle. At one year, the burdock's root is the edible delicacy *gobo*. There is also second-year burdock, which is much tougher and not considered very good for eating. By then, the large leaves of the plant have sprouted two-foot-tall stalks, so it's easy to tell which plant has a first-year or second-year root beneath it. He used a trowel to dig up one plant. The root emerged, along with a hunk of earth and miniature roots that came off in showers. Once Tim had shaken it relatively free of dirt, he held the small, carrot-shaped root for us to see. Compared to the rest of the plant, it was tiny. Although it wasn't commonly eaten, the rest of the plant—its large leaves and crisp stems—was also edible, he explained.

In the produce aisles of grocery stores, I rarely found root vegetables that were still attached to their leaves. If you were looking for turnips, then turnip roots you would find in bins, trimmed at the stem. My first assumption was that the greens attached to these roots would not be that tasty, or even edible. But recently, I'd discovered this wasn't always the case. It had begun with beets; their mild-tasting leaves are actually one of my favorite leafy greens to sauté, much more delicate than the thick, dense leaves of kale, for instance. Biologically, beet greens are almost the same green as chard, and the beet's deep red stems provide added nutrients that are also found in beets. I'd also tried out carrot greens in recent months, which I cooked down with swathes of other greens following a recipe for the Cajun stew *gumbo z'herbes*. I began wondering how many other vegetables had another edible part to them, as yet unknown to me.

Someone else in the group eagerly accepted this burdock root, and after Tim pulled up another plant, he handed the next root to the first bidder. I didn't get to snatch a *gobo*, but that was all right; by the time we had toured for an hour, I had tasted more plants than I expected I would be able to keep track of. Most of them were of the leafy-green variety, with similar looks and tastes, and to further complicate things, I hadn't brought enough bags to properly separate them. So I decided to go easy on my gathering this first time around, gradually inaugurating my stomach to the various new plants. I already had a good handful of dandelion leaves, some cloverlike sprouts called wood sorrel, which tasted lemony and sweet, and lots of the spicy poor man's pepper.

With all these edible leafy greens came several red flags, though. We passed a poisonous plant called the Star of Bethlehem, which resembled the thin, cylindrical shoots of the ubiquitous wild onion and could easily be confused for it. Another common plant called the pokeweed was edible only around this time of the year, as a leafy green, but later on it would become poisonous. I thanked my lucky stars I was getting my introduction to foraging from an expert, instead of foolishly going off on my own.

"I want to talk a little bit about the philosophy of the forager," Tim said, once we had found a grassy spot to sit down and take a break. We had all taken a seat in a patch of shade on a hill overlooking Grand Army Plaza.

"The difference between the forager and the consumer is about accepting what nature has to offer, rather than demanding what you want to take from it. You all know that today, you can get foods shipped in from halfway around the world at the corner store. But that isn't what this is all about. The forager must bend with what the earth allows, and its cycles."

At this point, I wanted to raise my hand and ask if this wasn't why humans had created agriculture, to grow what made the best sense for us, and not have to spend our days foraging and hunting. But as he continued to speak, with obvious passion and a unique sense of appreciation for the spontaneities of wild nature, I decided not to interrupt. Eventually, I think I got his point about foraging. It was done in defiance to the standard, and often hazardous, ways we had treated the earth in order to produce our food. It was an attempt to prove that the wild still held a bountiful harvest, and it was a celebration of that. Moreover, it was healthy (as long as you didn't eat the Star of Bethlehem). And some people, like Tim, were living off of it for a very significant part of their diets, even in urban areas. That part was particularly enlightening. I didn't know many other people ate from the wild, especially in densely populated places like Brooklyn, but judging from the size of my bags from a couple of hours of foraging, I figured it could easily be done.

"Does anyone want any cookies?" Madeline said once Tim had finished his talk. "I just found them, this whole wrapped package of them, outside on my street. Somebody must have put them there; I don't know why." She broke the seal on a package of oatmeal raisin cookies and passed them around. I took one, shrugging. What an odd combination, though, I thought, to be eating such factory-processed food that was found on the street, and at the same time, nutritious wild food from the city.

When I left after our tour split up, I had two plastic bags full of weeds that I hoped I would be able to tell apart from one another. At the beginning of the tour, Tim had advised that for any wild plant we were trying for the first time, to eat just a tiny taste of it the first day, then wait twenty-four hours. If nothing happened—no allergic reactions or unpleasant side effects—then it was fine to go ahead and eat more. I definitely wanted to follow this bit of wisdom. With everything jumbled together, though, I had to spend a while separating the leaves into bunches. But biting into them revealed a new strategy: I was learning to identify these plants by their taste alone, rather than by their names or appearances. With this skill, I felt like I was now becoming a foodie forager.

But one wild edibles tour wasn't nearly enough. I had gotten merely my first taste of Prospect Park that Saturday, and as luck had it, another foraging tour was taking place that same week. It was led by a man who had been giving wild edibles tours of New York City and its surrounding tristate area's public parks since the 1970s. He went by the name of "Wildman" Steve Brill.

If you search "wild edibles" in Google you're likely to come up with Brill's website first and foremost. So naturally, I had stumbled upon it when doing a little research before Tim's tour. It's a jungle of a site, filled with illustrations, folksy allusions and jokes, and plenty of photographs of the wild plants commonly found in the area, at any given time of the year. But the website on its own isn't really meant to be a guide to eating wild edibles. Steve Brill takes dozens of beginner foragers into parks and wildlife reserves throughout the spring and summer months each year, on average more than once a week. The photos, tips, and plant profiles on Brill's website are a great reference if you have already done a little bit of foraging first. The real experience, and the much more animated one, is Brill himself on his tour.

That Sunday, I stood in the same spot in Grand Army Plaza, waiting for my tour guide. Because he gives tours so often, Brill asks guests to bring a suggested donation of $10 and to RSVP by phone before showing up to his tours. I did as instructed, and when I spotted a tall, gangly man in his fifties walking up to the crowd sporting beige, safari-bound khaki shorts, a tucked-in T-shirt, large glasses, and a straw hat fitted snugly over a terry cloth sweatband, I knew immediately that it was Brill. This time, the tour group of fifteen to twenty people really ran the gamut in age. There were plenty of middle-aged couples with toddlers, a few middle school kids, a handful of young adults including me, and some senior citizens.

The toddlers were the most verbose. It had been a while since I'd last been in close proximity to a bunch of children for an extended period of time, and their constant squawking seemed exaggerated and endless. But the Wildman, the father of a toddler himself, was a natural entertainer and great with children. Corny jokes rolled out one after another, from the minute he began the tour. And the Wildman's jaunty step and rapid-fire chatter didn't fade at all throughout its two-and-a-half-hour course.

One of our first stops was beside a cluster of short sprouts with small yellow clusters at their heads. The tightly bunched heads almost looked like a miniature version of a broccoli crown.

"Hedge mustard," the Wildman declared. Following his cue, I picked one from the ground and tasted its small, flowering head. A second after chewing it with my front teeth, a strong, spicy mustard taste spread throughout my mouth.

"I think it tastes a little bit like Chinese hot mustard," said the Wildman. I wasn't sure if that was exactly the right comparison, but the weed tasted so distinctly flavorful, I couldn't imagine why our ancestors wouldn't have chosen it to cultivate thousands of years ago along with other mustards. I grabbed a number of these and tucked them into a plastic bag—I had remembered to take a bunch of bags this time.

"Uh-oh, and you see those?" the Wildman said, pointing to a tall, leafy green. "This is deadly nightshade. It's pure poison. You can touch it, but whatever you do, don't eat it."

On Tim's tour, too, I had been warned of the deadly nightshade plant. We were standing right by a patch of it when he was introducing us to common plantain, and he'd pointed out how similar the two plants were in appearance. Mistakes could be fatal even if eaten in small doses.

The Wildman now illustrated this point with a musical interlude. "If you eat this, the next thing you'll be hearing is this—"

He cupped his mouth into a hollow drum and clapped on his cheeks eleven times, patting out the dreadful tune they play in movies when someone has died. The children squealed in delight. Their parents snorted with laughter, none too fazed by the deadly plant. We trod on.

Next we came across a patch of tender-looking greens with distinctly heart-shaped leaves. Here and there, small blue-violet petals decorated their slender stems.

"These are violets," the Wildman told us. "Violet leaves are great at this time of the year, since they're very young. They get much thicker and tougher the longer you wait, but now they're nice and tender. Try," he said, and picked up a handful to pass around. Everyone bent down and began gathering the leaves.

"You can also eat the flowers, in case you didn't know. It makes lovely tea. Now, there's a story about violets," he said. And the Wildman began a drawn-out tale, told with a true storyteller's flair: A few years ago, while taking a group on a tour of a park, he met a lady who was particularly interested in everything he said. They kept in touch afterward, and a few months later, they began to court. A full year later, once the violets had begun to sprout again in the spring, they were married. After another year, they gave birth to their beloved daughter and named her Violet, after the very plant we were eating.

The Wildman elaborated on a lot of the plants I had seen on my foraging tour the day before, too. It was a good refresher course for so many of these common weeds. The chickweed, he pointed out, not only was an edible leafy green but made an effective poultice for rashes, or itches caused by bug bites. When its juicy stalks were split, you could rub them directly onto your skin. Even though I didn't have any itches, I tried it out on my leg. The cooling sensation from the plant's liquids felt refreshing. He also had some differing thoughts on some of the plants I was becoming familiar with. Dandelions, for instance, were much too bitter in his estimation to eat at this time of year. In March, the leaves were tender enough to eat raw, but now they were thicker, tougher, and more sharply bitter. He recommended cooking them at their present stage.

"Now, does anyone know why they're called dandelion?" he asked our group. A few guesses from the group later, he provided the rationale: "It translates to 'tooth of the lion' in French. *Dent de lion*. Because of the way the leaves are so sharply serrated."

One of my favorite discoveries of the day was wild garlic. Its long, slender grasses smelled strongly of onion, hinting at what lay just beneath the earth's surface. I could remember picking these out of my front lawn as a kid as well. But what I didn't realize then was that when these were pulled up from the earth slowly and carefully, they retained their small, bulbous roots, which were essentially small, bulbous cloves of miniature garlic. I stuffed a bunch of these into my bag. As they grew fairly rampantly year-round, I had the feeling I might never need to buy garlic again.

We came to a small cluster of spiky brambles near the Boathouse, situated by a scenic pond in the center of the park. We had stopped there initially to break for lunch, and afterward, the Wildman had sighted a black birch tree. The actual tree, not the leaves, turned out to be the draw of this particular plant. He carefully twisted off a small twig and split it in half, so that its young, rubbery bark pulled away from the greenish wood beneath. He sucked on the twig where it had broken.

"Now, can anyone guess what this tastes like?" Brill asked.

A few of us followed and broke off tiny twigs from the tree. Once I put it to my mouth, I immediately sensed a very familiar taste. My first thought was chewing gum—some type of mint. Then, on further thought, I guessed it was more like root beer.

"Sassafras!" I said aloud, naming the root that the popular drink's flavor was modeled after.

"Nope, it's not sassafras," the Wildman said.

"Cinnamon?" someone else guessed.

"Nope, it's not cinnamon, either," the Wildman said again. "Does anyone else have a guess?"

Everyone in the group sucked thoughtfully but shook their heads.

"It's wintergreen. Or winter mint. It comes from this plant," he told us. "Now, the important thing about this one is that it's also a mild pain reliever. If you chew on the stems a little, like this"—he demonstrated, with characteristic cartoonishness—"you get a mild dose of natural pain relievers. Also, if you steep it in tea, it's especially good for women around that time of the month."

A bunch of women on the tour immediately began twisting stems off the tree.

"Since it's a natural and safe alternative to aspirin, it's also good for kids and babies. When Violet was teething, she used to chew on this," the Wildman went on.

Since I love the flavor of wintergreen, I was a little bit more excited about steeping it in tea or something else to add flavor than about trying to cure my headaches with it. Though this was good to know as well—maybe I could cure a headache with a bowl of wintergreen ice cream sometime soon.

I had a question on my mind that I'd been trying to form the words for. I stepped up to Wildman as he was in the process of twisting a particularly toothsome branch apart, and asked him why all these plants, which were so great for eating or for other purposes, weren't mass-grown but only found in the wild.

"Well, because back when people decided to domesticate plants, they only picked some, and that was that, and the rest became weeds, and now we never think of them as food!" he replied. He'd shot this out so quickly, while tucking some of the birch into his fanny pack and getting ready to lead the group on down the path, that I felt like I had just asked the most obvious question in the world. His words made perfect sense, though, and at least now, the whole explanation seemed obvious.

As we were walking along the trail away from the black birch tree, the Wildman looked more closely at a bush next to it.

"Ah, this is a raspberry bush," he declared. "The raspberries won't grow until late June, though. So remember where it is—that's easy, it's pretty close to the Boathouse, just down the path a bit from it." I took careful note of this on my pad.

Just as with trash diving, there is some fine print associated with the act of foraging plants from the park. This was the subject of the Wildman's most drawn-out yarn of the day, told with a mix of wry sarcasm and bravado. It's against the law to "harm" the plants of New York City's public parks, and that meant Prospect Park, Central Park, and almost all the parks where he gives walking lectures on wildlife. In 1986, an inflamed New York City Parks Department held a sting operation to smoke him out. Evidently on a mission of epic pettiness (this was during the height of New York City crime), two park rangers dressed in plain clothes attended one of Brill's tours of Central Park, taking extensive photos and eventually calling for backup. Steve Brill was arrested, handcuffed, booked, and slapped with numerous charges. The story spread throughout all the major news channels and newspapers. NATURALIST ARRESTED FOR EATING A DANDELION, the headlines read. The parks department soon realized it had a PR disaster on its hands. But within a few weeks, they came to an agreement with Brill: They would drop the charges and allow Brill to continue giving his nature sessions in public parks under a set of sensible guidelines, mostly for the sake of the tour-goers' safety. Since then, he's taught hundreds of New Yorkers about the plants in their city's backyard.

As we were nearing the entrance to the park at Grand Army Plaza, having made a half circle of the park through winding paths, we passed a field of tulips.

"Don't pick those," he said to one toddler, who was eyeing them. "They're not perennials, so that's it if you take them."

The Wildman went on to explain that all of the plants we were harvesting that day were common perennials (meaning plants that live more than two years), able to be harvested multiple times throughout the year. They were hardy, invasive plants, a point driven home by their plentifulness. In some cases, picking them even encouraged their regrowth. Dandelion, for instance, is known for being especially well adapted to "disturbed habitats" not so kind to other plants, and for multiplying when it's fussed with. Also, it was important to pick plants only in places where there was a large bunch of the species in that one place. That would ensure that that particular patch would continue to thrive throughout its various stages.

Once the tour was complete, I had more than doubled the amount of wildlife that was already in my fridge. The wild garlic was one of the most useful finds of the day. I would use it in place of regular garlic throughout the month, and its thin, mild-tasting shoots were an easy substitute for fresh chives as a garnish. I concocted a simple salad of dandelion greens as soon as I got home and used garlic and the hedge mustard, minced up finely, to flavor the dressing.

*   *   *

About a month and a half later, while biking in the park, I passed the Boathouse and suddenly recalled the date. It was just then late July. I pressed the brakes and swerved onto the gravel path just behind the pond. When I came to the bush, sure enough, it was brimming with berries that were just beginning to turn from bright bloodred to dark purplish-black. I picked some and found that the darkest ones of the bunch were the sweetest and fell off the branch the easiest. This must be a black raspberry bush, I concluded. I took the blackest ones of the bunch and put them into my emptied water bottle.

Exhilarated by the discovery, I went home and ate a bowl full of homemade ice cream with raspberries on top. For the next few weeks, I made several trips to the same raspberry brambles, observing each time the berries that had gradually turned deep black-ripe and seizing on the opportunity every time.

Knowing about the hidden raspberry bush somehow felt incredible, like I had my own little secret tucked away in the park. It also felt like a thing of the past. People must have had the same feeling, I thought—that personally fulfilling connection with nature upon finding one of its choicest treats, for as far back as human history dates. There is something dangerously beautiful about wild foods when they're not deadly. Perhaps because there's that risk attached to wildness that makes discovering something as delicious as the common raspberry in a forest ten times more magical than finding it in any other setting. There is also a preciousness about foods that can be sniffed out only by hand—wild mushrooms like truffles and chanterelles. I thought about the pleasant surprise that Thoreau must have had when he stumbled upon a cache of raspberries or another familiar food while living on Walden Pond. I could imagine the smug satisfaction it must have given people centuries ago, before the domestication of many of these crops. Raspberries have been growing wild in North America for ages. I wondered whether Pocahontas had led John Smith to the choicest fruits to pick in the New World, if they ever had a thing together at all. I wondered what would have happened if D. H. Lawrence's heroine, Lady Chatterley, had found a raspberry bush while embracing the wilderness instead of her gruff groundskeeper. Would she have left Wragby to become a confectioner instead?

While I was lost in this state of fantasy, picking black raspberries from my "private" bush one afternoon, I suddenly heard a voice behind me.

"Hey—why are you picking them berries?"

I turned around; the voice belonged to a fifteen- or sixteen-year-old boy wearing long jean shorts and sneakers that looked about five sizes too big for his feet. Just behind him, a teenage girl sitting on a bench was craning her neck to watch us.

"Because they're good," I said.

"You can eat them?" he asked, eyes wide and a little frightened-looking.

"Yep, they're raspberries," I said.

"Those? You gonna eat those?"

I looked down at the container of berries I had just picked and scooped up a small handful. Their beads were full and shiny black in the sun. One of them made a smear of bright purple on my palm as I turned it over. I held out my hand for the boy.

"See? Want some?"

But the teenager scoffed at my offering, jumping back and making a face as if he had seen a putrefied maggot.

"No, thanks," he said. He went back to the bench and sat down beside the girl, who instantly started laughing.

Gee whiz, did these kids not know their asses from their elbows? I thought. These were raspberries, beautiful, black raspberries—and here they were free, free for the taking!

For the next few minutes I continued to search for the ripest berries to take home with me, but my quiet little reverie on raspberry picking had been broken. I could hear the girl and boy making cracks about me, being none too careful to go unheard. Giggling in spastic waves, they talked about how they would never, not in a million years, eat something they had picked from a bush.

"Like, not if I were dying, like starving in a desert, like not even then," the boy loudly cracked.

Back to reality. I was definitely in the twenty-first century, that was for sure.

Wild Dandelion and Pecan Turnovers with Lemon Béchamel

Wild dandelion has a sharp, peppery bite when raw and retains its bitterness when sautéed. The flavor of this vitamin-rich leaf, however, makes a refreshing alternative to bland spinach when stuffed inside a savory pastry crust. Best part: These turnovers are great to freeze and reheat in the oven whenever you want a quick "hot pocket." (MAKES 6)

FOR THE PASTRY:

1½ cups all-purpose flour
½ teaspoon salt
6 tablespoons cold unsalted butter, cubed
1–2 tablespoons cold water
Egg wash or milk for brushing (optional)

FOR THE FILLING:

6–8 ounces fresh dandelion greens, trimmed of long
    stems, soaked in cold water, and rinsed
⅓ cup finely chopped onion
1 tablespoon butter
½ tablespoon flour
½ cup heavy cream
Salt and pepper to taste
Pinch of nutmeg

FOR THE LEMON BÉCHAMEL:

1 tablespoon butter
1 tablespoon all-purpose flour
1 cup whole milk
Salt to taste
1 tablespoon fresh lemon juice

Make the pastry: Sift flour and salt and cut in butter in a food processor or with a pastry cutter until mixture resembles coarse crumbs no larger than a pea. Add cold water a small spoonful at a time, just until moist enough to form a ball. Cover with plastic wrap and chill while making the filling.

Make the filling: Heat up a large pot of water and prepare an ice water bath in a large bowl. Once pot of water is boiling, add the dandelion greens and cook for 1 minute. Remove with tongs and immediately place into the ice bath for another minute. Drain and squeeze excess water from dandelion greens. Chop roughly.

Cook the onions and butter in a saucepan on medium-low heat for about 4 minutes, until softened. Add the flour and stir thoroughly. Add the dandelions and stir. Add the cream and cook, stirring about 2 minutes. Season with salt and pepper to taste and pinch of nutmeg. Taste, adjusting seasoning as desired. Remove from heat and let cool.

Preheat oven to 375 degrees. Divide chilled pastry into 6 equal balls and roll each one out to about a 6-inch oval. Fill one side of each oval with an equal allotment of the filling. Fold over the other side of the pastry, and crimp the edges shut with a fork. Brush tops of pastries with optional egg wash or milk (for a golden color). Place on an ungreased baking sheet and bake for about 25 minutes, until edges are lightly browned. Remove from oven and let cool 10 minutes before serving.

Make the sauce: Melt butter over medium heat in a small saucepan. Add flour and stir constantly for about 2 minutes to make a roux. Add the milk, increase heat to high, and stir constantly, being sure to scrape around the sides and the bottom of the pan, until mixture begins to bubble and thicken, about 4–5 minutes. Remove from heat. Season with salt to taste and add the lemon juice. Drizzle sauce on a serving plate to place the turnover on top of.

Roasted Potato Salad with Beet Greens and Stems, Wild Garlic, Chives, and Hedge Mustard

Beet greens and stems are a good reminder that even though some parts of a vegetable are not as popular or as commonly eaten as the ones we're most familiar with, they're still perfectly edible. In the case of deep purple beet-green stems, they're actually terrific—mild, crisp, and nutritious to boot. This light potato salad uses minimal dressing, with herbs from the park. Be sure to consult a wild edibles expert and have some experience in identifying the plants before picking, though!

6 medium waxy potatoes, such as red or Yukon gold
4 tablespoons extra-virgin olive oil
Salt and pepper to taste
Pinch of cayenne pepper (optional)
Greens and stems from 1 bunch of beets
2 teaspoons finely chopped wild garlic bulbs
1 teaspoon finely chopped hedge mustard flower
1 tablespoon balsamic vinegar
1 tablespoon finely chopped wild chives (the stems from the wild onion plant)
1 stalk celery, finely chopped

Heat oven to 375 degrees. Cut potatoes into roughly 1-inch wedges. Coat with about 2 tablespoons of the oil, and season with salt, pepper, and optional cayenne. Roast approximately 15 minutes or until pieces are lightly browned and crisped in some parts. Let cool.

Coarsely chop beet-green leaves and stems. Heat a tablespoon of the oil, and once it's hot, toss in the leaves and stems. Add the wild garlic and hedge mustard along with a pinch of salt and pepper. Toss for 1 minute, or just until the leaves are wilted. Remove from heat.

Trim the toughest, thickest ends from the beet-green stems and discard. Chop the remaining stems and leaves into roughly ½-inch pieces (or pieces about the size of your chopped celery). In a large bowl, whisk the remaining tablespoon of olive oil with the balsamic vinegar and add the wild chives. Combine the potatoes, beet greens and stems, and celery, and toss to coat evenly. Can be served warm, room temperature, or cold.

CHAPTER 7

Not Ordering In

LESS HASTE, LESS WASTE

By sowing frugality we reap liberty, a golden harvest.

—*Agesilaus*

The kitchen in the new apartment I shared with Ben was about half the size of the one that I shared with Erin. Everything about it was miniaturized: the stove, the sink, and the lone slat of counter space, which was about the size of a sheet of legal paper. It fit the one cutting board I had, and that was all. But like the rest of the appliances in the unit, everything in it was brand-new. And since Ben didn't use the kitchen for much of anything, aside from placing the spare bike part on top of the refrigerator now and then, it was also all mine. For the first time in my life, I had complete reign over a kitchen—no roommates to share cooking space with, no dirty dishes that I didn't play a part in creating.

Once I broke the kitchen into my cooking routine, it became clear that my cohabitation with Ben was going to need some guidelines. First, I would be the cook, plain and simple. Naturally I pegged Ben as the dishwasher at first, but it turned out he had a near-phobic aversion to doing the dishes. I had seen this disorder before in many others—roommates and friends. They abhorred washing dishes as if it were the filthiest task the human race could deign to complete. So they piled up their sinks with them, leaving the leftover crusts of food to fester there for days at a time. I soon realized that if I forced Ben to be the dishwasher, this is what would end up happening. So instead, I made him the official floor scrubber, bathroom cleaner, duster, sweeper, garbage taker-outer, and uncontested handyman of the rest of the entire apartment. The kitchen was solely my territory.

With this new sense of power in mind, my nightly cooking habits took on a more ambitious turn. One of the first dishes I made using the oven was a Hanukkah recipe I had read about in *The New York Times* for stuffed-under-the-skin chicken. I took my time creating the stuffing and carefully packing it under the skins of the quartered chicken pieces. I'd also gone on a last-minute run to the market that evening to find the smoked paprika that the dish required. By the time I put it in the oven, it was nine o'clock. By the time the toothsome chicken was suitably cooked through, it was eleven. Ben had already given up on it and ordered pizza. So I had stuffed-under-the-skin chicken for most of that week.

I resolved to cook more quickly on weeknights from then on. There were a handful of dishes and techniques I could rely on to achieve this—if I had leftover rice, I could always make a quick meal of fried rice with eggs and frozen peas. I could also do stir-fries or pasta with fresh vegetables and grated cheese on the fly. At the end of my meal I'd put away the leftover portion in Tupperware and bring it with me to work the next day. I'd also do the dishes.

Every now and then Ben would still order takeout just to satisfy a craving. Once his meal was done, he'd pile the remains in our small garbage bin: carryout containers, aluminum foil, waxed paper, sometimes a cardboard pizza box, plastic cutlery, unwanted sauces, menus, paper bags, and the plastic bags the paper bags often came in. On those occasions when Ben ordered takeout, our garbage bin was overflowing by the end of the night.

"Why don't you just tell them you don't want the duck sauce or the menu?" I asked Ben after he polished off a takeout tray of sesame chicken one night. I knew that I was treading dangerous ground whenever I contested his eating habits, as he played safe by not challenging mine. He shrugged and stuffed the squeaky container into the trash can, cracking its top to fit it all in. I already knew the simple answer to this question: It was easier not to. He was not one to make special requests when ordering his food. It was also of no immediate matter to me: Ben ordering more takeout meals meant fewer dishes for me to clean and more garbage for him to take downstairs.

This comparison summed up a previously undiscovered formula about not eating out: more dishes, less garbage. Now that I was cooking for myself and eating in, I had a lot more dishes to do. Dishes, of course, are meant to be used, washed, and reused, until they break (or go out of style, at which point hopefully someone else less discerning will get to use them). It was the equivalent of a handkerchief versus a Kleenex when compared to takeout boxes and bags. I had to sacrifice both the time and energy spent cooking as well as cleaning up after it, just the things the patrons of takeout or restaurant food save by their convenience.

But on the upside, I had a lot less garbage on my hands. It struck me then how much less trash I was producing since I'd stopped eating out. It wasn't just at home, either. At work I used to have a smelly pile of trash from my takeout lunch and sometimes breakfast wrappings in the bin under my desk by the end of the day. These days, I left the office with it virtually empty most of the time. I had stumbled upon a benefit of my original mission: By not eating out, my garbage footprint was now considerably smaller.

I thought about all the unwanted accoutrements that come with every takeout meal. Back when I was buying lunch every day at work, there were so many little things to throw out at the end of the unceremonious twenty-minute eating spree at my desk. Pushing the keyboard aside, I might have a small box of sushi one day. The molded plastic tray came with a lid that, once popped off, served as the dipping bowl for sauces. The soy sauce and wasabi came in individually wrapped packets, as did the pickled ginger and the pair of disposable wooden chopsticks. On the tray beside the sushi was a small green piece of plastic film that was cut along one edge to resemble spiky grass. Everything came inside a plastic bag, along with a stack of napkins that I used less than half of. Another day it might be a cup-sized portion of soup in a cardboard carton along with a double-wrapped half sandwich, a roll, and crackers, along with a spoon, salt and pepper packets, and another bag with more napkins.

The trash produced by food ordered by delivery was even worse. I rarely had my weekday lunches delivered, but when I was an executive assistant, I often had to order for my boss. Even if it was just coffee, the delivery man would arrive holding a big bag; inside it was a cardboard cup with a protective sleeve to keep you from burning your fingers, napkins, creamers, sugar packets, stirrers, and if the order was for more than one coffee, a four-cup holder—basically, a whole powder-room wastebasket's worth of trash. I wonder if it's not telling that the household trash cans of yesterday tended to be much smaller than today's mammoth tubs.

It's no surprise that Americans are the world's biggest producers of garbage. According to Elizabeth Royte in her book *Garbage Land: On the Secret Trail of Trash*, "Since 1960, the nation's municipal waste stream has nearly tripled, reaching a reported peak of 360 million tons in 2002." Interestingly, over the course of the same period the number of meals Americans ate in restaurants versus the number of meals they prepared and ate at home has risen nearly that much.

That isn't to say that the restaurant industry is solely to blame for all that garbage. A home-cooked meal is rarely garbage free, either (unless you harvest your own foods from your farm or garden, and compost the debris). But packaging now accounts for 30 percent of all landfill space in the United States, making it the single biggest category of trash. Packaging includes the boxes that frozen foods come in, or the cardboard containers hot French fries are served in. It's a sturdy, crisp shopping bag from a boutique, the elaborate box a bottle of perfume might come inside, the foam peanuts and crumpled newsprint that boxes are shipped with, and so on. Packaging is simply "trash waiting to happen," wrote Heather Rogers in *Gone Tomorrow: The Hidden Life of Garbage*. And it's an essential part of the takeout or delivered restaurant meal.

Cans, bottles, egg cartons, and shopping bags from grocery store purchases all add to the national waste stream. But individual takeout meals that feed one person at a time come with a lot more disposable paper and plastic goods per serving. It's been estimated the U.S. population tosses out enough paper and plastic cups, forks, and spoons every year for them to circle the equator three hundred times. And many of them are unwanted and never used, like the sauce packets and extra menus that Ben would routinely throw out. All the extraneous trash waiting to happen, so to speak, also takes massive amounts of energy to produce, and some materials they're made out of, like plastics, don't ever properly decompose.

So the more whole foods one cooks with, I found, the less packaging is produced. Foods like fresh produce generally go into plastic bags by the handfuls and can be used for several meals. Dry grains like rice and flour can make dozens of single servings at the price of one bag, waste-wise. Processed or prepared foods from the grocery store, however, come with more packaging. Sometimes they're individually wrapped inside boxes, like snack brownies and cereal bars, or come with disposable trays, like frozen dinners. Often, they're portioned off for one serving only, such as small cups of yogurt. I realized that the more I cooked from scratch, with whole foods like vegetables from the Greenmarket, or flour for bread, the less packaging I would go through as a general rule; the more processed the food, the more waste it creates.

In her book, Royte decided to weigh all the garbage she alone produced on a daily basis, and she was surprised to see how much solid bulk she tossed away on her first day. The trash included an empty wine bottle, a milk carton, and a peanut butter jar, dense objects that, for their purposes, would have been made to last more than one use in an earlier time. I had plenty of these containers around my apartment, too, waiting to hit the recycling bins or trash cans once they were used up. But I was still convinced that eating in created much less trash than taking out. For example, I had the same bottle of soy sauce in my cupboard that I'd been using for months. With all those packets, containers, and plastic cutlery (which Ben would never use when there was a real fork around), takeout could easily create double the amount of trash of a home-cooked meal, I projected.

I suddenly remembered some of the horrors of modern-day catering. When I was working at the publishing house, I ordered business lunches twice a week for meetings. I'd order the meal for the group and unload it in the conference room. A basket of paper-wrapped half sandwiches came wrapped in cellophane and decorative ribbons—an actual wicker basket of them. The wraps were wrapped in paper, and each sandwich half was speared with a wooden toothpick. The side dishes came in sturdy plastic serving bowls, with sturdy plastic serving spoons and tongs, some that were extra and never used, and a bowl of salad always came with three or four tubs full of different types of dressing (most barely touched by the end of the meeting). There was a large plastic platter of cookies, brownies, and other desserts, also wrapped in cellophane. Everything was thrown out after the meal—from the baskets to the tongs. (Weren't tongs and serving spoons meant to be made with quality, to be used in kitchens for close to a lifetime?) All of these disposables were too big to fit in a single tall garbage bin in the office kitchen. And the next week, the same exact order would be placed again, with the same amount of trash.

At another company I worked for, the upper management had a fondness for ordering from a shop that served individually boxed sandwich halves. After conferences, the kitchen was filled with leftovers, stacks of cardboard boxes with a cellophane window built into one edge that showed the insides of the particular sandwich half that it held. Most people took two or three boxes at lunch to fill up.

Fancy packaging from high-end restaurants may be one thing, but even fast food or the cheapest takeout place offers a pile of inedible waste with every order. In the *Omnivore's Dilemma*, Michael Pollan recalls the allure that fast food at McDonald's held for him as a child, noting that the food was wrapped up like "little presents" and that he didn't have to share any of his own items with his sisters. This speaks to a strong attachment we must have as a culture to wrapped-up food, just like we want our presents to be nicely wrapped.

So, I concluded that not eating out had whipped me into a lean, mean, less-garbage-making machine. But by how much less? I wondered. Was there a way to find out, maybe by comparing the total waste of an average cooked-at-home meal to that of one average takeout meal? I decided to follow Elizabeth Royte's example and do a mini-weigh-in myself.

Of course, there is no such thing as a perfectly "average" or "normal" homemade meal or takeout meal to make this comparison airtight. But just for curiosity's sake, I thought I might try to make the exact same dish I could buy from a takeout restaurant. For this I went with an easy category for me: Chinese stir-fry. I decided I'd place an order for a single lunch-sized serving of chicken with broccoli and white rice, and make the same simple dish at home for one. Then I'd weigh all the garbage produced from each version and see which took the heaviest toll.

To get started, I first purchased a kitchen scale. Earlier that week, I'd picked up a head of broccoli from the Greenmarket, which was wrapped in a single plastic bag in the fridge. To get the chicken, I went to a small butcher shop in my neighborhood. I pointed to the boneless chicken breasts behind the glass case, and the butcher raised an eyebrow when I told him that I wanted just one. Shrugging, he wrapped the half pound or so of meat in butcher paper and slipped it inside a small plastic bag. The rest of the ingredients I'd need to make this dish I had at home already: rice in a large plastic bag in my cupboard, sauces in bottles and jars, some garlic. This was just the kind of dish I'd make all the time: a stir-fry with one type of meat and one veggie. You could make four portions of the same, satisfying thing in under one hour, easily.

Around this time, I was becoming more wary of not only how much waste I was creating, but how environmentally friendly the actual foods I purchased were, too. I'd read *The Omnivore's Dilemma* and was avidly devouring magazine articles and websites having to do with the sustainable food movement, which was then not yet really a movement. I felt guilty as I walked home from the butcher. I would have bought some chicken from the farmers' market if it had been open that day, at a stand that sold cage-free and humanely raised animals. I had read up on horrifying facts about chicken coops where the animals spent their short lives squashed together, and was sympathetic to these and other conventional meat animals' poor health and living conditions. I'd also read *Fast Food Nation*, and the *E. coli* in hamburger meat that had created a scare, described in that book, was now turning up in vegetables like spinach. As time went by, I would find out about the problems of runoff from those great big feedlots, how it was contaminating water supplies, and how monoculture (the practice of planting only one plant variety), favored by industrial agriculture, threatened crops and biodiversity. It seemed like most of our food supply was being controlled by very careless corporations. In middle school, I'd overhear students crack jokes about the gray hamburger patties in the cafeteria. As long as I was in a place to make a decision about what to purchase and eat and what not to, I'd stick with the more responsibly raised meats, I'd decided—which happened to be tastier and less "gray" than the others.

All this new food awareness was gradually weighing in on my food-buying choices. Since I was buying raw ingredients to cook with, I was faced with decisions like whether to buy organic, humanely raised, or pesticide free all the time. This was another unexpected result of my not-eating-out mission: I was now forced to think about where that meat or that vegetable came from and how it was grown. Eating in restaurants, you don't often have that choice as a consumer. More and more, restaurants tout the names of the farms or purveyors where their ingredients came from. But this trend is mostly among more upscale eateries, often expensive ones, too. And that was something I really couldn't afford all the time. I figured that with the money that I was saving by not eating out, I could afford to be choosy and to buy based on principle. Hence, eating in, and cooking everything, was the catalyst for my interest in healthy, sustainable, seasonal, local, and generally more earth-friendly food.

I added another feature to my blog to showcase this in every recipe I posted. I called it the "Green Factor," and it rated the environmental friendliness of all the ingredients in the dish, combined. After every Green Factor rating, I tried my best to explain why it was rated so, digging into the implications of all the foods, how and where they came from. Ultimately, I stopped eating meat as frequently, since the pastured meats I now wanted to strictly support were more expensive, and I didn't feel that I was sacrificing my health by having meat only once or twice a week. On the contrary, you could argue that less meat in our diet keeps humans and the earth healthier. That chicken breast that I got from the butcher for my weigh-in experiment had been the first piece of meat I'd bought in a week.

Once home, I chopped up some garlic and a few slices of ginger from a knob that was drying in my cupboard. I couldn't remember exactly how these had been packaged when I'd gotten them. I no longer had the original bags, but I guessed that I had bought them originally in plastic ones. Still, I was using so little ginger and garlic for one individual-sized portion of chicken and broccoli that these bags would be almost negligent in my waste weigh-in.

Calculations got trickier when it came to the sauces I put in the dish. I added a few splashes of soy sauce to marinate the chicken, along with a spoonful of cornstarch. While the chicken was cooking in about a tablespoon of vegetable oil, I added a splash of Chinese rice wine, followed by another few splashes of soy sauce and some jarred hot sauce. All these things came out of glass bottles or jars except for the cornstarch, which was in a small cardboard box. All these ingredients, too, had been in my kitchen for the better part of a year. How many one-pint servings of chicken and broccoli, then, could each bottle make? The task of weighing out the refuse for my single serving proved excruciatingly difficult, especially since most of these bottles in my cupboard were only partially full. In the case of the rice wine, I thankfully used up the last two tablespoons or so from the bottle, so the weight of the bottle was easy to calculate. But the soy sauce bottle was about half full, so I had to divide the weight of the contents printed on its label by half. Following numerous tedious calculations, I sat down to make the following list:

¾-POUND CHICKEN BREAST:

>   Butcher paper from chicken = 0.25 ounce (perhaps mostly because it was wet)

½ POUND BROCCOLI:

>   Plastic bag from the broccoli (did this really weigh anything? It didn't register on the kitchen scale . . .) = 0.005 ounce

1 TABLESPOON SOY SAUCE:

>   Total weight of empty bottle = 15.5 ounces
>   Number of 1-tablespoon uses per bottle = 34
>   So total glass waste of a 1-tablespoon serving (15.5 ÷ 34) = 0.45 ounce

2 TABLESPOONS RICE WINE:

> Total weight of empty 24-ounce bottle = 16 ounces
> Number of 1-tablespoon uses per bottle = 28
> Number of 2-tablespoon uses per bottle (28 ÷ 2) = 14
> So total glass waste of a 2-tablespoon serving (16 ÷ 14)
>   = 0.43 ounce

1 TEASPOON HOT CHILI SAUCE:

> Total weight of empty 18-ounce plastic jar = 5 ounces
> Number of 1-teaspoon uses per bottle = 102
> So total plastic waste of a 1-teaspoon serving (5 ÷ 102)
>   = 0.05 ounce

1 TABLESPOON CORNSTARCH:

> Total weight of empty cardboard box of cornstarch: 2
>   ounces
> Number of 1-tablespoon uses per box = 56
> So total cardboard waste of a 1-tablespoon serving
>   (2 ÷ 56) = 0.035 ounce

1 TABLESPOON VEGETABLE OIL:

> Total weight of empty (because I drained it!) 24-ounce
>   plastic bottle = 1 ounce
> Number of 1-tablespoon uses per bottle = 28
> So total plastic waste of a 1-tablespoon serving (1 ÷ 28)
>   = 0.035 ounce

**TOTAL GARBAGE WASTE FOR SINGLE SERVING OF HOME-COOKED
CHICKEN WITH BROCCOLI: 1.255 OUNCES**

For the next part of the weigh-in, a couple of days later, I picked up the phone and, with a paper menu in hand, dialed the number of the nearest Chinese takeout restaurant. I ordered a pint of chicken and broccoli, served with white rice, and a can of soda. Then I waited.

An order of plain old chicken and broccoli from a slipshod Chinese takeout restaurant with fiberglass between the counterperson and the customer would not ordinarily have been my meal of choice for compromising my not-eating-out mission. This sacrifice was purely for the purposes of the weigh-in. Still, as I walked down the street to pick up my order a few minutes later, I realized how strangely excited I was about eating it. I'd had this same dish countless times throughout my life, near identical in flavor and appearance, from countless Chinese takeout places that were nearly identical in appearance as well. By the time I finished my lunch, which was quite a lot for one person, I was strangely satisfied. The meal wasn't great—actually, it was a lot worse than I'd expected it to taste: too sweet, the sauce thick and gloppy from too much cornstarch. But maybe that was a good thing for now. I'd be able to keep eating in a little more confidently now than if it had been better.

I made sure the kitchen scale was set at zero before I weighed all the disposables from the takeout meal. On went the foam tray, now emptied, along with the fork, stack of napkins, extra sauce packets, paper bag, and the plastic bag that had held everything. The takeout place had given me a can of soda as part of the lunch special, so after it was emptied I placed it in the scale's basket as well, along with the straw and wrapper. The number on the dial was difficult to read, but it told me that the total weight was slightly more than 3 ounces all together, somewhere between 3.25 and 3.5. My $18 investment in the kitchen scale and $5 takeout lunch had been justified: the Chinese takeout meal weighed significantly more than the 1.255 ounces I produced in cooking the same portion of my homemade version. (I decided to leave the soda can's weight out of the total for this, too, since I didn't drink soda with my homemade version of the meal.)

As I was placing the Styrofoam takeout tray onto the scale, squinting to read that it weighed just under 1 ounce, I began to feel like this was all slightly ridiculous, my weigh-in. I also began to wonder whether its weight was really the end of this story. Or whether it was the most important one.

Let's start with the plastic bag that the takeout meal came in. Granted, in addition to the plastic takeout bag, I had also used a plastic bag to take home the broccoli from the Greenmarket. But flimsy plastic bags in general amount to a whopping mass of waste throughout the planet. Even though many Americans have replaced them with reusable cloth totes when doing their shopping, they're a tough staple to do without in a lot of cases, like with fresh meats and produce. The reusable bags have made great strides in recent years, and more and more people than ever bring them to grocery stores instead of opting for the store's plastic or paper. However, the trend hasn't become so popular in the takeout food world—or, for that matter, when shopping for anything else.

Sometimes when I need a snack at work, I head down to the nearest fruit cart on the street. The same vendor always tries to offer me a plastic bag to carry my purchase of one single piece of fruit. He isn't making a special case; everyone else I see is offered one and almost always accepts it. In the same vein, the ubiquitous coffee-and-bagel carts in New York City are notorious for handing customers a single cup of coffee in a brown paper bag, with a pile of paper napkins. In most cases, the bag becomes trash the moment it leaves the vendor's hands. I can't figure out the reason for all of this—if it's meant to protect the customer from handling a piping-hot cup, then what's the use of the ultrathick stack of napkins?

These carts are placed close to office buildings for convenience, too. The cart nearest my office is about six or seven paces from the building door. I've caved to that temptation and grabbed a bagel or croissant on occasion. The first few times, I felt guilty chucking the brown paper bag the minute I got upstairs, so I began waving away the bag whenever a vendor snapped one open to put my purchase in. So what if people saw me holding a cold bagel on the elevator, I figured? It's a bagel, not a 40-ounce bottle of malt liquor.

Every lunch hour I saw coworkers coming back to their desks carrying bags that hold a single plastic case of tossed salad, or pre-pared, buffet-style food. The way I saw it, a paper bag is no easier to clutch than the container the food is typically wrapped in already. As long as there aren't eight things being carried in the bag, it didn't really offer much more ease.

One logical answer might be the need for someplace to put the forks, napkins, and other utensils. I didn't see these as very difficult to carry in addition and, what's more, plastic cutlery is completely inferior to actual flatware. I tried to keep my own metal fork and knife at my desk at work, and I washed them every time I was done using them. They were pretty simple to keep, and I didn't have to deal with the flimsy prongs of the plastic fork struggling to do its job.

Moving on to the foam tray that held the bulk of my takeout meal: It's no news that the polystyrene foam packaging material is nonbiodegradable. It's been banned in the cities of Berkeley, California, and Portland, Oregon, since 1990, and it continues to be checked off by cities throughout the United States, including virtually every major one in California. There was a movement against polystyrene foam packaging when I was small, probably back in the early nineties when it was being banned in other places, and I remember my grade-school teachers instructing us to avoid using this nonbiodegradable packaging material at all costs. That's the last memory of public outrage over polystyrene foam packaging that I can recall. But these days I see it being used for takeout foods and drinks more than ever, from Dunkin' Donuts coffees to Jamba Juice smoothies—and now, Chinese takeout food.

But the use of polystyrene foam packaging is not just an environmental concern; it's a major public health concern. Polystyrene foam can leach the chemical styrene, a known carcinogen, into the food it touches, and with enough exposure it can cause damage to the human reproductive system. Researchers estimate that a polystyrene foam cup can leach up to 0.025 percent of styrene into the beverage it is holding in a single use, and the amount that it leaches increases when the food or beverage in question is hot or high in fat. It's debatable whether eating or drinking out of polystyrene foam containers can add up to enough styrene exposure to cause significant damage. But the long-term effects of styrene exposure, observed mainly through workers exposed to it in plants, have been undesirable.

The toxicity of polystyrene foam underscores a much bigger, developing problem in today's world—of untested and potentially hazardous chemicals lurking in nearly every manufactured product we touch. There has been a lot of hubbub over the dangers of the common plastic polyvinyl chloride (PVC) and phthalates, the family of chemicals often used to soften it. PVC may be used to make everything from plastic cling wrap to refrigerators, disposable drinking cups to reusable water bottles. But recently, the issue gained attention when it was discovered in baby toys such as teething rings. Like polystyrene foam, the amount of toxic chemicals these plastics can leach increases with heat. Everyday inks and dyes are under scrutiny as well: In one Italian study, researchers discovered that inks containing toxic chemicals were being printed on common cardboard pizza boxes, and they concluded that with the high heat levels inside the boxes, these chemicals could migrate into the food, although it is unclear what, if any, effect this could have on humans.

One of the most frustrating parts of this problem might just be that as consumers, we simply don't know what chemicals are in the products we're using. Unless we take it upon ourselves to do some investigative research and send plastic toys or food containers to a lab for inspection, there's no way to discern between a plastic fork laden with PVC and one that's not. There are sixty thousand chemical compounds on the market that have never been tested for safety that could be making it into our everyday products, according to Mark Schapiro in his book *Exposed: The Toxic Chemistry of Everyday Products and What's at Stake for American Power*. In contrast, ceramics, glass, and many types of metals have been used since the beginning of time to serve food. So with that in mind, I much prefer to eat my soup out of some type of ceramic dish when I can.

Leaving aside the unwanted sauce packets, extra paper menu, and napkins from my weigh-in for the moment, we get to the aluminum soda can. The government has tried to take measures to encourage aluminum recycling, offering a five-cent deposit in the states of New York, Maine, Vermont, Massachusetts, Hawaii, Iowa, and Connecticut (as my Chinese takeout can of Diet Pepsi had clearly engraved on its top). But collecting cans for their deposit value may soon be a thing of the past. According to the Container Recycling Institute (CRI), aluminum recycling rose significantly in the 1970s and 1980s, due in large part to the mandatory deposit legislature in nine states. Since 1992, however, when recycling reached a peak of 68 percent, the rate has been dropping steadily. Today, 50 percent of aluminum beverage cans in the United States are never recycled. And of course, we're producing more of them than ever.

Recycled aluminum cans have been demonstrated to be just as strong and durable as cans made from virgin materials, and they require one-twentieth of the energy to manufacture. The states with the highest deposit refunds, ranging from 2.5 to 10 cents a can, have the highest recycling rates. Michigan currently has the nation's highest rate, recycling more than 95 percent of aluminum because each can's redemption value is 10 cents.

In New York, the 5-cent refund has remained stagnant since the bottle bill that ensured a recycling redemption was first passed in 1983. Just imagine if a slice of pizza cost the same today as it did in 1983! Clearly, this incentive to recycle has not kept in line with inflation. Furthermore, New York doesn't reward the return of the empty containers of noncarbonated beverages such as bottled water, sports drinks, teas, and juices, as states like California, Maine, and Hawaii do.

Finally, on to the disposable chopsticks: Nearly every Chinese restaurant in America (and around the globe) has them, and they all get thrown out after one use. China produces 45 billion pairs of chopsticks each year, which accounts for an annual loss of roughly 25 million trees and a deforestation crisis that in 2006 prompted the Chinese government to place a 5 percent tax on disposable chopsticks, in the hopes that businesses would begin using and reusing washable chopsticks instead. And yet, most still haven't.

Suffice it to say, what began as a weigh-in of a takeout meal versus a home-cooked meal gave me a lot to weigh over. To be sure, I may have made the waste materials involved in wrapping a takeout meal sound frightening, destructive, and deadly. In truth, most of the exact same materials found in my batch of Chinese takeout garbage are found in grocery store and not-eating-out purchases, too. Many households purchase cans of soda, and microwaveable meals might come in PVC plastic trays. Eggs come in polystyrene foam containers sometimes, as well. And if you don't bring a reusable tote to the grocery store, you'll end up with a lot of double-bagged-plastic waste. These materials are all used in daily life for many purposes. But back to the argument about eating more whole foods rather than processed, or buying in bulk, or making more foods from scratch: The little differences in the amount of these materials that are wasted can really add up.

Many people have brought up the argument that eating at restaurants at least in theory is more efficient than cooking at home, conserving more resources and energy since restaurants cook larger quantities all at once. I've heard it complained more than a few times that people purchase groceries for one meal, and then end up with a lot of leftover ingredients that they don't know what to do with and eventually throw out, too. It's understandable, but the solution might just be to get more experienced at cooking and at grocery shopping. The argument has also been made that it takes more energy and resources if you're cooking for a single household—or person—at a time than for a restaurant full of people. It's also more cost-effective to purchase food in bulk, as restaurants do, which is part of why they make a profit from serving you.

These ideas are completely valid, and they might lead one to suggest that eating in sit-down restaurants only is the earth-friendly alternative to buying individually wrapped takeout from a restaurant. But I for one can't afford to do this (nor is this the most realistic option for most people).

Now that I've probably made all takeout restaurants on the planet look like accomplices to pure evil, I'll admit, I had plenty of cravings for all my old standby orders, especially throughout that first fall and chilly winter of not eating out. Sitting in front of the TV with takeout meals had been a rare indulgence for Ben and me when he lived at his old apartment (for some reason, we always sat on the floor with our takeout boxes spread out before us, as if they couldn't all fit on his dining table). If there wasn't enough in my cupboards, or if it was raining or freezing out, it was all too tempting to pick up the takeout menus to choose something to have delivered to my old apartment door, too.

Once in our new apartment, every time Ben came through the door with takeout, bathing the apartment in the scents of chicken *shawarma* or enchiladas, my mouth would water uncontrollably. It was also becoming increasingly dangerous to go out with friends and stay out late because there was always that point in the night when somebody wanted to get food. I learned to settle for a bodega snack if I was also hungry at times like those. I'd get chips or over-salted nuts, maybe an ice cream bar. But the allure of a late-night slice of hot pizza still remained, untouchable.

So to satisfy my cravings, I set out to re-create a few of my favorite takeout restaurant foods. I missed sushi, so I tried making my own seaweed-wrapped *maki* rolls. It seemed daunting at first: The rice needed to be carefully mixed with vinegar and then kept damp. The nori wrappers were unfamiliar to the touch and easy to tear. I scoured the Internet for tips on this technique, and for Christmas, I hinted to Ben that I might want to own a sushi cookbook, a hint he took. I also got myself a simple straw mat, sold at most Asian markets, that was used for making *maki*. After trying it out once, I realized that it was really easy to get the hang of. And almost any vegetable I had on hand tasted good in a *maki* roll. The nori is first placed on the straw mat, then covered with an even layer of sticky rice. From there you could place any slivered vegetables at the bottom. At first I had put mostly fresh vegetables, such as julienned cucumbers and carrots. Then I began experimenting with more cooked ingredients instead, or in addition. For rolls, I fried long slices of Japanese eggplant that had been dipped in a flour batter and a sprinkle of salt and cayenne pepper. I placed fresh spinach leaves on top of the rice that had been stuck to the nori seaweed, piled on the fried eggplant pieces in a neat bundle at the bottom edge of the square, and spread mayonnaise on top before rolling the rice and seaweed into a neat, tight log. It turned out that I didn't need the raw fish after all to sate my craving for sushi—the sushi rice and seaweed took care of that for the most part. All I needed were the rice, vinegar, nori, and a few vegetables, and I was set. I began making fresh cucumber rolls and, a couple of times, lightly steamed asparagus or roasted okra pod rolls to bring with me to lunch. I found that a package of nori seaweed wrappers goes a long way—there were usually between thirty and fifty sheets in each. Also, that *maki* rolls were a great food to transport wherever you needed to go, like work.

Because I was cooking so much, I was also producing a lot of organic waste—onion and garlic peels, husks and stems of vegetables, and so on. I began storing these in a sealed plastic container, and on Saturdays I would take them to the composting center I was fortunate to live a short walk from. I would try to use every part of a plant—or an animal, for that matter—as much as possible. I'd do different things with broccoli stems once in a while and even learned to make orange-peel candy once. I had no delusions of low-impact grandeur with these experiments. It was more of a way of fooling around with whatever stuff I had on hand, making the most of it. But I liked that they didn't end up going to waste.

By early spring, there was one staple of cheap, greasy, takeout food fun that I was still struggling to get right: pizza—perhaps the most iconic takeout food of them all. But I was determined. I wanted to eat pizza. The more I tried and failed at making a decent crust, the more I yearned to run to the pie shop down the street and just gobble up a thick, oil-slicked slice. It didn't matter how good the rest of the ingredients on it were. I wanted to bite into a slice that tasted and felt like a poofy, chewy, crispy-on-the-outside and maybe slightly charred-on-the-bottom actual pizza crust.

As I discovered in my early forays with bread baking, it is all about science. And I am just not a very precise-minded cook. The fun shuts off in my system after approximately four and a half minutes of repetitive kneading. I still wanted to make a good crust for my pizza. But I didn't want to spend an eternity getting to that point.

I'd heard of people buying dough on its own from pizza shops before but had never done it myself. So on my first visit, ever, to the nearest pizza shop in my new neighborhood, I walked in with trepidation. I waited while someone ahead paid for her order and walked out with a large cardboard box smelling like just what my appetite was asking for. Then I asked the man at the counter if he sold uncooked dough.

Expecting at least a quizzical stare, I was surprised when he immediately responded, "How many? One?"

I guessed that he meant enough dough for one large pie, so I nodded yes. He turned around and took a metal plate with a round pat of dough out from a shelf in the kitchen. Then he asked if I was going to use it that night, to which I nodded again.

"If not, then you should put it in the refrigerator," he instructed casually. He slipped the dough onto a paper plate and tucked it inside a white paper bag.

"Two dollars," he said.

I handed him two bills and took my purchase, silently cursing myself for the takeout bag and paper plate.

Once I got home, the pizza making got under way. Since this dough had already been kneaded and allowed to rise for however long the pizza shop preferred to do things, it needed only to be stretched out on a pan, topped, and baked in a hot oven. Ben helped me forge the dough into a floppy rectangle of somewhat uniform thickness, even taking a few attempts at tossing it in the air first. Luckily, the dough didn't fall on the floor. Next we placed it onto a rectangular cookie sheet, for lack of a round one or some other pizza-specific baking pan. I spread on some simple tomato sauce I had simmered earlier that week from a can of plum tomatoes, and spiced it up with a little more crushed red pepper. On top of that I layered on shredded mozzarella. Ben and I arranged some jarred jalapeños and slices of lightly browned Italian sausage on top—this was Ben's favorite pizza-topping combo.

The result of this pizza night was even more satisfying than I would have liked. I just wanted to keep eating, no matter how full I was. The pizza so nearly resembled the actual takeout experience, only it was better tasting, with all the toppings we'd added. I ate half the cookie sheet–sized pie in one night. Between the two of us, we finished it off.

I had aimed fairly low, hoping only to re-create an average slice of New York City pizza, more or less like the ones sold where I had purchased the dough. But what I came away with that night of our first pizza binge was something more than I'd bargained for. I always hated shops that used too little sauce, so I spread on a thick, oozing layer that seeped into the dough and made some parts a little sodden, though not in an unpleasant way.

After this success, I made pizzas every now and then. I tried to make them healthier by adding less cheese and more vegetables—sliced bell peppers, broccoli, zucchini, or whatever I had in the fridge. I used pesto and tapenade instead of tomato sauce sometimes, and learned to fashion other flatbread-like foods from the pizza-shop dough, like an olive oil and herb-rubbed, feta-topped Middle Eastern–style *za'atar* bread. It took about twenty minutes to make, from raw dough to a fully cooked, takeout-like snack.

Even though I had learned to cook weeknight meals pretty quickly, my nightly exploits in cooking were far from done by the time I put the last dish on the drying rack. I'd end up blogging about my recipes late into the night, which annoyed Ben, because I'd keep the lights on in our little apartment, and my tapping on the keyboard kept him up.

By this point, my blog was no longer just about cooking home-made meals for fun or necessity. It had become an obsession, and it was taking over a good deal of my leisure time. I was posting recipes, tips, and reasons for not eating out on my blog that were intended to engage the practical-minded, busy, working foodie. I was no longer the model for that audience. I was still working nine to five, and I could have kept my little cooking adventures in line with the rest of my life. But instead I was using all my energy and free time to write, photograph food, and come up with new recipes. How could I stop? I was having more fun with this project than with anything I'd ever done in my life.

I, for one, was perfectly happy.

~~~~~~

BLT *Maki* Rolls

The procedure might sound complicated, but after a couple of tries it's easy to turn out maki with any combination of fillings. This one rolls together the famous cold sandwich fillings, and a little bit of garlic mayonnaise really makes it sing.   (MAKES 3 ROLLS)

  1 cup uncooked sushi rice
  ¼ cup sushi vinegar*
  ¼ cup mayonnaise
  1 teaspoon rice vinegar (or substitute white vinegar)
  1 teaspoon sugar
  1 garlic clove, minced
  3 square sheets of nori seaweed (can be found in packages at most Asian groceries)
  10–12 leaves of romaine lettuce, thick ribs removed
  6 strips bacon, cooked to crispy and drained on paper towels
  1 large, firm tomato, cut into ½-inch strips

Rinse and drain the rice, and cook in a rice steamer according to your machine's regular instructions. In the meantime, spread about half of the sushi vinegar into the bottom of a large square or rectangular baking pan. Transfer the rice to the pan and gently mix with a soft rubber spatula, while you fold in the rest of the sushi vinegar. Do not overmix, as you don't want to break any of the grains. Cover the pan with a wet towel and let cool to room temperature before using.

In a small bowl, combine the mayonnaise, rice vinegar, sugar, and minced garlic into a smooth sauce.

Place a square of nori on top of a sushi-rolling mat (these are ideal because their long slats of wood distribute pressure throughout the length of the roll). Wet your fingertips, and place little handfuls of rice evenly on top of the nori square. Spread until you have a reasonably even, light layer of rice. Arrange a few lettuce leaves in a single layer on top of the rice. Pile a neat, small line of bacon and tomato strips about ½-inch from the edge closest to you. Spread a neat, thin layer of the garlic mayonnaise across the fillings. Lift up the

----
*If you don't have sushi vinegar, you can substitute 3 tablespoons rice vinegar, 1 tablespoon water, and 2 teaspoons sugar, dissolved over heat.

straw mat on that same side, and roll until the nori covers the fillings. Without pressing too hard, continue to roll, lifting the straw mat out of the way as you go along, until the entire nori sheet is rolled up. Press down a little bit on the finished roll to secure the ends. Using a very sharp knife, cut the roll into five or six pieces. Place the pieces cut-side-up or down on a plate. Serve with wasabi and soy sauce.

~~~~~~

Kale, Radicchio, and Sausage Pizza

Whether you're using unbaked store-bought pizza dough or your own, lots of fresh, chunky toppings are always a refreshing alternative. The flavorful combination and bright colors of this pie make it especially appealing; if your crowd has vegetarians, try this out with smoked mozzarella, and leave out the sausage.

(MAKES 1 APPROXIMATELY 9-INCH PIE)

4 tablespoons olive oil
1–2 Italian pork sausage links
2–3 oz. fresh mozzarella
Uncooked dough for one 16-inch pizza from a pizza shop
1 small head radicchio, shredded
4 large kale leaves, thick ribs trimmed, and chopped
2 oz. grated pecorino romano, or another firm, aged cheese such as Parmigiano-Reggiano
Pinch of red pepper flakes (optional)

Heat a heavy skillet over medium-high heat with 1 tablespoon of the oil. Lightly brown sausages on all sides until just firm, about 5 minutes. Transfer sausages to a cutting board and let cool. Once cooled for 5 minutes, slice links diagonally into ovals no more than ½-inch thick.

Preheat oven to 400 degrees. Spread pizza dough onto a pizza pan or cookie sheet and brush top with olive oil. Break the mozzarella into thumb-sized pieces and scatter across top of dough. Arrange sausages evenly across top, and top with radicchio, kale, and red pepper flakes. Sprinkle with the grated pecorino romano. Bake for about 20 minutes, or until edges of the crust are lightly browned. Remove from oven, and add an optional drizzle of good olive oil for garnish.

CHAPTER 8

Giving Thanks

COMMUNAL FEASTING WITH FRIENDS AND FAMILY

Dining with one's friends and beloved family is certainly one of life's primal and most innocent delights, one that is both soul-satisfying and eternal.

—*Julia Child*, The Way to Cook

For me, summer officially begins when the first backyard barbecue is thrown. It's the smell of charcoal and hamburger grease wafting down a residential block, mingling from various backyard grills. My first summer after beginning the blog, I took advantage of as many barbecue invitations as I could, held in friends' yards or on rooftop patios. As a guest, all you had to do was bring your share of beer and a side dish perhaps, and sit back as a long evening unfolded under the starless sky, which popped with the occasional illegal firework on any given night.

Not eating out in New York feels like a more natural thing to do in summer. Ben and I would pack a picnic and ride our bikes to a nearby park for an afternoon. I lived a short walk from my local farmers' market, and every Saturday when it was open, I would pick through the plentiful baskets, choosing what to make for the week's feasts, amid the bustling crowd of neighbors doing just the same. I'd ride laps around Prospect Park on weekends and pass massive family barbecues taking place on the lawn one after another, catching waves of jerk seasoning and clouds of hibachi smoke from the track. Block parties serving full trays of barbecued chicken, mac and cheese, and collard greens would clog up an entire block, at least somewhere, on any weekend of the summer, it seemed. A handful of girlfriends and I planned an elaborate picnic at a waterfront park in Brooklyn, and convinced some local acoustic musician friends to entertain along the rocks, before a backdrop of the Manhattan skyline.

Then, almost as soon as I could get into the swing of things, summer faded into fall. My work schedule went back into full throttle, with no more half-day Fridays. It got cooler. My bike spent more and more days against the wall of my bedroom, unused. The fresh fruits and ripe Jersey tomatoes at the farmers' markets dwindled. And then the forgotten hunger pangs for quick and convenient or long and languid restaurant meals came creeping back.

September marked the one-year anniversary of my blog and my not eating out. That summer, I had cooked up a storm. From picnic lunches to more elaborate projects, like a chilled watermelon soup served in a hollowed watermelon bowl I brought to one barbecue, I felt like there was no stopping my eating-in mission. I was only just getting warmed up, it seemed. So when I posted the twelfth "Reason for Not Eating Out" essay on my blog (each month, I wrote a post making one argument on the topic). I announced the one-year anniversary and the fact that I was going to push on with not eating out and blogging about it.

Ben seemed a little less jubilant about this decision than I was. He didn't complain outwardly, but I could tell he was tiring of my nightly typing ritual and my insistence on bringing homemade food along with me whenever I was going to be out for a long period of time, instead of joining him for a bite at a restaurant. As a consequence, I craved occasions when I could be around like-minded cooking enthusiasts, and my friend Karol and I went to some of our first local amateur cook-offs that summer and fall.

Then came my favorite occasion to cook with others: If there was ever a time of the year when it was inappropriate to eat out, it was Thanksgiving.

My friend Matt decided he couldn't wait to get into the spirit.

"A Fall Harvest Feast," he wrote in an e-mail. The idea was, since so many of our friends left town for Thanksgiving, we would throw an early Thanksgiving-like dinner party for a handful of close friends. Matt was Karol's best friend, and until then we had never really hung out when she wasn't around. But lately we'd discovered that we shared a common passion for food. Although he worked as a barista at a popular restaurant in Brooklyn, I hadn't realized before that he, perhaps even more so than Karol, was such an avid foodie. We'd get into heated discussions over the respective merits of peeling vegetables versus leaving the skins on, or oversalting (Matt was a proponent of using as little salt as possible).

"I really want you in on this," he went on. "We'll plan the menu early, so nobody will bring the same things. There should be lots of variety, like a Thanksgiving spread, only better." I wrote back, letting him know I was definitely in.

The Fall Harvest Feast would be held at Matt's friend Maia's apartment. Maia's specialty was Southern fare, and she planned to make biscuits and pie for dessert. Karol was also bringing pie, and when one other friend insisted on bringing her famous sour cream apple pie, it was clear that my pie-making expertise, passed down from Dad, wouldn't be needed. Instead, the general consensus among my friends had my name on the turkey.

We all agreed that the meal wouldn't be complete without a roast turkey. But no one knew the first thing about what to do with a whole, dead bird—actually, everyone else was frightened stiff about the notion of transforming it into a stuffed, thoroughly cooked main course. In their eyes, I was the only one qualified for the job.

How hard could it be, I thought? At Thanksgivings with my family, my dad was the designated turkey handler, from stuffing to carving. To feed a houseful of our extended family, and often guests, and have enough for leftovers for the next day, he generally cooked a thirty-pound bird. In recent years, he'd picked up the habit of brining the bird the night before, and this required a massive bucket and the space to keep it cool throughout the night. I had neither of those elements. But then, we weren't going to roast that big a bird.

"How big should it be?" I asked Matt a few weeks before the feast.

"I'd say at least twenty pounds," he said. Our guest list was still a little uncertain at this point, and besides, it was always better to have more than less. Plus, we had a huge advantage on our side: The restaurant where Matt worked prided itself on serving only free-range, pastured, grass-fed meats and poultry from upstate farms. Since he was friendly enough with the staff and their suppliers, he could order a bird wholesale, for the same price the restaurant would pay. Not only were we all thrilled about getting a free-range whole turkey for the first time, but it would be at a bargain price. We placed an order for the bird two weeks in advance, settling on a twenty-pounder.

At the same time my friends and I were planning the Fall Harvest Feast, my own family was figuring out what to do for our "real" Thanksgiving dinner, which would happen about a week later. Every Thanksgiving since I had been born, my father and his three siblings brought their families to their parents' home in upstate New York. Two years before, my grandmother had passed away, and earlier that spring, my grandfather had also passed, at ninety-two. Their big house in a sleepy suburb was on the market, and the four siblings were spread among three states. Between the funeral and taking care of the estate, they had seen each other several times that year already. So my parents decided to host Thanksgiving dinner at their house, in New Jersey. My aunt Ellen and cousin Phoebe, who lived in Connecticut, would come to our dinner. The New York contingent of the family would spend the holiday together at one of their homes. So this year's dinner would be a smaller-scale affair. But I didn't expect it to be any less extravagant a feast, since my parents always held court as the chefs of the family.

There would be another missing piece to our Thanksgiving that year. My uncle, whom I've always simply called Jo-Jo, the Chinese name for a mother's younger brother, always attended family events with us. He was very close to us; he had even lived in my parents' home until I was about five, before moving to his own apartment in Queens. This year, however, had brought another downturn for my aging senior relatives. My maternal grandfather, or Gong-Gong to me and my brother, had grown too frail to care for himself. He moved in with Jo-Jo that fall, and my uncle was doing his best to look after him with the aid of a social worker a few days a week. There was no way my grandfather could travel to New Jersey anymore, and since the social worker was off on Thanksgiving, Jo-Jo needed to stay with him in Queens. Of course, we planned to go see them the day after.

It is said that the act of cooking and eating together was the catalyst of civilization. The need to prepare food and to consume it is what tamed humans into living in interdependent societies instead of individually as hunter-gatherers. Agriculture centered us as home-dwelling beings rather than as members of nomadic herds. People settled down, built cities, and began taking up certain skills to fulfill various needs of the community—many of which, at least in the beginning, were related to eating.

Not only did communal supping forge communities and play a large role in defining cultures, but it also offered people something a little more than plain sustenance. Coming to the table for an unquestionably enjoyable act—eating—allowed for human interaction either meaningful or mundane—essentially, the opportunity to commune.

It's often lamented that in today's eat-on-the-go culture, so increasingly prevalent in urban areas like New York, we are missing out on something very valuable. We have yet to see what will become of us if the trend continues. But forecasts have been portentous: "Americans will once again become a lonely race of Mesolithic hunter-gatherers prowling the darkened city streets, wallets honed and sharpened, ready to pounce on the unsuspecting pint of pasta primavera and snare the slow-footed slice of *pâté de campagne*," Jeffrey Steingarten wrote with comic melodrama in 1988. Just think of it: When you sit at your desk eating alone, or eat as you drive alone in your car, you're chipping away at eons of development in human civilization!

I had a growing number of friends and acquaintances in Brooklyn, however, who were excited about cooking and feasting with one another. Potlucks and food parties that involved gathering together for anything from full dinners to just hors d'oeuvres were all the rage—even put together on the fly. Staying in and eating something delicious had become, to my great fortune, a common way of hanging out.

Earlier that fall, my friend Becca and I paid a visit to a monthly communal dinner buffet called GRUB. It was housed in an industrial warehouse loft in Brooklyn called Rubulad, inhabited by a loose collective that often hosted parties, music shows, and other events in the space. Much of the food prepared at GRUB dinners was freeganed, too.

Becca was running late, so I arrived at the building before her. Once I climbed up the long staircase to the loft, the first thing that greeted me was a rocking horse dressed up in carnivalesque beads and brightly colored Christmas tree lights hanging from a wall at the top of the landing. In the windowless first room there was a small stage with a sequined purple curtain, empty in the half darkness. I had been to Rubulad once before, to see a music show at night. Then, the place was so bustling with bodies and I had walked through so many twisting, pitch-black hallways and separate rooms to get to the area where the band was playing that I had no idea what it really looked like. In the daytime, it bore a resemblance to an abandoned funhouse ride.

I went ahead into the main living room. Several people were standing around, talking, and in the spacious but ramshackle-looking kitchen, there were about ten or so people busy cooking. Each one seemed hard at work in his or her own station—some were chopping, others sautéing, some kneading dough. Several people were standing to the side and talking. I didn't see anyone I knew, so after a quick walk-through, I headed for the fire escape, where I saw some folks standing outside. After calling Becca, who assured me she was five minutes away, I was feeling a bit awkward, so I lingered on the far side of the spacious fire escape while pretending to be sending text messages on my phone. The pair that had been standing outside moments ago had dashed down the staircase to what looked like a puppet theater in the courtyard. A minute later, two more people stepped out onto the fire escape. I recognized one as a well-known graffiti artist I had met a couple of times, and the other as a photographer. The photographer looked my way and smiled.

"Cool shoes," he said, nodding at my pink Keds.

I smiled and thanked him. After a brief pause, he went back inside. I realized that if there had ever been a good opportunity to mingle with this crowd, I had just missed it.

Things didn't get much better once Becca arrived. We struck up a conversation with one of the girls cooking in the kitchen, but as it was her first time cooking for the event, she didn't have much to say about it. At one point Becca was rudely shrugged off when she asked another girl if she could take pictures.

Once the food was all prepared and set on a table in the living room, everyone lined up to fill their plates. Becca and I sat down on a couch to eat. My plate had four dishes, squashed together: a potato gnocchi covered in tomato sauce, a tofu dish with a sweet-and-sour sauce, a heap of salad heavy on the shredded carrots and fennel fronds, and a mixed veggie side that resembled ratatouille. We were told in a brief announcement before dinner was served that most of it had been freeganed, except for some purchased ingredients like spices or flour, and all of it was vegan.

There were at least forty people at the dinner that night, in various rooms and even on the rooftop. Though Becca and I enjoyed watching the meal being cooked and eating it, we left without making any lasting contacts. This was mostly our faults, but we sensed an exclusive vibe from some of the characters there. When we were finished eating, we turned our attention to a commotion in the center of the room. A girl clad only in a bra and jeans was wrestling with a guy, and they stumbled into the room laughing and squealing. They suddenly crashed onto the floor in a heap and then continued to roll around on their backs, cackling. Becca and I looked at each other and silently agreed it was time to go.

The bigger a dinner gets, the less intimate the experience, I left the event thinking. I always preferred smaller gatherings to big ones anyway, at least as long as good people and good food were involved.

As the Fall Harvest Feast approached, Matt, Karol, Maia, and I realized we were looking at about twelve to thirteen guests in all. It seemed like an easy number of mouths to feed. Twenty pounds, once you subtracted the bones and entrails, might not be a huge amount of bird. But we were planning to pull out all the stops with the side dishes and desserts. Matt had a pumpkin succotash in mind, in addition to a vegetarian stuffing prepared outside the bird. Karol wanted to make some healthy sautéed greens along with her decadent dessert pie. Aside from some obligatory potatoes, which Maia would prepare, we needed more sides to fill out the spread. So Matt called on me to whip up another dish, three days before the event.

I couldn't promise one, I told him. I was already making the bird, my own stuffing, and the gravy with the turkey drippings. I didn't see how I was going to manage something else in the same day. What's more, there wasn't enough room in Maia's oven for a twenty-pound turkey, not by a long shot. She also needed it to bake her biscuits and dessert. I would have to roast the turkey in my own home kitchen, and then cab it over to Maia's for the dinner. The cooking part for me sounded pretty lonely.

I also had a technical glitch or two. I didn't have a roasting pan that could possibly fit the bird, nor any basters, brushes, or kitchen twine for trussing it. Also, my hopes of brining the turkey overnight had evaporated, as Matt would be picking up the bird from the restaurant the morning of the dinner and delivering it to my door right away. I began hitting the cookbooks and Internet sources on turkey roasting, and I called my parents for some general advice on what I'd need to keep in mind.

I asked around to see whether any friends had a big enough roasting pan that I could borrow. No one did—not even Sean, whom I could usually count on for the obscure kitchen tool. As it turned out, he didn't let me down. The next day, he called me while shopping at Target to say he'd found a pretty big roasting pan there on sale for $12. He offered to buy it to save me the trouble, and I'd pay him back. Once I got the roasting pan home, I decided I could do without the basting equipment. Instead, I put my focus into what type of stuffing I would make.

Stuffing is one of those fun dishes where you can really create any combination of flavors and it'll still probably taste great. A little sweetness with savoriness is a hallmark of great stuffings, as far as I'm concerned. My family's version at Thanksgiving always had dates, along with celery and onions. After some pondering, I decided to make mine a little spicy and smoky, too, by adding chipotle. For the sweet component, I chose to add a very fall-harvest-y fruit, apple. I was going for Mexican flair with this stuffing, so I used chopped corn tortillas instead of basic bread—a risky move since I had never tried it before.

During these preparations on the day of the feast, Ben was mulling about at home. I'd wanted him to come to the Fall Harvest Feast, but he declined, saying he wasn't feeling up to it. At noon, Matt arrived at my door with the turkey. He, Karol, and Maia had swung by the Union Square Greenmarket that morning, too, and the trunk of their borrowed car was filled with makings for the dinner. Ben helped me carry the enormous vacuum-wrapped bird into the apartment, and with a heavy plop, I eased it onto the cleared strip of counter space. Once it was taken out of its packaging and placed in the roasting pan, I could tell a few things were different about this turkey compared to the ones I'd seen over previous Thanksgivings. It had a longer, somewhat leaner overall shape, less rotund. It somehow looked more birdlike, more like an animal that had been living a short while ago, rather than a fully roasted, reddish Thanksgiving centerpiece. The legs had already been somewhat trussed, secured with a big piece of skin right below the cavity, saving me the trouble of tinkering with twine.

Following the cues I had gathered from my turkey-roasting sources, I patted the bird down with paper towels and began seasoning it, both outside and in the cavity. Next I filled up the cavity with my stuffing. I had exactly five hours until I needed to be at Maia's place, so I popped the bird into the oven and hoped everything would go all right.

There are two camps of home cooks: the ones who follow a recipe word for word, no matter what, and the ones who sense how much of what is needed in a dish or how long it needs to cook. This disparity can be easily observed when cooking a Thanksgiving turkey. One type of home cook stands by as a turkey roasts and thinks to open the oven door only when the designated amount of time at the exact temperature that the recipe indicated has expired. The other type smells, hears, or sees something going on in the oven that lures them into checking it. My father inhabits the former personality; my mom, the latter. Over the phone, my dad had instructed that it would take at least four and a half hours to cook a twenty-pound bird. But only three hours into roasting, with basting every half hour or so (with much difficulty, since I had to use a large soup spoon and tilt the roasting pan to scoop up juices every time), my turkey was looking fairly golden brown and smelling wonderful. I had taken the advice I'd read somewhere to crank the oven to 500 degrees for the first ten minutes of roasting, to create a crisp, browned skin. This method probably shortened the necessary cooking time. Still, the turkey had an insert that would pop automatically when it was supposedly cooked through. I didn't have it in me to trust the plastic device, so after the bird looked positively done—beautifully done—at about four hours, I removed it from the oven and placed it on the stove to admire for a good, long minute. Its skin was glistening a warm golden brown, looking crisp to the touch along the center of the breast and at the crests of the drumsticks. I had stuck a few lemon slices and sprigs of thyme underneath the skin of its breast, and they were visible beneath the orangish skin, which had turned slightly translucent and had molded around them. It looked like the cover of a fall cooking magazine. Just then, the white plastic insert shot out.

I grabbed Ben for a hand at heaving the bird out of the pan so that I could begin making the gravy from the juice. He had stayed at a good distance while I took over the kitchen the entire day. I asked him again why he wouldn't come to Maia's. I was sure there would be a person or two he knew there. He used the defense of saying that he wouldn't be upset if I didn't want to come along to something where mostly his friends were involved. I argued that since Karol was such a close friend of mine, she was his friend by now, too. He pointed out that he'd come to so many other cooking events with me and Karol. I knew Ben wasn't crazy about Matt, even though he'd met him only once or twice, and I accused him of this, too. I also got down on him for never wanting to come to my family's Thanksgiving dinner, since they were so close. But Ben was loyal to spending his Thanksgivings with Richard and Sam, as he had been ever since moving to New York City six years ago for college. The three of them and a host of other friends whose families also lived too far away to justify a plane ticket for the short holiday annually gathered at Richard and Sam's apartment for a Thanksgiving feast. There was no pulling him away from that tradition.

In the end, no one left this fun little conversation happy, and I got into a cab to go to Maia's alone, with the fully roasted turkey, gravy, and my extra side. Yes, I had found time to prepare another side, while cooking the turkey that day. I wanted it to be a surprise for the others.

Cooking was in full swing when I arrived at Maia's. A spare door had been propped up on the floor with piles of books and covered with a tablecloth to create the dinner table. It had already been set with appetizers and a plate of Maia's perfectly golden, fluffy-looking biscuits.

Maia and Karol were scuttling about preparing their dishes in the open kitchen, and I squeezed in to warm the gravy and prepare the rest of my side course. Matt was fussing over his pumpkin, bean, and corn succotash, which was served out of an enormous hollowed half-pumpkin bowl. The pumpkin bowl was too large for the dish, so Matt carefully carved off some of its height at the top so that he was left with a ring of pumpkin. He wore it around his neck for most of the night. On the stove, an enormous pot of mulled apple cider was steaming. The drink of the night was a hot toddy, mixed with Bourbon and topped with mint sprigs, and I helped myself to one. After an hour or so of cooking around the kitchen and living room, we all sat down to help ourselves to a meal.

Even the vegetarians in our group joined in the chorus of aahs as the turkey was ceremoniously placed on the table. I began scooping the stuffing from the cavity into a bowl, though, and some turned away with uncomfortable expressions. Someone had brought paper turkey frills to place on the ends of the drumsticks. Once they were slipped on, they instantly made it look like something out of a comic strip. Lined up on the table were both Matt's vegetarian stuffing and mine, the pumpkin succotash, garlic-sautéed kale, mashed potatoes, gravy, an elaborate ravioli dish that Matt's friend David was still assembling, and my extra side of the night: a salad of roasted beets and fresh orange wedges with fresh mint leaves and candied orange peel. After all that, we'd have to save our appetites for the desserts: Karol's chocolate peanut butter tart, Maia's Indian corn pudding, and Jessica's sour cream apple pie.

My only concern was whether the turkey was thoroughly cooked. Matt helped me carve the turkey, and after the first few slices of breast meat, close to the surface, I held my breath. But one after another, the slices came out clean, ivory colored, and moist.

"I can't believe it's cooked," I said.

"And it's so good," Karol said, mopping up some gravy with a piece.

After having seconds of both white and dark meat, I knew there was something very different about this turkey, both inside and out. It had a prominent, savory flavor, and its meat was utterly moist throughout. I'd never go back to regular grocery-store turkeys again, I vowed. (It was too late to order one for my parents' upcoming Thanksgiving, though.)

After all the frustrations I'd been through with Ben during day, it felt great to be with friends who really appreciated the work I'd put into the food that I made. I couldn't remember the last time I'd felt that kind of genuine respect from Ben for something I had cooked. Then again, he saw me cook every single day, and my friends were reacting to a rare treat.

There was so much food, especially so much turkey thanks to the huge bird that Matt had gotten, that we had enough for continuous munching throughout the night, even after we declared ourselves full several times over. The desserts were polished off the quickest. Karol's tart, with its chocolate cookie shell, smooth peanut butter cream filling, and milk chocolate topping, didn't last very long. I had more than my share of the wonderful sour cream apple pie—and of the perfect complement to it, Bourbon-spiked apple cider.

Once we'd dug far enough into the turkey to reveal the wishbone, we carefully removed it. Matt and I decided to face off over the age-old wishbone pull. We each gripped one end and pulled. As our shaky feet began to lose their balance and we stumbled about the room, it was clear that this bone was too rubbery to break apart. It had barely spent any time outside the still-warm turkey. We continued to twist and stretch at the ends for what seemed like five minutes before giving up. A truce.

I don't have a clue what I had been wishing for anymore, but looking back, I don't think there's anything more I could have wished for on that night. I had everything that I loved about life: good people (and not too many of them) and really good food (too much of it, but that was okay). It was a wonderful night. Also, some of the people I became closer with that night at the Fall Harvest Feast, Matt and Maia especially, have remained some of my very best friends.

A week later, it was Thanksgiving morning. I had taken the train to New Jersey the night before and arrived late, along with my brother, my aunt Ellen, and my cousin Phoebe. But I woke up early, fixated on food preparations, and walked downstairs to my parents' kitchen in my pajamas. I put a big pot of coffee on. In the fully stocked fridge, I found a package of Greek feta, a somewhat squashed tomato, and a full carton of eggs. There was a wholesale club–sized bag of yellow onions in a drawer at the bottom of a kitchen cupboard. I decided to make a big frittata for breakfast, to share with everyone once they had woken up.

In *The Physiology of Taste*, Jean Anthelme Brillat-Savarin wrote, "The preparation and distribution of food necessarily brought the whole family together, the fathers apportioning to their children the results of the hunt, and the grown children then doing the same to their aged parents." It's funny, even though Brillat-Savarin was writing in eighteenth-century France, he might as well have been describing the Thanksgiving dinners of the Erway family tradition. That is, if you can call a thirty-pound turkey wrapped in plastic from the supermarket the "hunt."

At holiday gatherings with my family, rarely does cooking cease to be the center of activity. I don't see this as a strange quirk, or as archaic. Cooking and feeding one another are ways of playing out family roles as much as they are acts of necessity when you are with a big group of family members all at once. They were also an expression of hospitality for our guests. Right then Ellen and Phoebe were asleep in the spare guest room upstairs.

My mom came downstairs.

"What'cha making?" she asked. I had a large sauté pan of sliced onions on the stove, which I was in the process of slowly caramelizing before adding them to the eggs.

"A frittata," I replied.

"A what?" she said.

"This egg thing, sort of like a quiche but without a crust."

"Oh, yes, do that," she said. She looked at the clock. "Dad needs to wake up and start the turkey."

I suddenly remembered one of my favorite Thanksgiving snacks.

"Can we cook the gizzards now?"

"Yes, let's do that," said my mom. Nobody loved eating the entrails of the turkey as much as my mother and I. I particularly liked the neck. Boiled for at least an hour in plain water, and sprinkled with just salt, the tender muscles peeled off with a fork in delectable dark-meat shreds. It's a flavorful part of the bird and tastes a little like braised duck, if you ask me.

After a little while, my father came bumbling down the stairs, eyes bloodshot and darting as if he had just been dragged from a dream.

"Where's the turkey? Did someone start making the stuffing yet?" he said.

I helped bring the bucket that the turkey was brining in from the porch into the kitchen. My frittata had just gone into the oven, which my dad complained about.

"The turkey needs to go into the oven now if we're going to eat at three," he insisted.

"We're not going to eat at three; we never do. It doesn't matter anyway. We have plenty of appetizers. Breakfast hasn't even been served, and it's already ten," said my mom.

Indeed, we had a full day's schedule of food to pass through our mouths, and seemingly not enough time for it all. In anticipation, I started to make my next dish, a turkey liver mousse. I had never made it before, but I followed a recipe that called for chicken livers in a savory pâté-like spread.

An hour or so later, the frittata was taken out of the oven, and fruits and croissants were spread out on the kitchen table for breakfast. Everyone else had trickled downstairs in their pajamas, too. Although he loved to eat food, my brother wasn't terribly inclined to cook it. He was more interested in stealing time on the upright piano whenever he was at our parents' house.

"That's Chris's song," I said to Ellen, who had joined us in the kitchen for breakfast. "He composed it."

"It sounds lovely. Play some more," she shouted into the living room.

After showering and dressing, I went back downstairs to help prepare sides and serve midday appetizers. I copied Sean and Meredith's baked-Brie-and-mango-spread dish, which turned out to be a huge hit. The turkey liver mousse came out nicely, too. I had sautéed the livers with onions, a fresh rosemary sprig, and a splash of white wine, and then removed the rosemary and blended the mixture with chunks of cold butter. With all the cholesterol naturally in liver, it was a rich and incredibly fattening snack. After snack-time, I was already full, with a couple of hours left till dinner.

As we sat on stools around the kitchen eating Brie and crackers, my aunt began telling me about a self-help book she was reading. Ellen had separated from her husband earlier that year, and she'd recently begun seeing a new guy. The book was called *The Five Love Languages*, and it described five distinct ways people showed affection for each other in relationships. The point of understanding this, Ellen explained, was to see whether your methods of communication work with, or are appreciated by, your partner. Reading a quiz at the beginning of the book was supposed to show one which "languages" he or she uses most: acts of service, giving gifts, physical affection, and so on. Ellen said that the one she rated most important to her was acts of service—helping out around the house, being there to support each other, that kind of thing. The one she ranked least important was giving gifts. What did I think my favorites were? she asked. I thought about this for a while.

"Well, can't giving gifts be sort of similar to acts of service?" I asked. I moved on to the pâté, spreading it onto the remainder of the cracker that I'd just eaten part of with Brie.

"How so?" she asked.

"I don't know. I guess I'm thinking of cooking something really special for someone—which is kind of like a gift, in a way. But it's also . . . a meal, or necessity, too. Right?" I said.

Ellen shrugged. "I guess so. You should read the book. I'll lend you my copy when I'm done."

My cousin Zoe arrived as we were finishing the last of the cooking. Zoe lived in New York City and was in her first year of residency as a doctor, so she wasn't able to travel upstate in time to make it to her parents' Thanksgiving dinner. She almost couldn't make it to ours. We had thought that her brother, Elliot, who also lived in the city, was spending Thanksgiving with his girlfriend's family. Then at five o'clock we got a call from Elliot, who was driving down the New Jersey Turnpike with his girlfriend, Meredith. What exit were we? he asked.

"What? What?" my mom sputtered. "Elliot *and* Meredith are coming?"

"Yeah, they should be here in about twenty minutes," Chris said as he hung up the phone.

"Guess we should bring out the extra leaf for the table," said my dad.

"Do we have enough food?" My mom panicked.

"Of course we have enough food," I told her. Aside from the basics—turkey, stuffing, potatoes, and green beans—I was braising some Brussels sprouts in white wine and shallots and roasting a root-vegetable medley with celeriac and sweet potatoes, my dad was making an acorn squash dish he'd seen on a cooking show, and we had five—yes, five—pies, which were baked the night before with the help of Phoebe and Chris.

Okay, maybe we could use some more potatoes. I got started on boiling more potatoes to add to the mound already keeping warm in the oven. When the garbage disposal clogged with potato peels and whatever else had been in the sink before them, Chris was called upon to get on his back on the floor, unscrew the pipes beneath the sink, and scoop out the mess. That was another thing he was good at: fixing just about every mechanical and technical issue the family encountered.

There was a full crowd seated around the dinner table when it came time to eat. With Elliot and Meredith, there were nine of us total, not much smaller than our family Thanksgivings in years past. We served the food in the kitchen, buffet style, and we all carried our plates to the table. Our group was small enough, though, for everyone to hear the same conversation at once. Compliments on the food went around the table as we ate and talked. At one point, Elliot asked me how my blog was going, and how long I was going to keep writing it. I told him that I didn't intend to stop anytime soon.

"That's seriously amazing," Elliot said, after I confirmed that I'd keep not eating out as a general rule. Elliot had grown up in Manhattan, and he probably cooked for himself the least out of all the people that I knew.

"Come on, don't you ever want to cheat every once in a while?" he asked.

I nodded. "But it's weird . . . ," I went on. "Even when I do, it's like, I can't even imagine doing something like ordering out. If

I'm really in the mood for something, it's usually for something I can make, like a simple steak, or a bowl of noodles or something. I think about how quickly it can be ready on a plate. It's like I've forgotten how other food tastes or something. I don't know."

This was something that I couldn't quite explain at the time, but I think my palate had changed a little. I didn't crave restaurant food anymore the way I used to. Even though the temptation was always near, I'd prefer something home cooked to takeout if given the option.

Elliot looked confused for a moment. "Well, that's awesome. You must be saving tons of money," he said.

I told him about the Fall Harvest Feast I'd had with friends the week before.

"You must have gotten some practice," he said, slathering a strip of turkey with gravy. "Everything is so good."

"Oh, I definitely agree," Zoe chimed in.

"Best Thanksgiving dinner ever," Ellen said. Mouths full, everyone around the table nodded.

After a long, leisurely dinner we all retired to the living room to stretch out. Desserts wouldn't come until later, when we had regained our appetites. So Ellen suggested a game of cards. My mother had a different idea.

"This!" she said, proudly holding a bright blue case of mah-jongg tiles. Recently purchased in Chinatown, the mah-jongg tiles had been bringing my mother back to her roots lately. I'd played the game a couple of times already with her; it was easy to pick up, and actually a lot like many Western card games, so long as you could differentiate the numbers and characters on the tiles. Mah-jongg was actually a lot like rummy. Players had sets of tiles before them, which they tried to group off into three of a kind or three in a row. We'd take turns picking up tiles from the table and discarding them. Once a tile was discarded on the table, the next player had the option of picking it up to complete a set—calling out *"Pung!"* when this happened. And instead of saying "rummy," when a player had a winning spread, he or she would call out *"Hu-la!"*

We pulled out a card table and gathered around it. My mother,

Chris, and I were each seated at one of the sides of the table, and my aunt and cousin pulled their chairs close together and teamed up on the last. Mah-jongg is a four-person game, and the four sides of the table are thought to symbolize the four winds: north, south, east, and west. The familiar crackling sound as the plastic tiles were poured in the center and turned over one by one signaled the start of a long succession of games. After some pointers and practice rounds, Ellen and Phoebe were following just as well as the rest of us. At fourteen years of age, my cousin was downright scary-smart.

"*Pung!*" she cried, grabbing a tile that my mother had just placed on the table.

"That's the second time I gave you *pung*," my mom sighed.

The next day, after all our guests had left, my parents, Chris, and I drove to Jo-Jo's apartment in Queens. We brought the mah-jongg tiles, as well as some makings for wontons. It would be a simple late lunch or early dinner, and a third Thanksgiving for me.

We sat around Gong-Gong's easy chair in Jo-Jo's apartment. My grandfather refused to eat most of the time, shaking his bony hand in protest when Jo-Jo tried to feed him. But whenever he tasted something good, I noticed he always let up a little. We had stuffed and folded the pork and shrimp wontons in the kitchen ourselves, with the help of Gong-Gong's helper. "Auntie," as we respectfully called her, had taught us the classic Shanghai style of folding the dumplings in square, store-bought egg-noodle wrappers. Once Gong-Gong accepted a spoonful of wonton in soup, he eagerly took another bite, and another.

We'd gone to Jo-Jo's apartment to see Gong-Gong several times that fall, as his condition worsened. Since his hearing was so poor, at first Jo-Jo and my mom would communicate with him by writing on a dry-erase board in Chinese characters. "Do you want soup?" they might write, or more seriously, "Do you remember Wei Kai Lin?" (my Chinese name). After a while, it became less and less clear that he even remembered my mother anymore, and he couldn't maintain the attention span to read writing.

My mother brought the mah-jongg tiles to play once again that evening. Once the tiles were poured onto the table with a familiar crackle, Gong-Gong perked up a bit. He eyed the tiles attentively as we pushed them around for a while. We didn't end up playing a real game, but for the rest of the evening, as we sat around Jo-Jo's apartment talking, my grandfather plunked and picked at the pieces on the table, as if trying to recall what was supposed to be done with them.

"*Pung,*" I said at one point. He looked up in wonder for a moment, and I thought I saw his eyes shine with clarity, as if the clouds in his memory had temporarily parted.

Sweet, Salty, and Sticky Roasted Squash Seeds

A great snack to put out before the big Thanksgiving meal. If you've got squash on your menu at any occasion in the fall, instead of tossing the scooped-out seeds, try out this caramely, slightly spicy use for them instead. Keeps great in a jar for up to a week.

(MAKES ABOUT 1 CUP)

1 cup squash seeds (pumpkin, butternut, acorn, etc.)
1 tablespoon butter
¼ cup firmly packed brown sugar
¼ teaspoon salt
¼ teaspoon cayenne pepper

Preheat oven to 300 degrees. Make sure the squash seeds are dried completely, with bits of pulp removed. Heat a large skillet and toast the seeds in it for a couple of minutes over high heat. Melt the butter in the skillet, and toss in the sugar, salt, and cayenne pepper. Turn seeds onto a lightly greased baking sheet and spread in an even layer. Bake for about 40 minutes or until crisp. Let cool completely and remove with a spatula.

Turkey Liver Mousse with Pistachios

This is an easy, yet luxurious snack, and a good way to use the liver that comes with whole turkeys. Crushed pistachios add texture to the mousse as garnish, and you might want to serve individual crackers with the mousse spread on top, finished off with a small sprinkle of the pistachios. Try using cognac, sherry, or dry Madeira or Marsala wine for a change in flavor.

(MAKES ABOUT ⅔ CUP)

1 stick unsalted butter, cut into cubes
2 small onions (or 2 medium shallots), finely chopped
2 turkey livers
1 sprig fresh rosemary or thyme
½ cup dry white wine
Salt and pepper to taste
Handful gently crushed, shelled pistachios

Melt about 1 tablespoon of the butter in a small skillet. Add the onions and cook over medium heat until translucent, about 8 minutes. Add the turkey livers and cook, stirring occasionally, for 4–6 minutes, or until the insides are just pink and no longer bloody. Add the fresh herb sprig and the wine. Season mixture with a few pinches of salt and pepper. Cook until wine is nearly completely reduced.

Remove the herb sprig and transfer mixture to a food processor. Add a few butter cubes at a time and pulse until smooth and uniform. Taste for seasoning, adding additional salt and pepper as desired. Transfer to a small serving bowl or ramekin, cover with plastic, and refrigerate 1 hour before using. Serve with the pistachios sprinkled on top.

~~~~~~

Chipotle Cornbread Stuffing with Apples and Chorizo

This is an improved version of the chipotle stuffing I served at the Fall Harvest Feast, with cornbread instead of corn tortillas, and chorizo. A good handful of fresh herbs goes a long way in this recipe, so if you don't have fresh oregano, substitute with parsley, thyme, tarragon, or a mixture.

(MAKES ENOUGH TO STUFF A 15–20 LB TURKEY)

1 tablespoon vegetable oil
1 link chorizo sausage, finely chopped
1 large onion, chopped
2 celery ribs, finely chopped
1 clove garlic, minced
Salt and pepper to taste
1–2 tablespoons chipotles in adobo sauce, pureed in a food processor or blender until smooth
4–5 cups cornbread (preferably stale), cut into 1-inch cubes
2 Granny Smith apples, peeled and cut into 1-inch cubes
2 tablespoons fresh oregano, chopped

Heat a large skillet with the vegetable oil and add the chopped chorizo. Cook over medium-high heat, stirring occasionally, until lightly browned, 2–3 minutes. Transfer to a bowl, and in the same pan, add the onions, celery, garlic, and a couple of pinches of salt and pepper. Cook for another 2–3 minutes. Return the chorizo to the pan and remove from heat. Sprinkle the chipotles and toss to distribute evenly. Fold in the rest of the ingredients gently, so as not to break up too many pieces of bread. Taste for seasoning before stuffing into a turkey to roast.

CHAPTER 9

Going Solo

"Watch out; I hear they spit."

The camel I was sitting on abruptly stood on its hind legs, pitching me forward with a jolt that brought my face to the bristly hairs on its head. A moment later, it began to climb onto its forelegs and bumpily rose to a standing position.

"Why don't they tell you when they're about to do that?" I exclaimed.

I turned around and just caught a glimpse of Jordan's camel doing the same thing, almost knocking her sunglasses off her forehead.

"Aaah!" she squealed.

One by one, the camels seated in procession just behind her began to stand up, shifting their riders forward in their seats. There were twelve of us backpackers in the group, each mounting camels for the first time. When the camel at the end of the line sat aloof, refusing to move, one of our Berber guides walked over to it and spoke gently to its face. He patted the camel a few times. Grudgingly, it rose.

Then we were off—into the dunes of Erg Chebbi, in the Western Sahara of Morocco, for a night of camping in tents under the stars.

It was January, and my good friend Jordan and I were in the middle of our ten-day trip to Morocco. Jordan and I had been trying to plan a vacation together for the last year or so, hoping to relive some of the traveling adventures we'd shared when studying abroad in Europe my junior year of college. Now that we were both living in New York and working steady jobs with paid vacations, we decided to pick a place where we'd never been before and just buy tickets. We finally decided on Morocco; it was a country and a culture that we knew next to nothing about. What better reason than that, we thought, for us to go?

After spending three nights in Marrakesh, Jordan and I signed up for a three-day trek to the desert, passing the rugged Atlas Mountains and sepia kasbahs famously made popular by Hollywood films shot on location in this exotic landscape. In our van were ten other travelers, between the ages of twenty-two and thirty-two. They hailed from Spain, Australia, Quebec, London, Italy, Korea, and Japan. Two days into the trek, we were just like old friends.

The trip had been filled with stunning landscapes, architecture, and culture shock, but for me, it was also a fascinating gastronomic odyssey. From the start of my blog, I'd accepted that when I traveled out of New York City, and certainly outside of the country, I would allow myself to eat out for practicality. I took full advantage of this liberty while traveling through Morocco. There was nothing quite comparable to Moroccan food, I learned. It had dramatic extremes, from heavily spiced, slow-cooked tajine stews to fresh, barely seasoned vegetables and salads. Jordan and I had taken a casual cooking class while touring Marrakesh, and I already couldn't wait to duplicate back at home the dishes I'd learned about.

So after a near-perfect vacation with Jordan—the only imperfect part being an accidental thirteen-hour layover in London's Heathrow Airport, which was sort of fun and memorable in its own way—I came back to New York, going on less than three hours of sleep in the past twenty hours or so. But I arrived home in the afternoon, and I didn't want to mess up my return to work the next day by going to sleep right away. Instead, I wanted to surprise Ben with a fabulous Moroccan meal when he came home from work.

I had to get to work quickly. It was three thirty by the time I arrived home, and I had to pick up some groceries first. I was set on cooking the same two dishes we'd made in our cooking class, the Moroccan menu staple, tajine chicken with olives and piquant preserved lemon, and a side dish or warm dip of roasted green bell pepper and tomato, called *taktouka*.

I didn't have time to hunt down salt-preserved lemons in

Brooklyn, nor the time to cure them myself, so I settled for fresh lemon instead. I wanted to serve the tajine with freshly baked bread, as was always done in Morocco. But there wasn't enough time to turn out a loaf of no-knead bread, which needed to be set out overnight. So instead, I got to work actually kneading a loaf of bread—something I'd rarely done before. After eight minutes of kneading the dough, I was about ready to collapse into a deep sleep. But I managed to shake off the sleepiness and move on to cooking the tajine, since it needed to simmer a while. Red onion, garlic, and several spices later, the terra-cotta tajine that I'd brought back from Morocco was slowly cooking the chicken and olives inside. I got to work on the green-pepper dip next, the *taktouka*. Gripping the peppers with tongs, I held them over a high stove flame until their skins became blackened and crispy all over. I then covered them in plastic wrap to let the skins become soggy and easy to scrape off. Next I thinly sliced the roasted flesh of the peppers and sautéed the slices in a pan with chopped fresh tomato, onion, garlic, and spices. The tomatoes broke down into a loose sauce with just barely visible cubes of onion that coated the sliced peppers. The tingling smells of paprika and roasted peppers wafted to my nose as I stirred them in the pan, just as we had in the cooking class. Really, it was a lovely dish.

When Ben got home at seven, the apartment was engulfed in the aroma of cumin and coriander from the chicken. It was just finished cooking, and I hadn't had a spare moment to rest yet. But the food was all ready to eat: a freshly baked loaf of bread, the warm *taktouka*, and the lemony chicken and olive tajine. I was proud of this feat, and, once I tasted the results, I was duly impressed with the outcome. Stained yellow with turmeric, the chicken meat fell cleanly from the bone with the touch of a fork. The salty olives were soft and warm, and the onions and garlic had cooked down to a thick yellow sauce that was perfect for soaking the bread.

I tried to tell Ben everything about my trip over dinner. I was winding down from my third or fourth wind and got hit with another fatigue spell once there was a full meal in my belly. Ben was reticent throughout the meal. There had been a strange look of shock on his face when he walked into the apartment and saw me. I had been standing in the kitchen, as usual, which was situated awkwardly close to the door. The scenario was exactly the same as it had been countless nights when Ben came home from work: a cutting board and knife planted in front of me as I chopped up vegetables or dropped some pasta noodles into a bubbling pot. This time, the preparation was all done and I was just clearing some bowls and dishes into the sink.

Ben listened to my tales about riding camels and tasting the food in the stands of Marrakesh, and politely complimented the dinner I made. I showed him the terra-cotta tajine and told him about how well I had learned to bargain with the street merchants by the end of the trip so that I'd gotten it for a steal. He had very little to say about his week, by contrast, and seemed reluctant to go into detail about it. I got a strange feeling from this, but by eight thirty, I didn't have the energy to talk for much longer. After finishing the dishes, I fell into a deep, long night's sleep.

"How's your jet lag?" Ben asked on the phone the next day as we chatted from our respective office cubes.

"Better," I said. "Gone, I think."

"That's good. Hey, do you think we can talk tonight?" he asked.

"Sure. What's up?"

"Well, I just think a lot of things have changed . . . you know?" he said.

"Hm. What things?" I asked.

Ben hesitated. His next words came out nervously. "I think we should just talk later."

I laughed. "Whoa, you're scaring me now; what's up?"

There was a long moment of dead silence on the other end.

"Okay . . . let's talk, then," I said.

I was disturbed after the phone call, but I had no clue what he could be getting at. Something must have happened, but I wasn't sure what. Whatever it was, there was no use dwelling on it or trying to guess, so I just went on with my day as usual.

I left work at six and got home, as usual, about fifteen minutes before Ben. As I dumped my things on the dining table, I looked around the apartment once more. Yesterday, when I'd first arrived home from my trip, I did notice a few changes around the apartment. No major rearrangements of furniture, just little touches: A neat stack of magazines was placed on the coffee table with the TV remotes placed on top just so. A rug had been turned ninety degrees to make the room appear longer. My empty flower vases were nowhere to be seen.

But none of this could have prepared me for the topic of conversation that began a few moments after Ben walked in. He seemed stressed, nervous, and uncomfortable. He began by restating that some things "had changed." I waited for more.

"Don't you think so, too?" he pried.

"What things? I have no idea what things you're talking about."

He went on. It was a lot of little things, not any one big thing. But for him, at least, they were enough to make him decide that he wanted a major change. After three hours of back-and-forth debate, frustration, and utter confusion, at least three things were clear. One, Ben and I were breaking up. Two, he would take the apartment for the rest of the lease while I found someplace else to live. Three, I was no longer going to Richard and Sam's wedding in Mexico next month, and Ben would eat the cost of my plane ticket.

The next night I went to see Erin sing with her band at a small bar, and all my friends were there. I think they were just as blindsided by the breakup as I was, which felt somewhat comforting. Erin had just stared for what seemed like a full minute after I told her the news.

"But why?" she finally demanded to know.

There was little I could tell her. Immediately, my gut had told me that Ben's decision had something to do with a certain coworker whom he'd been spending a lot of time with lately. But he had hotly denied this, and my accusations got us absolutely nowhere over the course of the fight. I put this suspicion aside and didn't offer it to my friends at Erin's show. Just as soon as their initial shock had worn off, they were quick to jump to my ego-boosting aid. I'd be better off now, they assured me. Somewhere in the back of my mind, I believed this was true, too.

That week, as I began hunting for a new place to live, Ben avoided being in the apartment as much as possible, staying with friends on most nights. All of a sudden, I was cooking weeknight meals for just one.

My mom and Jo-Jo had planned to come over for dinner that weekend after my trip, to see my photos, claim their souvenirs, and enjoy a homemade Moroccan dinner. It was also going to be a late birthday celebration for Jo-Jo. But the day after my return from vacation, Gong-Gong was taken to the hospital with a case of pneumonia. He was moved to intensive care the next morning. My mother called me that day to tell me the news. The doctor didn't want to keep our hopes up. He was doubtful my grandfather would live much longer than a few days, in his fragile state. My mom spent the next day in his hospital room along with Jo-Jo. Later that night, with Jo-Jo beside his bed, he passed away. He was eighty-two years old, and my last living grandparent.

We decided to still do dinner at my apartment that Sunday. Gong-Gong's funeral wouldn't take place until a few months later, when his ashes would be placed to rest in a temple. For the time being, they would be held in the crematory, and to pay respect to the dead, my uncle was observing a Buddhist tradition of abstaining from meat for eighty days. He encouraged me to go ahead and cook anything I wanted on Sunday, and he would just eat whatever vegetables were there. But I decided to prepare an all-vegetarian feast. Fortunately, this wouldn't be too difficult with Moroccan cuisine.

I planned to make the *taktouka* again, this time with better bread, a spicy braised eggplant dish, and a savory vegetable couscous. Our Marrakesh cooking-class instructor, Mohammed, had begun his lecture by explaining that couscous was Morocco's national dish and its importance could not be understated. Classic vegetable couscous was a focal point of the Moroccan table, from wedding banquets and holidays to everyday meals, and a proper feast wasn't complete without it. Since it took so long to prepare, Mohammed recited only a recipe for seven-vegetable couscous during class, which we jotted on notepads.

As he described the painstaking process of gently massaging the grains by hand, setting them out on a wide, flat surface, then kneading them again to give them the proper texture and firmness, I could hardly believe what I was writing down. Wasn't couscous just supposed to be drenched with hot water and left to sit for five minutes until done? This sounded like an obscene amount of prep work, and for what payoff, I didn't know.

I didn't understand what all the fuss was about over couscous then, and Jordan and I certainly didn't get it when we were served a bland, dry couscous on our first day in Marrakesh. The British and Australians in our cooking class didn't seem to understand, either, and one of them commented on how the vegetables in couscous he had seen were so overcooked as to look "sad." But at a rooftop restaurant during a stop in the mountains, I decided to give the dish another try and noticed a distinctly satisfying lightness to the flavors in it that time. Then, after cooking my own vegetable couscous at home following Mohammed's directions, I think I finally got it.

Couscous was not something to be tucked away underneath chicken or a lamb chop, or swept to the side of the plate in a measly portion. It was in itself the main attraction in Moroccan meals, when cooked with the right care. Mohammed's recipe began by searing a bit of shoulder meat (preferably lamb) with bones in a large pot, for flavor. To that he added a sliced onion and spoonfuls of spices, followed with a chopped tomato. After twenty minutes of cooking, the pot was filled with cold water, large chunks of turnip, parsnip, and carrots, and a bunch of fresh cilantro and other herbs as desired.

In the meantime, the couscous was sprinkled with just a tiny bit of water and oil, gently mixed by hand, and spread flat on a plate to dry. Next, one had to break up the clumps by hand thoroughly, then transfer the little grains to a steamer rack placed on top of the pot. The idea is that the grains, held together by moisture to prevent them from slipping through the steamer rack's holes, would absorb the soup's flavors as it steamed above it. I didn't have a steamer and substituted a metal colander that fit nicely on top of my biggest pot. And even though I was worried because the holes in it were quite large, true to Mohammed's instructions, the couscous didn't fall through much at all. By the time the couscous was fully cooked half an hour later, my entire apartment smelled of the most wonderful broth in the world.

That leftover broth turned out to be my mother and Jo-Jo's favorite part of the meal. Because of Jo-Jo's fast, I skipped the addition of lamb shoulder for flavor in the recipe. Still, those turnips and root vegetables had simmered for a deeply savory, soothing stock with a rich golden hue and almost floral subtleties in flavor.

Steamed with this stock, the couscous fell to the plate in moist, yet separate grains and had a delicate firmness of texture. Mimicking what I'd seen done in Morocco, I'd piled the couscous in a great, pointed dome and arranged the cooked vegetables around it like campfire logs. I poured a ladle of hot broth over the heaped dish, and then it was ready to serve.

After polishing off this course, along with the roasted-pepper dip, eggplant, and half a loaf of homemade bread, we sat around the small kitchen table in my apartment with the scraped dishes. My mom and uncle helped themselves to seconds and thirds of the vegetable broth and held their soup bowls close like cups of tea as we continued to talk. Ben had made a point of staying out of the apartment that evening, and I'd told them that he was merely out with friends.

Looking down at his bowl of soup, focused in thought, my uncle uttered his first words about Gong-Gong's death. He had been in the hospital room with him when the nurses told Jo-Jo it was almost time. Gong-Gong's heart reading had dropped to its faintest, most infrequent beat. My uncle had gotten down on his knees to pray to Buddha.

He looked up again, but not directly at either of us. "I think it was good. It was a good ending," he said.

Throughout that night, I never brought up the fact that Ben and I were splitting up and that I was looking for a new living arrangement. I didn't think it would have been appropriate. That night was Jo-Jo's. But the next day, on the phone, I told my mother the news of our breakup.

"I knew it," she said.

How, I still don't know.

"I just knew," she repeated.

I had another cooking commitment to attend to that week. Just before leaving for Morocco, I'd gotten a heads up from the editor of one of my favorite food websites, Mark Douglas from "Culinate." He'd asked me to participate in a food-blogging contest they were holding, focused on chocolaty recipes. The prize for this contest was a trip for two to the annual Death by Chocolate food festival at the COPIA: The American Center for Food and the Arts in Napa. To compete, any food blogger just had to come up with a recipe that appropriately fit the theme, "Death by Chocolate," and write a post on it. I'd promised I wouldn't disappoint.

I initially thought I'd be inspired by Morocco and have a chocolate dish ready to concoct once I got back, perhaps with unique spice combinations. As I mulled over this and other possibilities, I searched the website, rereading the entry rules. A graphic on the contest page read in bright pink, "Treat your sweetie! Win a trip for two."

Clearly, I was in no place to treat any sweetie. Maybe I'd just sit this one out, I thought. But I did like the idea of eating spoonful after spoonful of something chocolaty until I hurled. Did it matter what?

It suddenly came to me. *Pain au chocolat.*

In French, this would mean "chocolate bread" or "bread with chocolate," and *pain au chocolate* is a buttery, croissantlike pastry filled with chocolate. Maybe I'd make something involving bread and chocolate, I began thinking. And then call it "pain with chocolate"—and that's the English, not the French kind of "pain."

Of course, this dessert wouldn't be as straightforward as a chocolate croissant. What, then, should I make? Chocolate bread pudding? Too boring, I concluded. Some kind of chocolate-topped bread crostini? Not impressive enough.

A chocolate trifle, I finally decided, with tiers of deep, dark chocolate pudding and torn white bread pieces instead of the traditional sponge-cake bits and vanilla pudding. Then, how about tossing in some more chocolate bits, in chunks throughout? And just as the classic trifle takes a drizzle of brandy or sweet liqueur, this one would have chocolate liqueur to meld it all together. A classic English trifle with a twist: *pain* instead of cake. And chocolate instead of fruit.

I baked a loaf of white, basic no-knead bread before getting the plan under way. Next, I whisked together a batch of dark chocolate pudding. I purchased some chocolate liqueur to drizzle in between the layers, and some rich dark chocolate to chop up and also shave as a topping for the finished dessert. Finally, I'd need a traditional glass, footed trifle bowl to serve and photograph the dessert in. I called up Sean and asked whether I could borrow his trifle bowl.

"Sure," he replied.

I took pains to photograph the cooking process and to shoot the final, ceremonious heap in the trifle bowl. Within the recipe's post, I described making the dish in all its painful glory, peppering the entry with deliciously morbid insights on breakups and the gloom of Valentine's Day for the singleton.

While the judges took a day or two to read the entries, I had a good look at all of them myself. I found myself drooling over the chocolaty recipes and photos on the other blogs, some of which looked very professionally made. But something told me that my post had a little more meat on its bones than the other ones, a bit more story, even if it was decidedly unromantic.

Mark Douglas wrote to all the finalists to tell us that a winner would soon be contacted by phone. That same day, I had just submitted an application for a one-bedroom apartment I was hoping would soon be all mine. It was February, and even though the last few days had been freezing, after work I decided to get off at a subway stop a little farther than usual from my home to enjoy a long walk through the brownstone-lined streets. It would be one of my last walks through Fort Greene while I could still call it my home. The apartment I had applied for was a ways east in Brooklyn, in Crown Heights.

As I walked, my cell phone rang. It was Mark Douglas.

"So, you know you won?" he said.

"No way!" I yelled. I felt like dancing in the street.

I'd need to book the plane tickets first, he instructed, as flights were beginning to fill up. I would be receiving all the details about the hotel and rental car that came with the prize trip from COPIA soon. Mark would also be attending the chocolate festival that weekend and hoped to round up a small group for dinner on the last night.

"I'm real curious to see who you'll bring along as a date," he chided, right before we got off the phone.

I'd laughed along, pretending that my plus-one was up for contention. But really, I knew all along whom to bring.

"Mom, we're going to Napa," I said a little later over the phone.

"What?" she shrieked.

"Pack your bags. It's next weekend."

A week and a half later, we were driving from Napa Valley to San Francisco in a rental car. Our day had begun early, with a delayed flight due to snow in New York. We landed in California with just enough time to make it to a guided tour of Bay Area chocolatier Charles Chocolates, first up on our chocolate-filled agenda. Chuck Siegel, founder of Charles Chocolates, walked us through the facilities, handing out choice bits and even letting us dip gloved fingers into slowly churning tanks of fudge. It was all very Willy Wonka–esque, but by the chocolate factory tour's end, what my mom and I could really have used was some lunch. So we decided to take a detour and spend the rest of the day and night in San Francisco.

Shortly after my parents married, they had lived in San Francisco for several years. There my father completed law school, and my mother worked odd jobs while acclimating herself to her new country of citizenship. My parents had met in Taiwan; my dad had gone to work for an import-export company in Taipei, as a bilingual associate (he spoke Mandarin and held an Asian studies degree) who would act as a sort of Western culture go-to person for the company. One of the first colleagues he met at the office was my mother. My mom had never dreamed of living in America, or anywhere else, really, before she'd met my dad. But a couple of years later, she was married, an American citizen, and living in San Francisco.

I'd been to San Francisco only once before, so my mom was eager to show me around the city she remembered so fondly. We went to Chinatown first and walked into the first Cantonese noodle shop we saw. It was only a couple of weeks since my Morocco trip, and stepping inside a restaurant again felt funny and frivolous. I wasn't used to sitting before a steaming bowl of wonton soup anymore, at least in the States, but once it was brought to our table, the vapors flooding my nostrils with the scent of stock, a rush of familiarity swept over me.

The month had been a wacky one in more ways than just a deviation from my usual eating habits. Just the night before our flight, I'd picked up the keys for my new one-bedroom apartment in Crown Heights and moved out of my old one for good. I'd hired movers, who dropped all my furniture into the new living room, and I left the boxes in the middle of the living room floor. I was a single girl now, with my own apartment.

The soup and congee that we'd ordered was comforting and fueled us for a lengthy walk around the city. I didn't realize how much I missed the run-of-the-mill Cantonese noodle shop. It wasn't just the food that mattered—it was everything: the roasted ducks and chickens hanging in the window, the butcher skillfully hacking into them on a block just behind the panes. The sound of other customers slurping loudly at the next table. The way our orders came rushing to our table about one and a half minutes after we'd placed them.

Afterward, we took a trolley downtown and shopped for a while, my mom pointing out familiar buildings and streets from her past. I'd made reservations for dinner that night at a restaurant that an old friend of mine from college co-owned with his brothers. It was located in the avenues, outside downtown, and its specialty was Japanese-Korean fusion. After dusk, we headed back to Chinatown by foot to retrieve our parked rental car.

"I used to walk up this street to our apartment every day," my mom recalled as we hiked up a steep cliff of a street. I was huffing and puffing after two blocks' worth.

"Really?" I was surprised. New Yorkers did a lot of walking, but they had no hills like these to deal with. Despite its steepness, the street was busy with locals, tourists, cars, and trolleys, heading both up and down.

"Oh, yes." My mom nodded proudly. "And I would sometimes carry groceries or my laundry right up this hill. I was your age then," she added after a pause. "Twenty-six."

Now, I thought I was pretty fit for chugging groceries around on my bike back in Brooklyn. But I could never imagine taking them up this hill. Or just climbing it, all the time, with or without a heavy load. I remembered that my mom also couldn't speak English very well back then. I suddenly felt very small, walking beside her.

The dinner at my friend's new restaurant, Namu, was much more impressive than anything I could have imagined a Japanese-

Korean fusion to be. Plus, my friend spoiled us with extra sides, drinks, and specials. We had black cod ceviche served in fried wonton cups, grilled okra with *shiso* aioli, bourbon and Korean chili-spiced baby back ribs, and cups of sweet sake. It was a unique culinary experience. The best part of all was being treated like family, despite it being a busy night at the restaurant. I felt a little guilty about my not-eating-out habit. What if a friend were to open a restaurant in New York, and because of my wack principles, I wouldn't support him or her by dining there? That wouldn't be very nice, I considered. I was glad the dilemma hadn't happened yet.

The next day was a whirlwind of activity, from sipping wines at a handful of vineyards in Napa Valley to tasting every manner of chocolate possible and taking a truffle-making class at the Death by Chocolate festival at COPIA. My mom and I also found time to stop for lunch at the Culinary Institute of America's Greystone restaurant, in Napa. There, I'd attacked a foamy soufflé of cheese that was baked on top of my French onion soup. My mom had ordered a light seafood cioppino, which came with a separate jug of hot broth to pour over the dish.

At the end of the day, we also enjoyed a long dinner with Mark Douglas and three other guests from the chocolate contest. We'd gone to Julia's Kitchen at COPIA, named after the culinary heroine. My entree was a very deconstructed bouillabaisse: a thin, tomato-based stew with fresh and barely seasoned seafood and a shower of parsley. I felt like I was becoming better acquainted with this California cuisine, something I knew about only from books and magazines.

The next morning, after a quick breakfast at our hotel, my mom and I headed for the airport. It had been a brief but packed two days on the West Coast, and I was sure that my chocolate cravings were sated for the next year or so. I also hoped that my restaurant-food cravings wouldn't come back to haunt me after all those great and guilt-inspiring meals we had. But as I drove us to the airport, thinking ahead about my upcoming week, I couldn't wait to get into the kitchen and start cooking again. I could almost feel the familiar grip of the spatula in my hand, and the motions of mincing garlic replayed in my mind.

"You know," my mom said, leaning back in the passenger seat,

"I think it's a good time for you to be living alone, have your own place. It will be good for you."

"Yeah?" I said.

"Jo-Jo thinks so, too," she added.

I was squinting from the sunlight, but something about what my mom just said made my eyes tear up a little, and I didn't want her to see. I focused on the road ahead, my hands firm on the wheel.

"I think it will be good for you," she said again.

Back in Brooklyn late that night, I walked into my apartment and plopped down my luggage at the door. The living room was still littered with boxes. It was about midnight, and after a long weekend away, I was tired and found myself missing my old home, and barely recognizing my new one.

When I sat down a few days later, trying to come up with my next "Reason of the Month for not eating out" blog post, I felt a little bit at a loss. I got up and walked around my apartment. There was a large stockpot on the back burner of my stove simmering with a big batch of vegetable stock I was making. It smelled wonderful, the carrots, celery, onion, and turnips slowly seeping their flavors into the hot water with a steady bubble. I went back to my computer and tried to write again.

I'd had such an overwhelming change of pace eating in restaurants in Morocco and San Francisco—I was lucky to have eaten at some pretty good places throughout, and this didn't exactly represent the typical restaurant-food experience for most people. But still, I began to question what I was gaining from this not-eating-out experiment that was so great in comparison to perhaps just eating in really great restaurants. Or, what was I taking away from this experiment that was so much better than what I could gain by traveling around and experiencing new foods all the time in different places?

But that wasn't the point of it all, was it? I wasn't ever trying to say all along that not eating out in New York was somehow unequivocally *better* than eating in restaurants. No, in a perfect world, a good balance of home-cooking passion and a hearty appetite for exciting and new restaurant food would do me just fine.

The problem was expense and practicality. By knowing how to cook all the time, I was saving myself a huge bundle. And I'd made it practical for my busy lifestyle.

I walked around my living room again, stopping to open the stockpot and stare at the vegetables at the bottom. The translucent, loose rings of an onion were flapping in the bubbles like a winged creature trying to take flight. I closed the lid and walked down the short hall to my bedroom. I opened the door—I'm not sure why I ever closed the door in the first place; it's not like I needed to for privacy—and stared at the messy room for a minute.

I sat back down on my living room couch and opened my laptop again. The screen flashed on with a slight beep and returned to my half-written blog post. I erased the text and rewrote the title. "Reason for Not Eating Out #19: Because You Can (Almost) Afford to Live Alone." In it, I estimated the food cost for an average month's worth of eating solely from grocery-store purchases. I compared that to an average month's worth of eating a combination of grocery store and restaurant food, in a breakdown that resembled how I used to eat before I began my blogging quest. The difference in spending, month to month, came surprisingly close to the couple of hundred dollars more I was paying in rent than at my old place, with Ben. It didn't make up the deficit for my own one-bedroom completely, but it made a compelling argument for sacrificing restaurant spending as a way to budget for something else—something more valuable, perhaps. And for New York City, space commands a very high value.

Ben and I saw very little of each other after the move. After tying up some loose ends regarding the apartment, my mail, and the like, we didn't really communicate. I guess neither of us felt the need to.

One cold night a couple of weeks after moving, I went out for drinks with Jordan and a few other friends. We'd gone to a nearby bar and had a good time. Once it had gotten late, we all took off in our separate directions. As I biked my short ride home, I thought about how I was going to put on a record and cook up a hot bowl of noodles with a splash of hot chili sauce in the soup once I got home. I wouldn't have a sleeping boyfriend to be sorry about waking up in the next room. I also wouldn't have a boyfriend who just wanted to buy a big bag of chips and sit in front of the squawking TV whenever we came home from a night out like this. Still, I felt a little alone in the world as I rode home, and also, freezing cold.

I no longer thought about Ben specifically these days so much as I felt a lack of some other entity, a confidant, someone to help pull along the weight of every day. This new sense of independence was compounded by the fact that I had no roommates. I had never before entertained this option in all the time I'd been in New York—mostly because I didn't think I could afford it. Even back when I was living with Erin, which seemed so long ago but was only a little over a year, sharing tight corners and trying to squeeze in personal peace and quiet now and then just seemed the natural course of living in the city. But here I was, in my apartment all to myself. And here, too, I would be cooking for one.

I remembered what my mom had said in the car when we were driving to the airport in California, and how confident she had been about my new living situation. This was a far cry from the mother who had told me almost four years ago, when I first moved to the city, that roommates were, if nothing else, watch keepers of one's life. They would be the ones to call if you got locked out; they were the key contact if anything should happen to you. Now she was saying something else. It had never occurred to me before that I might be doing myself a favor by living alone, or that I could have been depriving myself of some room for personal growth otherwise, much like I had stuffed all my old sketchbooks, musical instruments, and reams of writing tablets into a box at the tippy top of my packed closet, out of reach. Maybe I really would be better off, more productive, by not being around others all the time. I think that's what she and Jo-Jo meant when she said it would be good for me.

At the bar that night, instead of being stimulated by the prospect of meeting someone, I found myself thinking about how lame most of the city's male population was. It was sad, really, the way the drunkards had all sat around in big groups, staring down all-too-aware-of-this females and knocking back beers until they were loud and giggly. Maybe this wasn't so bad or unusual; maybe I was just seeing guys in a dull light right then and it would take a real diamond in the rough to change my point of view.

I rode past another bar on my way home and glanced at a crowd of smokers hanging out by the entrance. There were three scruffy dudes shivering in the cold in sweaters, corduroy jackets, and ripped jeans. I summed them up pretty quickly and suddenly felt gripped with a conviction: Whoever I was going to date next—whenever that would be—would have nothing to do with these types of overeducated, overly taste-conscious, regular losers and persnickety coffee-shop jerks. The type who fetishized some sort of hardscrabble New York lifestyle, barely making rent on tip wages while their parents back in some other state probably had enough money to buffer them, or at least buy them a winter coat.

Well, it turned out I was wrong.

~~~~~~

Roasted Green Pepper and Tomato Dip (*Taktouka* Salad)

This dish was taught at the La Maison Arabe cooking class in Marrakesh, Morocco. It can be served warm, room temperature, or cold, and it can be eaten with bread as a dip or simply alone as a side.   (SERVES 2–3)

> 2 large green bell peppers
> 2 tablespoons olive oil
> 2 garlic cloves, minced
> 1 heaping teaspoon paprika
> 1 teaspoon salt
> ½ teaspoon black pepper
> 3 large ripe tomatoes, cored, peeled, and finely chopped

Holding each bell pepper with tongs, blacken all sides of its surface over an open flame from a gas oven. Alternately, the peppers can be placed on a sheet and broiled on each side, or baked at 500 degrees, until their skin has crisped and blackened. Place peppers into individual plastic bags and close tightly to prevent any air from getting in. Let sit for 10 minutes. Remove peppers from bags and carefully peel away the skin with a dull knife (it should be soggy by now and slip off easily). Core the peppers and slice them into very fine, long slivers.

In a saucepan, heat the olive oil with garlic. Add the spices and tomatoes and cook about 5–6 minutes, stirring occasionally, until tomatoes have broken down and reduced to a thick sauce. Add the slivered peppers and stir for another 2–3 minutes. Serve immediately.

~~~~~~

Minty Moroccan Couscous Salad with Mint and Ghee

With vegetables, protein, and grains, this salad makes a great summer meal and travels well to potlucks and parties. The classic North African ingredients—olives, almonds, and raisins—add a warm complement to the fresh tomatoes, but the mint clarified butter (ghee) is the real secret to the dish's tastiness.

(SERVES 4–6)

2 tablespoons extra-virgin olive oil
½ large red onion, finely chopped
2 cloves garlic, minced
1 teaspoon each coriander and cumin seeds, toasted and crushed in a spice grinder (or use ground powders)
2 teaspoons turmeric
1 teaspoon paprika
1–2 teaspoons salt
½ teaspoon black pepper
2 cups uncooked couscous
1 cup vegetable stock or water
2 cups grape tomatoes, halved
½ cup raisins
½ cup roasted almonds, roughly chopped
1 cup pitted black Greek olives, roughly chopped
1½ cups chickpeas, soaked and fully cooked, or if canned, rinsed and drained
Juice and zest of 1 lemon
1 stick butter
4–5 tablespoons fresh mint leaves, finely chopped

In a large, heavy pot, heat the olive oil. Add about one-third of the chopped onions, the garlic, all the spices, and the salt and pepper, and stir over medium-low heat for 4–5 minutes, until the onions are soft. Add the couscous and stir to coat evenly. In a separate pan, bring the vegetable stock or water to a boil. Pour over the couscous, stir thoroughly, and cover the pot. Let sit for 5 minutes.

Fluff couscous and stir in the rest of the ingredients except for the butter and mint leaves.

In a small saucepan, slowly melt the butter. Remove from heat, and with a regular spoon skim off all the solid white milk fat that has separated to the top (it's okay if a tiny bit remains in the pot). Add the chopped mint leaves and let sit for at least 10 minutes. Drizzle the clarified mint butter over the couscous and stir thoroughly. It's best to let the couscous sit for at least one hour before serving, to let the flavors blend. Serve at room temperature.

CHAPTER 10

New Lows

THE SEARCH FOR THE PERFECT DATE MEAL

The way to a woman's heart is through the door of an expensive restaurant.

—Conventional wisdom / Refrigerator magnets / Coffee mugs

My first few weeks living in my new apartment, I spent most nights cooking boring, repetitive, and humble foods for myself. It was pleasant, if a little lonely. I didn't have to worry about another person around to disagree with whatever I felt like making. I didn't have another set of eyes in the apartment to watch me if I was frantically clanging and grabbing things around the kitchen, avoiding the splash of oil and dropping spatulas, or cursing because I forgot to add something to the pot. In fact, I didn't do much of anything frantically while cooking anymore. Who cared how prompt or good dinner was, when there was only myself to please? It turns out I was my own best personal chef. I'd spend a languid half hour stirring risotto, listening to the radio or records, watching everything going on in the pot. Somehow, everything I cooked in those first few weeks came out seamlessly, too, delicious even if simple.

On the phone one day, it suddenly occurred to my mother that I couldn't go to restaurants for dates.

"How are you going to date?" she exclaimed in between huge, incredulous cackles. "No one is going to be able to take you out!"

"Whatever," I said, rolling my eyes. My friends were supercool and creative, I tried to explain to her. And we don't care about institutions like the nice, civil restaurant date. I think this scared her for a moment even more than the thought of me never dating anyone again.

The truth was, I knew it was going to be different now, if I should meet someone whom I might want to date. But I hoped that my strange eating disorder wouldn't be seen as a handicap. Sure, it would be awkward to have to explain the whole blog premise to anyone who just asked me if I wanted to go grab a bite, and it was bound to cause a little hiccup in those precious few moments when a person first asks someone out. But men who were so uncreative as to not know what to do for a date besides go to a restaurant? I decided I had no need for them. Hey, maybe this could be something of a built-in filtering device, this no-restaurant thing.

I also felt like all of my previous relationships were founded on going to eat in restaurants. This didn't exactly bring a tear of nostalgia to my eye. In high school, my first boyfriend and I would drive to twenty-four-hour diners throughout New Jersey, which, no matter the town, always had the same Deco exterior and harsh fluorescent lighting. There we'd sit in a booth for hours, sipping coffee and plunking quarters into the jukebox. After he moved away for college, we began going to the big-box, chain restaurants like IHOP, which dotted the highways that then separated us. After a while, it became harder to tell whether we were going to any of these places for the irony or kitsch value as we had been at first.

In college I dated a vegetarian for a little while, and the idea of an exciting restaurant meal then was limited to a large foldout menu filled with fake-meat dishes at a Buddhist vegetarian restaurant in Chinatown. It wasn't bad, but personally I'd rather have gone to the better Chinese restaurant down the street and ordered a spicy and savory tofu dish, maybe garnished with traces of meat for flavor, like *ma po* tofu.

With Ben, it felt like the first six months of our relationship was a series of checking out one cute, hip new restaurant in Brooklyn after another. This common type of dating wasn't unenjoyable, of course, and it was definitely a good way of exploring the city. But after a while you might begin to wonder if there was any reason the two of you had decided to spend time together other than to try the next thing on the menu, or the next hot restaurant.

I was determined to find alternatives to the stale old ritual of going out to eat on dates. Dating while not eating out in New York was just the challenge I needed to try my hand at next, to make the experiment more complete. Now, who else was up for the challenge?

Around this time in late February and early March, I also found out that Ben had moved on to another relationship. I discovered this by accident; while clicking around on MySpace one day at the office, I saw that the relationship status on Ben's profile had gone from "single" to "in a relationship."

My hands froze as I stared at the screen, and I felt a nasty surge of nausea rise in my throat. I knew at that moment whom it was with: that coworker of his, who had become so chummy in the last few weeks of our living together. The three of us had even hung out together several times. There was no doubt in my mind that she, who incidentally was ten years my senior, was the person he was now proudly in a relationship with.

I spun around in my seat. The queasy feeling in my stomach persisted as I stared for a moment straight ahead into space. That space was actually the back of my coworker Keith's cubicle, and his computer monitor was right then tuned to Facebook. I got up and went to the ladies' room, half expecting to retch into the toilet. But nothing came.

"I feel like I've been shat on by a million birds," I told Matt that evening. We were standing in my kitchen, getting ready to make an easy dinner and crack open a bottle of white wine that was sweating on the counter. I'd invited a few friends over for a simple dinner a couple of days before, but everyone else had fallen ill or, in Karol's case, had literally fallen, while jogging, and was nursing a bruised knee.

"And this woman works with him?" Matt asked after I explained my discovery earlier that day.

"Yep."

He pulled the cork out of a bottle with a pop. "How old is she again?"

"She's thirty-five and miraculously still has acne."

"Well, cheers to that," he said, and handed me a glass. We clinked and both took a sip.

Matt thought for a moment. "Sometimes it's good to make a clean break, to have less reason to think about it. You and Ben haven't spoken in weeks, right?" he said. I nodded.

"With me and Jill, just the other day I got an e-mail from her, saying she was mad at me for something I apparently did when we were dating," Matt said. He went on to describe how his ex-girlfriend, Jill, had nagged him because she found out he had gone on a tour with "Wildman" Steve Brill recently, and one time while they were dating Jill had been talking excitedly about Brill's tours and Matt had shown no interest whatsoever.

"So three years after we broke up, I can still be a bad boyfriend," he concluded.

"That doesn't sound right at all," I said after a pause.

"Nope."

We spent the rest of the night talking about failed relationships and thankfully more pleasant topics, gossiping, cooking black beans and rice, and putting on CD after iPod track after record. By the end of the night, I felt about eight hundred times better than I had earlier in the day, almost jovial. I knew in my heart that I was over Ben already. But rejection, and especially betrayal, are hard things to swallow. They can be treated only by friends who know how to make light of the situation, I think.

That weekend, I went to a birthday party in Williamsburg. When I left the party, it was only eleven thirty or so, and the spring night was mild and crisp. I was in good spirits, enjoying the air against my face after having been inside the stuffy bar. So I picked up my phone and dialed Karol, who lived nearby and who I could bet was hanging out somewhere in the neighborhood. She was. She told me to come meet her at a bar where she was playing pool with a couple of friends.

Almost immediately after joining them at the table, I met Nick. He and a friend were standing by the pool table watching Karol's game, since they had written their names on the board to play next. He had shaggy dark hair and a two-day scruff, and he leaned in and started talking to me suddenly as if we were old pals. He stuck around over the next hour or so, and we chatted in between watching and playing rounds of pool. He said he was in New York for the summer only, heading off to grad school in Chicago in the fall. In the meantime, he was working at a coffee shop and picking up freelance translation jobs on the side. I told him what I did and mentioned my food blog. As a way of explanation, I'd handed him my minicard for the blog.

Around two or so, Karol and I were still hanging out and shooting pool, but Nick's friends were piling into a car outside. It had begun to pour; splatters of rain and lightning were showcased through the windowpanes from where we were standing, and Karol and I resolved to wait it out before going home. We ended up staying for a couple of hours longer and at least that many more drinks.

When I got home, there was already an e-mail in my in-box from this Nick fellow.

"On the off chance that your handing me your card was motivated by something other than career advancement . . . ," it began.

It was short and to the point. Basically, he wanted to go on a date.

I told Karol about it on the phone the next day.

"So are you going to go out with him?" she said.

"I don't know. Maybe. What'd you think of him?" I asked.

"I totally can't even remember," she said, groggily. "But you thought he was cute, right?"

I had. It was just one of those things, plain attraction.

"But I have serious concerns that he may be younger than twenty-five," I said.

"Now *that* is highly possible," Karol said, with a firmness that made it sound like she was finally waking up a little.

My guess on Nick's age was based on the crowd at the bar that night, which was rife with barely of-age drinkers, and the fact that he was going to grad school in the fall. But here's why I decided that even though he might be young, immature, or for all intents and purposes just not Mr. Right, I'd still go on a date with him: He was leaving New York at the end of the summer. So, what did anything matter, really? It actually sounded great—there'd be no pressure, no worries, nothing. Except for figuring out what to do on a "date."

Instead of a restaurant, maybe it was time to move the all-important date meal to a home setting. What would be the perfect date meal? I began to wonder. It's a term you hear thrown around a lot, though when it came to the actual food I could think of no limitations to or clear objectives regarding what was on the plate. Was it something elaborately planned, executed, and plated just so, or a slap-dash, easy meal so there was enough time left for the really fun stuff? Was it a bloodred, juicy steak? A communal bowl of spaghetti to slurp at like Lady and her Tramp? Seafood didn't smell to me right for this category. Neither did anything that was too cheesy or garlicky. I could see how a really rich, chocolaty dessert could be defined as romantic, but that was no main course.

One of my favorite short stories, "The Nice Restaurant," by Mary Gaitskill, is about a couple dining out one night. The woman, Laurel, is said to be much older than her youthful, energetic companion, Eric. While they are sitting in the restaurant together, Eric says of Laurel: "Your face was just wildly expressive right then." She replies, "I just got sucked into the whole you know, nice restaurant thing, then got disgusted by it all too quickly."

Then, after a leisurely meal, the narrator concludes this about Laurel's feelings toward Eric: "She absolutely loved him. Even though she knew they wouldn't be dating longer than a few months."

I think the story is saying, in a way, that the nice restaurant dinner is sort of like a cad: It has the power to temporarily seduce, transport, and haunt. But the effect is short-lived. You go to the restaurant fully aware of the limitations of its spell; you date him, even though you know he won't be there in the long run. But you do it anyway.

What I wanted was this, the reckless seduction, passion, however fickle it may turn out. The "nice restaurant" factor—but at home. I wanted to see my apartment transformed into this ultra-romantic place, too, so that the mood could exist in an enclosed bubble for that time and place. And I wanted it to be gone in the morning. Theoretically, this would be impossible to do, since my home would still be my home, and I'd have to do the dishes and take the trash out, just as usual. But, with a little imagination, I wanted something greater than the sum of the parts of an extraordinary meal to take place in my home.

Nick called me the next day. I had responded to his e-mail saying he could give me a ring sometime, adding that my number was on the card. It was Sunday, and my schedule that week was packed, so when he called, we decided to try to hang out the next weekend. We settled on Saturday but made no certain plans.

Later on in the week, Nick e-mailed me, asking for suggestions. I had a couple of ideas: there was a supper club that we could drop into for cocktails. I was friends with the group that ran it and had gotten into the habit of doing so, even without coming for the sit-down menu. Then, there was a new cocktail bar we could check out, I suggested.

He e-mailed back: "Do you ride a bike? What about a bike ride in the afternoon; then we could maybe check out the supper club, or the bar."

Wow, biking around for a first date is totally my speed, I thought.

"I have plans with friends until 5-ish," I wrote back. "But I'll be out with my bike anyway. Give me a call."

We met up at the entrance to Prospect Park, where I'd just finished picnicking with some friends. We didn't end up going very far. We began riding but stopped at the statues in Grand Army Plaza. There was a fountain with a statue of the sea god Neptune surrounded by mermaids, and we discovered the engraved figures of a horse-mounted Abraham Lincoln and Ulysses S. Grant on opposing sides of the arch's interior. It amazed me that I'd never thought to actually look closely at these sculptures, in all the times I'd ridden or walked by them.

"This is the arch that makes everyone in Brooklyn feel like they're in Paris," I said of the Civil War memorial that was the centerpiece of the plaza. It was just beginning to glow from blue stage lights set along its sculpted face, and we were standing underneath its huge, arched ceiling. I hadn't ever described that observation before; nor could I remember if anyone else had first made it, but the words spilled out from my consciousness as if they'd been there all along.

We also biked to the Brooklyn Museum a short few blocks away. The vast, curved stretch of front steps before the entrance was filled with people just leaving a big exhibit. The water fountains that lined the sides of the museum spouted tall shoots of water in procession that splattered to the pavement.

"So, what do you want to do now?" Nick asked.

I was out of ideas, so I went with the easiest answer. "Want to go get a drink?"

We settled down at a table in the backyard patio of a small nearby bar. Over our first drinks, Nick happened to mention the age of one of his siblings, so I casually asked him his age.

Twenty-four! My fear was confirmed. What was I doing, raiding the nursery? I mean, I was no geezer at twenty-six, but I didn't think I'd want to be hanging out with the twenty-four-year-old version of myself anymore. I looked around, panicked for a moment. I was tempted to run back to the relative safety of the inside of the bar, which was full of mature, safe, normal-aged strangers. But instead, I managed to swallow a sip of my wheat beer, getting a taste of the bitter lemon rind that had been hanging on the rim of the glass a moment ago but had sploshed into the drink when I picked it up with a jerk, and to listen to the rest of whatever the hell he was saying.

He had a five-year-old sister?! His parents, God bless their sprightliness, were in their late forties?? I finished my beer in one glug.

"Do you want another drink?" I interrupted. We both looked at his glass, which was just less than halfway full.

"Um, no—well, okay, sure," he said.

I went inside to the safety of the bar. I ordered another round of drinks from the bartender, silently cursing over the fact that he didn't offer to pay for them—the immaturity! When the bartender handed me my change, she flashed a quick smile. With thick dreadlocks and smart-looking glasses, she had a beautiful smile. She also looked exceptionally bored that night. She turned to gaze glumly at the customers seated around the bar, waiting for someone to need her service.

As I walked back outside with our drinks, I suddenly felt very lucky to be where I was right then. It was unusually warm that spring night, and I was celebrating that by having drinks on a patio and having a conversation with someone who was completely new to me. What did it matter if he was two years younger? Maybe *I* was the one who was being immature about this age difference.

We ended up staying at the same bar until well after midnight, talking, drinking, and at one point breaking out the Trivial Pursuit game that was stashed on a dusty shelf. Starved, we feasted around eleven o'clock on some flatbread with herbs I had baked that morning and took to the park with me earlier in the day, wrapped in foil. I'd crunched down on an apple a little while before that and noticed Nick watching enviously as I did. Luckily, I had plenty of the herbed bread with me in my bag to share. So this was not eating out in New York while dating, I thought. Not a very glamorous example, I had to admit.

"What else do you have in that cavernous bag of yours?" Nick asked.

I pulled out a blueberry cereal bar: dessert.

Outside, as we were unlocking our bikes to leave, I strapped on my helmet and heavy bike lock.

"Well, it was nice hanging out," I said.

He paused as if I were going to say more.

"It was nice hanging out, too," he said.

With that, I waved and pedaled away. I could feel Nick's eyes on me as I turned a sharp corner and rode out of view. He'd seemed stunned when I said good-bye without any mention of hanging out again. But even though I'd had a good enough time, I wasn't sure how much I really wanted to hang out with him again. Plus, I couldn't wait to go home and make some noodles.

The following Wednesday night, I was standing in my kitchen, licking ice cream off a spatula. I'd just churned up a batch of fresh basil-infused ice cream and was trying it for the first time. My cell phone rang at ten thirty. It was Nick, and he said he had been hanging out with friends in the neighborhood. He asked if I wanted to grab a drink somewhere. I hesitated. First, it was a weeknight. Then, I had to clean up this ice-cream stuff. But earlier, I'd picked up a six-pack of beer, and I was downing one at the moment. So I offered him some beer and ice cream at my place instead.

About twenty minutes later, Nick pulled his bike into my apartment and awkwardly left it at the door. I offered him a beer and a bowl of basil ice cream. He glanced at the pots of herbs I had placed on my windowsill, which included basil.

"I've never heard of basil ice cream before," he mused.

"It's not that unusual," I said. "Actually, my friends and I had some once, at a restaurant, one of the last times I went to one. That was about a year ago—no, more like two." I suddenly realized how long it had been since I had been served a scoop of ice cream in an unfamiliar bowl.

We settled at the table and talked for a while. We quickly got on the topic of philosophy, as Nick had been reading a lot lately to prepare for grad school. I'd taken only one crash course in the subject in college and had a pretty limited knowledge of Western philosophy, so I was attentive to Nick's ramblings, even though, deep down, I couldn't help thinking the study was just a lot of hemming and hawing without action.

I noticed that Nick didn't really finish his ice cream, and that irked me a little. I finished mine and went for seconds. It had a very strong presence of sweet, Italian basil leaves, from soaking a couple of handfuls in the milk and cream. It was deep, almost jade green in color.

After a very long time talking, I looked at my watch. It was almost two in the morning.

"Well, you probably need to get up for work in the morning," Nick said, taking the cue.

Finally, I thought to myself. I was afraid he'd never say it.

"Thanks for coming," I said.

He got up to get his bike, and I followed him to the door. But then, as we stood and looked at each other for a moment, I had a feeling the night wasn't over.

Like a pair of tigers, we both sort of lurched at each other's faces at once. The kiss lasted long, too long, and I was standing too close to the hallway to my bedroom. Something came over me—a tide of recklessness—and as we gravitated through the hallway, cloying and dropping clothes, shoes, I almost felt like I was in a movie of someone, or something, not like myself.

But, when I woke up the next morning to go to work, with another body beside me, it was clear that was not the case.

Back to the perfect date meal: Perhaps the right meal really could make or break a date. What would that be? I was fond of making beautiful, picturesque, and dainty one-person courses for myself, whenever I felt like I needed a special treat. I was also fond of making ice cream. When would I have the chance to put it all together, a complete meal, for someone when it really mattered?

I shuddered, thinking of all the times I had tried to impress Ben with a romantic, home-cooked meal. I also had a strange feeling that I never wanted to see Nick again. Suddenly, all I wanted to do was cook a perfect datelike meal for myself—and myself alone.

That night, I came home with a single chunk of tenderloin wrapped in butcher paper. (I'd asked the butcher not to bag it further.) I turned the television to the news as I put on a pot of water to boil, adding two red potatoes. I had some wasabi mayonnaise in the fridge from a previous *maki* roll–making mission. Also there was a wedge of plain white cabbage, along with the usual jars and bottles of Asian condiments. All together, I had the makings of my perfect meal.

I was planning to blog about what I made for dinner—a perfectly seared, ten-minute tenderloin steak, marinated in soy sauce and sesame oil beforehand, a spicy braised cabbage side, and creamy, wasabi-spiked mashed potatoes. But when I was done eating and rinsing the dishes clean, I walked into the bathroom and began to run a hot bath. Afterward, blithe and bleary from the bath's soporific effects, I turned in early. It was perhaps the single greatest meal in the history of one-person dating, and the greatest single-person date.

Nick had followed up with an e-mail earlier that day. In it, there was a link to a website.

"Read the part about the Italian name for basil," he wrote.

I clicked on the link and found a page that described various beliefs and legends about the sweet basil plant. First, there was a Hindu story about basil. The next legend was the one from Italy. My eyes scrolled through the text, catching, "it is used in love spells," and "a pot of basil on a windowsill is meant to signal a lover."

Hey—that was where I put basil, I thought.

Then I read the kicker: "In Italy, sweet basil is called 'kiss me Nicholas,' 'bacia-nicola.'"

The moment I put the name together with who the message had come from, I let out a huge cackle. I continued to giggle, intermittently, throughout the day. At the same time, there was a deep feeling of discomfort growing inside. It wasn't that I was ashamed of anything we'd done—there was no harm in it, as far as I was concerned. But whatever attraction I'd once had for Nick just seemed to have disintegrated, in a mere day. That wasn't what was supposed to happen, right? Maybe it was all because of the basil.

There were other things bothering me about Nick, too. Over the course of our conversation the night before, he'd mentioned that his parents recently struck it rich with a new business of theirs, and how *embarrassed* he'd felt about their success in front of his friends. He also glorified his job at the coffee shop as if it were the only humane place to work, making slight jabs at the cubicle nine-to-fivers. I could hardly care if he disapproved of my work environment, or his own family, but I felt a bemused reproach toward his more-proletarian-than-thou attitude.

That Saturday, after politely but pointedly avoiding making plans with Nick during the week, I went out to celebrate my friend David's birthday. We began the night early. By nine o'clock, we were all pretty tipsy and had each played at least one bad game of pool each. At that point half the party decided to break off and hit up the restaurant next door for a quick, late dinner. This, I'd learned, was one of the dangerous aspects of not eating out: When other people feel the need to eat, like, really stuff themselves with tons of food, I can't participate in the obvious fun of overeating while drunk, unless it's something I brought, or junk food from a convenience store.

Luckily, both Matt and Jordan had also already eaten, and we stayed behind to drink and play pool. Jordan turned in a little while later, not feeling too well, so it was just Matt and me until the rest of the party returned.

Of course I'd told him and the rest of my friends about my rendezvous with "the twenty-four-year-old," as they referred to him. Everyone had been pretty amused by the tale. After a trip to the ladies' room, I came back to find Matt waiting for a drink at the bar. I poked around in my pockets for extra cash and felt my cell phone instead. On impulse, I picked it up and rang Nick's number. It rang. And rang. And rang. And went to his voice mail. I closed it without leaving a message. Matt had just turned around with his new drink to watch me put the phone back in my pocket.

"Did you just call the twenty-four-year-old?" he asked.

"I think so."

Matt threw his head back and laughed. "Why?"

"I have no idea. I don't even want to talk to him," I said.

"And you even put on makeup to make the call," he said, pointing to the lipstick I'd smeared on a minute before in the bathroom.

This was weird but true. Suddenly, I couldn't stop laughing— about how worked up I'd gotten about "dating" again, how I was going to make it "perfect" with some sort of food. How basil had gotten the best of me, and how I truly didn't know why on earth I'd just phoned the guy, for no reason at all.

We gradually stopped laughing with a heavy sigh. Matt shook his head as we looked around the crowded bar. Its walls were lined with arcade games, and by that hour, ten thirty, it was teeming with Williamsburg regulars and the usual flock of guys who'd traveled from Manhattan in the hope of impressing girls with their arcane Pong skills. I was beginning to feel a bit claustrophobic, and I could tell Matt didn't care for many of the characters who were surrounding us. A guy standing at the bar next to us kept glancing our way. Matt shot a wry look at him, and he walked away.

The next day, and the day after, I'd receive calls and e-mails from Nick, asking to hang out again sometime. But after responding politely once, I let the communication wither away. I just wasn't feeling it anymore. He took the hint and stopped calling shortly after.

I realized that my great date meal plan had been a flop. But sitting at the bar, staring glumly at the crowd beside Matt, I couldn't bring myself to care about date meals anymore.

"Matt," I said, "let's have more cooking nights. Like Friendsgiving—just friends. Just for fun."

"Sounds awesome," he concurred.

Soy-Sesame Filet Mignon with Sautéed Cabbage and Wasabi Mashed Potatoes

This is one of those quick, simple, but luscious and inventive "perfect date meals" I had been dreaming up. Unfortunately, I never got to make it for any home-cooked date, though I have for myself and thoroughly enjoyed it. I think that the ease of preparation and the classic elements—steak, potatoes, and vegetables—make it a good fit for cooking at home with someone special. Plus, a hint of hot wasabi powder never hurts to spice things up. (SERVES 2)

2 beef tenderloin steaks (filet mignon)
2–3 teaspoons soy sauce
1–2 teaspoons Asian sesame oil
2–3 medium red potatoes
¼ cup whole milk or half-and-half
1 tablespoon butter
¼–½ teaspoon wasabi (Japanese horseradish) powder
Salt to taste
About 2 cups cabbage, shredded
½ red bell pepper, finely sliced
About 1 teaspoon fresh ginger, cut to matchstick-sized
    slivers
2–3 tablespoons vegetable oil
1 scallion, finely sliced
¼ teaspoon white pepper

Marinate the steaks in the soy sauce and sesame oil, spreading the marinade evenly with your hands. Cover and chill while you prepare the rest of the ingredients (up to a few hours).

Boil the potatoes until tender. Drain, and return to the pot. Add the milk, and mash with a large fork or potato masher. Add the butter, wasabi powder, and a couple of pinches of salt. Taste for seasoning, adding additional wasabi or salt as desired.

Combine the cabbage, bell pepper, and fresh ginger in a bowl. Heat a large, heavy-bottomed skillet with the oil. Once pan is very hot, place the steaks in the skillet. Let cook a minute or two until nicely browned. Reduce heat to medium-low, and flip steaks. Cook another 2–4 minutes, until the other side is browned. When steaks are medium-rare, they should feel slightly firm to the touch. Continue cooking to desired doneness. Remove steaks and set aside. Immediately add the cabbage mixture to the pan and cook on medium-low, stirring frequently, for about 2–3 minutes. Season with salt and white pepper to taste. Serve alongside the mashed potatoes and steak.

~~~~~~

Fresh Basil Panna Cotta

If you don't have an ice-cream maker, you can always make individual custard cups of fresh basil panna cotta. The recipe's name means "cooked cream," and the recipe's almost just as simple as that. Like the ice-cream version, it's tried, tested, and true for inspiring a little romance (for better or for worse).   (SERVES 4)

> 1 packet unflavored gelatin
> 2 tablespoons water
> 1 bunch fresh basil leaves, rinsed well
> 2 cups heavy cream (or substitute whole milk for up to ½ cup)
> ⅓ cup sugar

Dissolve gelatin in water and set aside. Reserve one or two large basil leaves for the garnish. Combine the cream, sugar, and the rest of the basil in a medium saucepan and bring just to a simmer. Remove from heat and cover to steep for 20 minutes. Strain the leaves from the cream mixture and stir in the gelatin. Divide equally among four ramekins, cover with plastic, and chill at least 4 hours or overnight to set. Roll up reserved basil leaves and slice thinly into chiffonades. Place a pinch of the chiffonades on each of the ramekins to garnish.

Underground Eateries

SUPPER CLUBS AND THE EXCLUSIVE SOS

The first time I went to an underground supper club was back in January of that year, 2008. It was the Whisk and Ladle Supper Club, the Williamsburg-based operation run by four residents of a large loft apartment in a converted industrial building. I'd heard about it from a casual friend and fellow food blogger, Amelia, who often cooked with the group. We'd run into each other a few times at various food-related events that year, and she urged me to come by sometime. At Whisk and Ladle, she explained, the bar area was open for drinks after the sit-down dinner was served. So I could drop by without sitting through (and paying for) dinner to check it out.

When I arrived, around eleven o'clock, dinner service was still in full swing. The loft's open kitchen was separated from a vast dining area by a wooden staircase that led to bedrooms overlooking the entire space. A few waist-high brass candleholders lit the lobby area, and a small side table held a placard with the night's menu. Just before the kitchen, a rope-and-wooden-slat swing hung from the ceiling. About thirty guests were seated to the far left of the loft, at three or four long tables. The kitchen was full of cooks and their presumed friends scurrying about, plating dishes and bringing plates or glasses to the dining area. I spotted Amelia in the kitchen, wiping her brow with the back of her hand and squeezing some sort of plastic bag with the other. She walked over when I waved. Taking my hand, she immediately piped a spurt of pea green substance the texture of toothpaste onto my finger.

"We made edamame paste," she said. "Try!"

I found myself licking creamed edamame off my hand before I could even say hello to anyone. Smooth, with a buttery richness that coated my tongue, it had the concentrated flavor of fresh edamame beans.

"Wow!" I said.

This state of awe pretty much remained with me throughout the night. After meeting a couple of the roommate-chefs, I settled at the living room area's makeshift bar to let them get back to work. The bar was manned by Nick, one of the roommates and a professional bartender by trade. I was his first cocktail customer of the evening, and he was more than gracious about fixing me a drink. Written on a folded card set at the bar were the drink specials he'd come up with for the evening. After he briefly explained each of them, I chose a Bourbon-based drink with Japanese-twig tea and fresh lemon. A few moments later, he poured me a shot of roasted peanut–infused vodka that he'd been experimenting with lately. It tasted of peanut shells at a ballpark in liquid form, in a surprisingly good way. While I was sipping and chatting with Nick, Amelia came over and brought me a bowl of soup from the kitchen, apparently extra stock from the evening's first course.

"This is Danielle's green-apple soup," she said, referring to one of the resident-cooks I'd just met. Even though I had already eaten, I took a curious sip. Lukewarm, it was still good enough to finish. The thick soup was creamy and tangy at the same time, topped with julienned Granny Smith apples and shaved Parmesan.

Eventually the diners, finished with their desserts, flowed into the room. Soon, everyone was drinking and chatting with one another. The cooks, finished with serving for the night, were lapping up leftovers with their hands and coated spatulas. Interestingly, the night's main course had been bear meat, and there was a lot of buzzing around the room about how the new dish had turned out. The cooks had ordered the meat frozen from Exotic Meats USA, on a whim, and were cooking with it for the first time that night. I didn't try any but heard that it was pretty tasty. I got to sample the dessert, as well as an extra serving of the salad, which was simply flat-leaf parsley sprigs with farmer's cheese, dressed in a light vinaigrette. I think I took a turn on the rope swing toward the end of the night; I also managed to break one of their plates. Luckily, no one seemed to mind this at all, and overall, I had a terrific time at

Whisk and Ladle meeting new people and tasting their food. I'd been a little unsure about arriving at the supper club all alone, but after that night, I knew there was something completely different about this type of experience from what I'd found at the normal bar, restaurant, or club.

I'd heard whispers about secret supper clubs popping up sporadically in several cities, but before going to Whisk and Ladle, I didn't really understand what they were. I'd heard of the Ghetto Gourmet, which started in San Francisco but had grown several offshoots in other cities, including New York. From descriptions of the club on its website, it sounded like a Bohemian gathering of friends serving humble, homemade food to diners sitting on cushions tossed about one big room. I didn't know anyone personally involved in Ghetto Gourmet, and through their website I couldn't tell if the New York City–based chapter was still in operation. Come to think of it, the GRUB dinners at the Rubulad warehouse might be described as a supper club.

Unlike those dinners, however, Whisk and Ladle and the supper clubs I visited afterward operate on a much more formal level. To attend a dinner at Whisk and Ladle, for instance, one needed to hear about the club by word of mouth first. Then prospective dinner guests would sign up for the group's e-mail list, and when a dinner was announced (roughly twice a month), guests had to RSVP for a seat by e-mail well in advance. If accepted, the diner would receive an e-mail with the secret address and directions to the dinner shortly before its scheduled date. Because Whisk and Ladle had become such a popular underground phenomenon in its two years of serving dinners, only about a quarter of hopeful diners who RSVP'd would score a seat. The menu was listed in each e-mail, usually consisting of five courses with wine and beer, and a cash cocktail bar would be open before and after the dinner. There was a set price, which was usually around $50, depending on the night's delicacies. I'd heard rumors about some unorthodox reservation-taking habits—like members deleting a chunk of the RSVP e-mails at random, reading only the rest, or choosing certain reservations over others at their own discretion rather than on a first-come, first-served basis.

Supper clubs, "underground restaurants," or RSVP-only dinner parties for strangers in a home setting are a fairly new trend. But they're a largely undefined trend, too. In the recent book *Secret Suppers: Rogue Chefs and Underground Restaurants in Warehouses, Townhouses, Open Fields, and Everywhere in Between*, Jenn Garbee wrote that there is a lot of variation among the numerous supper clubs that have cropped up in the last decade or so around the country, according to the ones she visited or investigated. She determined that there are no distinguishing rules, limitations, or factors behind supper clubs, except that they are not restaurants.

My fascination with supper clubs was complete. I attended a full dinner at Whisk and Ladle later that spring and visited two other underground supper clubs in the city that I'd hunted down.

The first one was held in a quaint two-bedroom apartment with a beautiful backyard, in my old neighborhood of Fort Greene, Brooklyn. Called Ted and Amy's Supper Club, it was run by resident Kara and her friend Adam, a former chef. They'd named the club after Ted Allen and Amy Sedaris, their two favorite food idols, respectively, but the stars had no connection to the club.

I had planned to go to the supper club with Amelia, but when she came down with a cold the day of and couldn't make it, I called up Matt. When I arrived at Kara's brownstone by bike, Matt was already hanging out with other guests in the backyard, with a glass of wine in hand. The supper club had sent out a reminder e-mail that day with a brief sentence about each of the dinner's ten guests, which we had provided earlier that week. But I hadn't had a chance to tell Kara and Adam about my last-minute date switch. I was relieved to see that they were so laid-back, though, welcoming Matt inside once he simply announced that he was my "alternate."

Unlike Whisk and Ladle's closed-off cooking process, the guests at Ted and Amy's Supper Club seemed to be pretty welcome to help out in the kitchen. At least, they were invited to help if they were willing. While watching Adam grill up some mango chicken sausages, I noticed he was having a difficult time flipping them on the grill without them tearing. I stepped over and offered to help, and together we quickly pried the sausages from the blazing grill before they became too burned. We concluded that they were sticking because of the extra sugars in the sausage from the mango, and because they were so lean. The grill needed to be oiled well beforehand. I was a little cautious about overstepping my role, since Adam was after all a trained chef, but he seemed truly grateful for the extra hand. After the main course had been saved, we relaxed with a clink of our beer bottles.

After a thoroughly enjoyable dinner of grilled sausage and vegetable skewers, grilled corn on the cob with the charred frays of husk protruding from the plate, savory black beans, and a yogurt and blackberry panna cotta dessert, I had made several lasting friends and even earned an invitation to come back and cook with the group. The ambiance of Ted and Amy's dinner was less formal than that of Whisk and Ladle's, and the number of guests was small enough that we could all engage in the same conversation.

After I wrote a blog post about my supper at Ted and Amy's, I was invited to a dinner by another supper club, this one, called SocialEats, located on the Upper East Side of Manhattan. The eight-person dinner was a casual, modest affair, perhaps even more so than Ted and Amy's, hosted by a husband-and-wife team who were lawyers by day but passionate about cooking at home. They also dined at the same table as the rest of the guests, as at Ted and Amy's, and since roughly half of the eight people at the table already knew one another, it felt a little bit more like a traditional dinner party.

During the long subway ride back to Brooklyn after the dinner that night, I began thinking about how I would invent my own supper club. Mine would be different from each of these, somehow.

It was May. On one of the first warm Friday nights of the spring, warm enough to warrant the first barbecue of the season, I found myself on Matt's rooftop patio in Williamsburg. We had just finished taping a first-ever video for my blog. Matt had by then begun a new job working as a freelance videographer and was eager to create more videos to add to his reel. On a lark, I had decided to submit an amateur video for a new television show on the Food Network. A friend of mine, Darin, was a producer for the new show *Ask Aida* and encouraged me to make a video in which I ask the show's host about a cooking-related dilemma. The basis of the show was that the host, Aida Mollenkamp, would then solve the problem through her culinary expertise.

My particular dilemma, however, was a little outside the realm of basic kitchen skills.

After several cuts due to mess-ups and giggling, I stood in Matt's kitchen and told the camera, "Recently single, and on the rebound, I've been thinking about what to cook on a date."

I went on to ask Aida what types of foods or dishes might be considered aphrodisiacs, so as to seduce a potential (and potentially disinclined) lover. Matt and I wrapped up the shooting around early evening, just as the sun was beginning to set. We ate dinner on his roof, some simple pasta with asparagus that I'd brought along to stage in the video. A little later on, we were joined by Karol and Jordan, and that night we managed to attend a series of rooftop and backyard cookouts. There were three parties going on in Matt's building and the building next door to his (which was easy to get to by climbing over a rail between the roofs), and we hopped to and from them for the rest of the night.

At some point during these festivities, the idea for SOS was born. We were all four of us single, and all eager to meet new people as well as cook and eat together more. I wanted to create a supper club, but with some sort of twist. The name "Singles-Only Supper Club" popped into my head. The idea was, we would invite only guests who were single, in the hopes of seducing them with aphrodisiac food. Each one of us would invite one guest of the opposite sex whom we were interested in dating. The person should not be someone we knew very well—least of all, someone we had a history with. This would be something of an exercise in working up the guts to ask someone to come to a small dinner party. Also, the other guests wouldn't know what we were up to—except that we were having a small dinner party. No mention of the real meaning behind the acronym SOS would be uttered around them.

We even tossed around the idea of reviving the "key party," a phenomenon of 1970s upper-class circles that involved a bowl where the men would place their keys. At the end of the night, each woman at the party would reach into the bowl, scoop up a set of keys, and go home with the owner of them. The ritual was often played out with married couples seeking a little sexual adventure, so it was risky business when it came to personal feelings. But while we were willing to take the risk of causing jealousy and ill will among ourselves, we weren't willing to take the risk of going home with one another. As much as I loved Matt, I wasn't about to sleep with him. At least, not under my normal, non-aphrodisiac-influenced circumstances.

Through e-mails over the next week or so, we tightened down the idea further. I sent an overly formal e-mail to my coconspirators, Karol, Matt, and Jordan, laying out the game plan and offering my apartment for the first dinner. I came up with a code name for myself in all SOS-related correspondence and encouraged the others to do so, too—just another ridiculous element of our scheme.

I also came up with a menu for the first dinner. It began with a salad featuring fresh, lightly blanched asparagus. It was in season, first of all, but most important, my research had identified it as a supposed aphrodisiac food to many cultures. Second, I'd make a lobster risotto—just because it was luxurious and something I'd always wanted to try—with another aphrodisiac food, fennel. For the main course, I decided on beef cheeks, braised in a red wine sauce for hours, and served with a pomegranate juice reduction on a bed of mashed butternut squash. (For some reason, the words *beef cheeks* struck me as racy.) Pomegranate and butternut were both known to raise heart levels and enhance "performance." There would be a dish involving eggplant, another supposed aphrodisiac. For dessert, a buttery-sweet amaretto ice cream would be in store. In many cultures, it's thought—and this is likely due to the word's similarity to *amore*, or *love*—that the almond liqueur or almonds in general were romantically inspiring.

Underground supper clubs may sound like novel, urban inventions, but they have more in common with period feasts than with anything restaurant-like. The tradition of feasting, elaborately and over long, leisurely hours, has moved for the most part from fine homes to restaurants. Even wedding banquets are rarely held in homes today. Modern supper clubs aim to bring the grandiose dinner back into a private setting.

In *The Invention of the Restaurant*, Rebecca Spang described what would become the most notorious private banquet in eighteenth-century Paris, held by an affluent eccentric named Balthazar Grimod de la Reynière. The dinner was exclusive to a select number of distinguished guests, who were unsuspecting of the evening's full extent; at his dimly lit chateau, they made their way to the dining room through a long, sinewy hallway and a series of chambers. A black-draped coffin placed atop the dining table set the night's macabre tone. At the entrance, "heralds dressed in Roman robes examined the guests' invitations," and after further scrutiny, a pass code, and admittance, in the final stage of initiation, hired hands dressed as choirboys perfumed the guests with incense.

Of course, details of the dinner that Grimod held were known only by attendees and passed on by word of mouth. However, the gossip must have spread among the Paris elite, and Grimod basked in the mystery that he had created.

Similar to this, today's supper clubs thrive on the limited publicity creating a sense of mystery and legend surrounding their activities. Word of mouth is very much the prevailing—and preferred—modus operandi. The Whisk and Ladle owns a website under its name, but it's sparse, and hardly an exact detail is mentioned—no names, locations, or exact dates. Visitors can simply register to receive e-mails from the club, whenever they are sent out. That places like Whisk and Ladle have a high stake in their secrecy comes with good reason, too: They're completely illegal. No food and health department ever checks their kitchen premises or their operation standards. But most important, no business plan was formalized to accept the customers' payments. Therefore, supper clubs usually describe their fixed dinner prices as "contributions"—a gratuitous offering, a willing exchange, rather than a strict payment. These are details that, like the dinner's location, are told to diners only in follow-up e-mails once their RSVP has been accepted.

You could consider all this and reach the conclusion that the people who start supper clubs want to make money, doing so by making food, but are too lazy to get a proper license and commercial space, and prefer to do things under the table in a manner that's more comfortable, not to mention financially beneficial to them. But money is beside the point for most of the people I've met who run supper clubs—and I've met at least a dozen of them by now. Many of them have no intention of ever opening or working in a real restaurant, instead aiming to create an intimate, alternate dining environment and do what they love to do—cook, free of the burdens of public scrutiny and financial incentives.

And they have their niches, as well: one supper club in New York is based around the premise of locally harvested, seasonal foods; another hosts dinners with a theme attached to each one, like the Roaring Twenties. A Razor, A Shiny Knife is a supper club based around the premise of instructional cooking demos, and guests are invited to get a hands-on education in the dishes that are served for the night. There are also supper clubs with little or no theme other than that no one at the table need any preexisting social connections; they're held in a setting resembling a home dinner party. In the fall of 2008, a two-night, hundred-guest dinner event was orchestrated among five supper clubs called Undergrounds Unite. The event was elaborate, large, and some say overpriced, at $100 a plate. But it was a unique milestone in the short history of the supper club trend. Unlike most big foodie events, however, it was kept very much out of the public eye, known to only those who attended it. None of it was spilled to the press.

You can see how some of today's supper club conspirators have that same glimmer of mischief that Grimod must have had. I can imagine that today's supper club hosts and hostesses must share some secretive delight in withholding details about a dinner until shortly before it is held, or in being choosy about who gets a seat. The word *club* connotes exclusivity, and within this private realm, it is true that pretty much anything can happen. At a restaurant, "The customer is always right" motto defines how restaurateurs run their businesses: to please the customer, bending over backward sometimes by changing menu items and other details given what's been most successful. At supper clubs, it could be more common that the creators shape their guests to fit their vision. At one dinner given by A Razor, A Shiny Knife, guests were instructed to come dressed all in white. The clean, sparse loft where the dinner was held was drenched in white, marked by a single long, twenty-two-person table draped in white cloth. Only the kitchen staff (including myself) was dressed in all black. With another supper club called the Underground Food Collective, based in Madison, Wisconsin, guests are often treated to surprise visits from the farmer, or winemaker, who produced some of the evening's delights. In the case of SOS, our guests—whoever they were—would be the unsuspecting guinea pigs for a highly aphrodisiac-charged, and hopefully delicious, meal.

One day while I was chucking spam e-mails from my in-box, I came to an e-mail with the subject line, "This is not spam, this is Morgan."

Who the hell was that? I paused for a moment at the DELETE button, then decided to open it.

"Hi, Cathy," it read. "We met while I was tending bar."

Oh, right, I remembered. A week or so earlier, I had met up with my friend Scott, a fellow food writer. He'd insisted on going to a certain upscale Manhattan restaurant for a drink because a friend of his worked at the bar and could make "a mean drink." His friend Morgan.

In the e-mail, Morgan complimented my blog and offered a recipe for a simple black beans and rice dish. I thanked him in a quick reply and told him I'd have to try the recipe sometime. I was used to receiving mail like this from blog readers or new acquaintances and did my best to respond to them all. His response the next day was followed, in a postscript, with a proposal: "Ever thought about Not Drinking Out in New York? If you're interested, I could do a cocktail demonstration sometime, and invite a few friends over. You could invite friends, too. It could be fun. Let me know."

I had to agree, it did sound like fun. I hesitated, then shrugged it off—after all, this was a friend of a friend. I wrote back enthusiastically. We chose a night the upcoming week, and I roped Karol into coming along with me for the cocktail tutorial at Morgan's place.

Up until then, home cocktail making conjured chilling visions of Sean and Meredith's floor of full liquor bottles. In the last few months of living together, Ben had become a bit of a fancy-booze collector, too. I'd kept my own apartment clean of bottles, to ward against such obsession. As a result, I didn't know much about making drinks.

The cocktail night turned out to be low-key, informative, and a lot of fun. We made basic, beginner-level cocktails like the old-fashioned, gin and tonic, and whiskey sour. Afterward, Karol and I found ourselves with a newfound appreciation for gin and ring-ing headaches, and I found my SOS date. That night, after making a few rounds of homemade cocktails, Morgan's four friends had taken off, and he, Karol, and I had gone to a nearby bar. Karol and I couldn't help but bring up the subject of our upcoming dinner, though we were tactful to not mention the full extent of SOS. Morgan jumped in to ask about wine pairing for the menu. We both shrugged, not having given it much thought until then. He then offered to act as sommelier, should we need one, and pair each dish with an appropriate wine. It sounded like a great idea.

There was definite chemistry between Morgan and me that night. Over the next few days, we kept up by e-mail and tried to make plans for the next week. It seemed natural to pin Morgan as my SOS "date," and I urged the rest of the team to hurry up and find theirs soon.

Karol was lagging, having asked one or two people who weren't able to make the date we'd eventually settled on. Matt was also shot down by his top choice. Jordan was thinking about asking a coworker of hers but couldn't seem to find the right way to do so. In the meantime, we talked about how to set the price for the meal. Through all my months of blogging, I had a good sense of what a small meal for two to four would cost. (Each recipe on my blog included a "Cost Calculator" feature in which I tallied up all the prices of the ingredients used.) But I had no idea how much this elaborate dinner for eight was going to be—and the wines added to the confusion. I hated above all the idea of overcharging guests at a supper club. The cash contribution at Ted and Amy's supper club and SocialEats was relatively fair, at $35 per head, but the $50 tag at Whisk and Ladle was a little steep. The whole concept of charging guests stank to me of "real" restaurants. However, it was also pretty unavoidable, if the club were to keep throwing dinners regularly. We went with $35 for each SOS guest, which in my estimation would cover the expensive ingredients I was planning to pepper my dishes with—a dollop of American caviar and crème fraîche on the lobster risotto, the lobster itself, the beef cheeks, the pomegranate. Along with some greens, the asparagus salad would have either chunks of avocado or else sautéed portobellos, both pricey items. But I wouldn't have wanted to do the dinner any other way than ultraluxurious, hoping to set a romantic mood.

Finally, Karol pinned down her "date," a friend/acquaintance named George, who worked at a bar that she frequented. As for Matt, he was determined to meet the girl of his dreams the weekend before the dinner. That weekend, the Whisk and Ladle Supper Club happened to be hosting a party in their loft. Not a dinner, it was their end-of-season shebang, called the Pink Ball. The exclusive invitation described a dress code of pink and white and promised live bands and DJs, aerial silk-rope dancers, and games like Twister and "musical clothing." I was allowed to come with only one guest, and since Matt saw it as an opportunity to meet his girl, I brought him along. I'd found a seventies pink-and-white printed dress and wrapped an old brown leather belt around the middle to cinch the waist. Matt bought an old ladies' pink pullover with snowflake embroidery, put on his roommate's white track pants, and tossed a pink scarf that I gave him around his neck. I thought we looked pretty amazing.

The party was crowded the minute we arrived. In the kitchen, we snacked on pink cupcakes with pink icing, and trays of homemade raspberry-pomegranate and fresh strawberry ice cream that were melting to a pleasing, sweet sludge. We moved on to the bar area, where Nick and a friend were serving four different pink cocktails with the likes of strawberry-infused vodka and guava nectar. We tried them all.

Before long, the party seemed to have bloated into an all-consuming mass of pastel-clothed bodies. One guy was even running around in nothing more than a pink loincloth. To add to my disorientation, everywhere I turned, I could have sworn that I recognized faces, but not well enough to know how, or from where.

"Are you that 'don't eat out' girl?" a tall, familiar-looking guy asked me.

"How did you know?" I asked. We'd met at Whisk and Ladle once before, he said, "when you were on the swing."

This explained why I couldn't place him at first. He was standing beside two friends of his, another Asian guy and a pretty brunette girl, both of whom I didn't recognize. Matt and I introduced ourselves to them. The girl, Lauren, started asking me about my blog, and I explained the concept while she nodded enthusiastically. She was wearing white jeans and a silky printed tank that hit below the hips. We ended up hanging out with Lauren and her two friends for most of the night, dancing and watching the bands and silk-rope dancers perform, twirling like acrobats from silk sheaths hung from the loft's ceiling. I could tell that Matt was really into Lauren, so once it got late, I decided to take off alone. The party was in no way winding down, but I also realized I'd had more pink drinks than I could rightly count. I could barely walk to the door and find my jacket.

I stumbled to a convenience store down the street to use the ATM for cash to take a cab home. I stood for a moment on the busy main drag of Williamsburg, which was flooded with people getting out of bars, looking to grab grub or a ride home. I waited as a couple of cabs went by, already filled with passengers. Then a familiar face approached me—it was Brian, who had just been at the Whisk and Ladle party, too.

"Hey, Cathy," he said. "Waitin' for a cab?"

We chatted for a minute on the street, glancing up and down the streets for yellow taxis. "I'm going in to grab a slice. Want one?" Brian asked, motioning to the pizza place next door.

"Uhh . . ."

"Come on, I'll get you one," he said.

"This is kind of against my religion . . . ," I heard myself saying. But I followed him inside, and as Brian signaled with two fingers to the counterperson, and was handed two white plates with steaming-hot, shining slabs of pizza, I felt my resolve immediately weaken.

The pizza was too soggy to fold in half. I couldn't actually lift it from the plate without it bending like a thin sheet of paper, so that all the cheese and sauce rushed toward the triangular tip. I ended up shoveling it into my mouth from the plate. We stood outside eating, watching the street. Though Brian was making some sort of conversation, I couldn't actually answer him since my mouth was working the molten cheese into fine, chewable pieces. Seeing that my mouth was unavoidably smeared with grease, Brian handed me a napkin, grinning politely at my hearty appetite.

Finally, an empty taxi stopped in front of me. I waved good-bye, thanked him again for the pizza, and got in. It was my first slice of New York pizza in more than a year. I was still working on the cheese when I noticed that Matt had called and texted a few times to see whether I was okay. I returned his messages while slurping my sloppy slice. The next morning, I found that my cell phone and purse had orange goo all over them. And I had a disgusting taste of pizza and pink booze in my mouth. Never again, I vowed.

Less than one week before our supper club was scheduled, panic broke loose. Jordan, who had decided to wait until the week before to invite her coworker, in order to make it seem more "casual," discovered from another coworker that he was gay.

"I got nothin'. Or no one, as it were," she wrote to the core supper club members (signed, "Fifi"). A few minutes later, I received an e-mail from Karol.

"Why don't you send a casual invitation about the newly formed supper club to a bunch of male acquaintances of yours? Hopefully ones who Jordan might like," she wrote, reading my mind exactly. I realized that, of anyone else in the group, I would be best suited to this task since the dinner was at my home and everyone knew how nuts I was about food. But I didn't feel up to playing matchmaker again; before Karol had gotten George to come, I tried to invite someone I thought she might like to dinner, as her secret SOS date. It was Adam from Ted and Amy's supper club. But I couldn't fathom inviting just Adam without also inviting Kara; it would seem rude. So I ended up inviting them both, and settled in to see what would happen. As it turned out, Adam already had plans, but Kara was eager to come. Of course, we were all happy to have Kara at our dinner, and one extra guest couldn't hurt. At the very least, it might make the game more interesting. But I was wary of things backfiring now. Plus, with all the recipe planning, food purchasing, and preparation to take care of, I was beginning to feel frazzled and overextended.

But I gave in. I wrote to about a dozen male friends of mine who I had a vague notion might be single. The first one who replied was Thaddeus. It was settled; he would be Jordan's "date."

I suddenly realized how brave all those people who held supper clubs, like Kara and the Whisk and Ladle residents, were. Who knew what types of people might come through their door, and into their very homes? What if they were lunatics?

The next day, Tuesday, I got an e-mail from Matt. Earlier, he had reported that Lauren had agreed to come to SOS, but since a friend of hers was in town from France, she'd have to bring him along, too. The four of us were just fine with this—a mystery man, why not? And from France, no less! Plus, it would even out the girl-to-guy ratio and bring our group of diners to ten.

Matt's message began, "NOOOOOOOOO! p.s. I told you she liked you better than me" (signed, "Dash Probington").

I scrolled down to see the forwarded e-mail below. In a previous message, Matt had offered to cover Lauren's $35 dinner price, and she'd followed by saying, "Oh, that's really sweet but I'm afraid I couldn't possibly accept it. Plus, my girlfriend would be really jealous if she found that a nice man such as yourself were treating me to dinner."

I cackled aloud. Perfect—Lauren was not only in a relationship, but also a lesbian. We really should have considered things like sexual orientation before starting our date seeking. I forwarded the message on to Karol and Jordan and giggled to myself the rest of the day.

The Saturday of the dinner, I spent the entire day cooking. I'd already braised the beef cheeks for six hours the night before and done some other prep work, too. I'd gotten the beef cheeks from a small butcher in the West Village, one of the only places that had them through special preorder. The cheeks were enormous in size, big juicy slabs of tough, red meat. I was shocked at first, not quite sure what to do with them. But I went with the normal route of braising stew meat, and cut them into larger-than-normal chunks. I patted them with a little flour and salt and pepper, and browned them in my Dutch oven. Then, once I had added red wine, a couple of carrots, onions, and celery, I brought the pot to a boil and stuck it inside the oven, covered, to braise the rest of the night.

The lobster was a lot trickier to cook. I picked up two live lobsters that morning from a seafood market in Chinatown. It felt ludicrous to tote live lobsters in a double-wrapped plastic bag on the subway home. I'd cooked live lobsters and other crustaceans before, on family vacations by the shore. I wasn't looking forward to killing the things myself, of course. But, I figured, this was the reality of cooking and eating animals, and somebody had to end their lives at some point. That whole week I'd scrounged the Internet for tips on the most humane way to kill lobsters. I found a lot of theories, and the one I most consistently saw (aside from slicing the head in half deftly with a sharp knife) was to stick the lobsters in the freezer for fifteen minutes before boiling them. This would put the animal into a state of "shock" and was thought to sort of anesthetize the creature before the otherwise agonizing boil. This seemed simple enough to me. Keeping the lobsters in all their baggage, I stuffed them into my freezer the moment I got home and slammed its door shut.

Really, no one knows what the least painful death for lobsters is, except for lobsters. Studies have shown it's impossible to determine, or we just don't have advanced enough science to figure out what goes through the lobster's limited brain. There are some who say that they might not even be capable of feeling pain at all. All we know, and all that the theories are based on, is intuition—from chefs, fishmongers, years of tradition, and experience with the animals. It's true that chefs have a special connection with animals they must kill before cooking. There's an intimate knowledge of the animal's reactions, and almost every chef seems to consider the comfort level of the animal when he or she puts it down.

I filled my largest stockpot with water and brought it to a boil. Fifteen minutes after they had been in the freezer, I took the lobsters out. Now, you have probably gathered by now that I'm not really a girly-girl about such things. But when I held the first lobster above the water with tongs (true to the advice I'd read, it had been extremely sluggish, almost to immobility) and saw it react by flinching its whiskers the moment its dangling claws touched the surface, *I*, for one, felt a sharp pain. I pushed the bugger underneath the water as quickly as I possibly could and clanged the lid on top. Because the pot wasn't big enough for both of these huge, gangly beasts, I'd have to cook them one at a time. After about ten minutes, I carefully lifted the first one out with tongs. It was morbid to see it now so bright red, and its weight felt completely different from the live thing it had been just minutes before.

I'd popped the other lobster back in the freezer while the first one cooked, lest it wake from its stupor. I took it out again, and as I peeled back the plastic bag, I was suddenly struck with a horrible thought: What if it saw the other cooked, red lobster, hanging out on my counter right before its death? How terrifying! I quickly hid the cooked lobster inside a bowl before taking the second one out. With the stockpot still going at a rolling boil, I popped the next victim inside. This one went in slightly better than the last; it barely moved. After it was boiled, I spent the next few hours cracking open the tough shells with a hammer and my fingers (for lack of a proper tool—my oversight). It was tough work removing the chunks of meat, and after that had been accomplished, I saved the empty shells and enormous heads to make a savory broth to cook the risotto with.

My apartment reeked of seafood all afternoon. After making a run to the grocery store for some last-minute ingredients, I came back and was hit with the scent of the seafood stock I was making. I worried that this might not be the most appropriate mood-setting aroma for the night. But by evening, it seemed to have left the apartment a bit, or at least I'd gotten used to it. By then, the room had overwhelmingly taken on the savory smell of the reheating wine-braised beef cheeks.

By seven, all the core supper club members had arrived and were giving me a hand with setting the table. Jordan had brought little glass vials with flower buds and place cards with each diner's name to set at the table. I was grateful for the help; I'd been cooking for several hours straight and my fingers were blistered and torn from all that hacking away and picking at lobster shells. Then the first guest arrived. It was Morgan. He was carrying a load of wine bottles and filled the fridge with the white wine.

"For a girl who doesn't eat out, your fridge is kind of empty," he noted.

I didn't realize it until then, but I'd been so swept up in preparations that I'd eaten hardly a thing all day. I was starving. I'd baked a loaf of no-knead bread to serve with dinner and broke a chunk off of it. Slowly, the rest of the guests trickled in: Kara, George, Thaddeus, Lauren, and her French friend François, who wore thick black-rimmed glasses that made him look sort of like the French version of Buddy Holly. I was nervous about how Jordan would react to Thaddeus, and rightly so, as it turned out. Shortly after he arrived, she whispered to me in a corner that she was not at all interested. Thaddeus was definitely the most dressed up for the evening, in a black suit with a T-shirt. Lauren appeared a completely different person from the party-outfitted girl at the Pink Ball, wearing camouflage cargo pants and a thin beige tank top, her long curly brown hair tied back.

By the time everyone had their first glasses of wine, we gathered at the table. We had to scrunch close together—too close, in fact, and as I had only a long coffee table that could fit us all, we were seated on pillows on the floor. I'd imagined this might be intimate, but in reality it was pretty awkward.

The first course was my amuse-bouche, or, put simply, the bite-sized appetizer before the formal five courses began. I'd put together tiny stacks of goat cheese, roasted red pepper, and basil on crisped bread slices, and placed them for a few moments under the broiler until they were warm and oozing, with the tops lightly charred. Next up, I served my asparagus salad. I'd blanched the asparagus, then tossed the sliced spears with avocado and watercress, dressed in a lemony vinaigrette.

I began to arrange soup dishes of the lobster risotto shortly afterward. I was so focused on serving everyone that I didn't get in on much of the table conversation. I was seated all the way at the end of the table, too, beside Thaddeus and across from Karol. Jordan had initially arranged the seating so that each SOS member was next to his or her "date," but after people started picking up the cards out of curiosity and getting them all mixed up, the seating arrangement got a little confused. Plus, both Jordan and Matt had already forfeited the mission of dating their "dates." Only Karol was still seated beside hers.

I looked curiously at Morgan, seated across the table. Over the past couple of weeks, we'd exchanged a number of e-mails and tried making plans to meet up, but they'd fallen through due to our different schedules. Still, there were pretty clear indications of flirtation on both sides. I wasn't picking up on any of it tonight, though. In fact, he seemed more interested in talking to Jordan.

After the risotto, everyone felt they needed to take a break before the next course. Without realizing that five courses plus an amuse-bouche is a lot of food, I'd piled a heaping scoop of risotto on each plate, big enough for a full meal itself. Each was topped with a delicate arrangement of the lobster claw and tail meat, drenched in hot butter, a dollop of crème fraîche, a miniature scoop of caviar, and a sprinkle of fresh fennel fronds. Everyone, including myself, was already stuffed.

Across the table, it looked like conversation had broken down into small groups: Matt and Lauren were chatting up a storm, pointing at photos on one of their cell phones. Kara, François, and

Thaddeus, to my left, had lifted themselves onto the couch. I guess kneeling on the floor for an extended period of time isn't exactly for everyone, especially guys. For a period, we had been talking about the meaning behind the logo on Thaddeus's T-shirt, but once that question had been sufficiently answered by Thaddeus, conversation dropped to a lull. George was being especially quiet, only talking to Karol in low tones every now and then. Karol, too, was being unusually quiet. And Morgan was still talking to Jordan. All at once, he addressed the group:

"You know what the greatest rock album of all time is?" he said.

"Uhh . . . no, what?" said Matt.

There were a few guesses around the table—*Nevermind? The White Album?* Personally, I had no interest in addressing such ultimatums. I wasn't sure what context the question had risen from, anyway.

"*Appetite for Destruction,*" Morgan proclaimed. "By Guns N' Roses."

Very slowly, the blank faces around the table began to nod.

"I'm going to plate the next course," I said, excusing myself from the table.

Clearly, the group wasn't really gelling in any sort of way. And there was nothing romantic going on, either. Karol had warned me that George was really shy and awkward around strangers, but it didn't occur to me that he couldn't make eye contact. At least everyone wasn't taking turns explaining what he or she did for a living, which was the boring state of conversation at some of the other supper clubs I'd attended. But nobody seemed to be terribly interested in talking to one another, either. Each time a new course was served, Morgan gave a two-minute lecture on the type of wine he'd paired the dish with, where it was made, and how. I got the sense from the lack of conversation afterward that nobody cared terribly much about wines or the subtle art of wine pairing. I was too distracted by hostessing to really think about the notes in the wines I was knocking back myself. I just hoped the main course— and some more wine—might spark up conversation a bit.

"Um, Morgan," I said, tapping him on the shoulder. "Did you have a different wine to pair the meat dish with?"

"Oh, yes. Right. It's up on the counter, the red wine," he said, turning away from Jordan a moment to address me. "Actually, I'll get it," he said, after a pause.

"Thanks," I said.

Matt walked by me on his way to the bathroom. I pulled him into the hallway for a moment.

"Can you believe this?" I hissed.

"What?" he said. I nodded in the direction of Morgan, who was gesturing as he talked to Jordan.

"Ah, forget him," Matt said. "Seriously, I think you can do better than him. *Appetite for Destruction*?"

I looked back. Jordan was giving wan nods every now and then. She'd hardly uttered a word all night, least of all to Thaddeus. She turned to gaze around the room and caught my eye for a moment. We exchanged hapless looks.

"So much for SOS," I muttered.

"It's taking on a whole new meaning," Matt said.

Karol came to the kitchen to give me a hand.

"What do you need me to do with this stuff?" she asked. I instructed her to put scoops of the butternut squash puree on the bottom of each plate; on top of each one I arranged a few nice-looking chunks of braised beef cheeks, and then ladled some of the pomegranate reduction sauce on top, followed by a sprinkle of chopped parsley and fresh pomegranate seeds as garnish.

"This looks amazing," Karol said.

I had to admit—it did look pretty impressive. The butternut squash was a rich, sunset orange color, and the pomegranate reduction, thickened with a touch of cream, painted the plate with splashes of deep magenta. We brought the plates to the table and rinsed out the white wine from everyone's glasses. Morgan gave a brief introduction about the red wine he'd paired the course with, a bold and fruity something or other, from someplace or another.

"Wow, this is really good," Kara said, digging in.

"I've never had beef cheeks before," Lauren noted. "They're really good."

"I think you just have to braise them forever, with wine. Everything tastes good if you cook it like that," I said.

"Yeah, but you made it *really* good," Jordan said. The compliments brightened my mood a little. I pecked around at my plate, too antsy to eat much, and worried about plating the next course.

I had run out of plates to serve everything on, so I'd need to wash the first set of plates, which were stacked in a splattered, messy heap in the sink. How did places like Whisk and Ladle serve all those diners? I couldn't wrap my head around how much work a supper club involved.

When the meat course was finished, or at least half finished, since most of the guests were beyond full by now, Karol helped me wash and dry a set of ten plates. The final course before dessert was something I'd devised called "East-West Eggplant." Each plate had one Japanese eggplant half placed down the center, which had been sliced lengthwise, seared on the cut surface, and roasted until soft inside. On one side of the plate, or on the "West," I'd piped a streak of classic, Italian basil pesto. For the other side, "East," I'd made a Chinese sesame seed paste and soy sauce–based sauce, with a bit of sugar and rice vinegar for pungency. The diners were meant to cut the roasted eggplant and dip it in either sauce as they pleased. From past experience, I had seen how basil could be a potent, effective aphrodisiac. I was now desperate for its charms. We carried the plates to the table.

"What are we looking at here?" François asked. I explained the concept of the dish to the group, and everyone nodded appreciatively.

"Cathy's mind, on eggplant," Matt pronounced.

"I love this pesto," Morgan commented. Good, I thought.

"Wow, but that 'East' sauce is incredible," Kara said.

"Yeah, I want to know how to make something like this," Lauren added.

If I'd had the patience to plate the dish with more care, I might have piped neat, elegant squiggles of each sauce to the left and right of each eggplant half. But as it was, I'd simply squeezed angry glops of the stuff on either side, so that the pesto resembled a pile of mangled seaweed, and the Asian sauce was a medium-brown, thick sludge. Anyway, that's how I saw it in my miserable state of mind.

Once everyone was done picking at their dishes, we all took them to the sink and got up to stretch a little. Dessert wouldn't be served until later on, if anyone had the appetite for it then. Somehow, almost three hours had slipped by already, and since we began the dinner a little late, it was almost time for people to start getting back home. We opened another bottle of wine. As a precaution, I'd stocked my kitchen with a few extra bottles. I was glad I had, since we had just run out of the specially paired wines. We put on some livelier music and tried to get a dance party going, but nobody was into dancing much besides the four of us core supper-club members. Finally, at around midnight, I put out bowls of the amaretto ice cream that I'd made earlier that week, each one topped with caramel sauce and a crisp amaretti cookie that I'd baked that day. I ended up talking a bit with Morgan as we all stood around the kitchen, chatting about the dinner and wines and so forth. When I cornered Karol about how things were going with George, she just shrugged.

"We're just friends, that's all," she explained. "There was never going to be any hope of anything else."

"I see," I said. I hadn't realized that this was in fact the case all along, but it made sense. Karol wouldn't have wanted to invite someone she wasn't comfortable with. George was nice, but they did truly seem to be on a platonic wavelength the entire night.

George was the first guest to take off for the night, explaining that he had to work early the next morning. Kara and Thaddeus were next to go, an hour or so later. We were listening to a dance-mix CD that Lauren and François had brought along as a gift. It was a pretty good mix, and we ended up staying up late listening to it as we chatted. Lauren and François also brought rubber bouncy balls to the party, for some reason, and we all enjoyed a run at popping them around the room.

"I'm way too full to dance," Lauren said, shaking her head when Matt tried to take her hand. "I think I might throw up if I tried to."

"So what does SOS stand for, anyway?" François asked at one point. It was the question we were all dreading earlier on, when it was just the four core members in my apartment. But no one had prepared a good answer for it then.

"Something-or-Other Supper Club," I quickly filled in.

"Really? That's all," he said.

"Yeah, whatever. We just wanted to have some friends over; you know, it's a supper club," Matt said. Thankfully, the topic was quickly dropped. Also, around then I remembered to put a bowl out for contributions. In all, I had spent somewhere near $200 on ingredients for the meal. I couldn't keep track of it all, actually. I'd gone so far as to purchase ingredients I didn't end up using—white truffle oil I thought might be nice for the goat cheese crostinis, a whole tin of caviar, only half of which was used. A whole bottle of nice, expensive amaretto liqueur to spike the ice cream with, instead of a generic, imitation-flavor brand. That, plus the wines we owed Morgan for, amounted to a loss for the four of us of $20 to $30 each. It wasn't so bad, compared to throwing a regular dinner party without asking for contributions. But I realized how grossly I'd underestimated the cost of the night.

Morgan was the last guest to go who wasn't a core supper-club member, at around three in the morning. Just before he left, I remembered that I needed to pay him back for all the wines. We stepped into my bedroom for a minute while I found my checkbook.

"Is that enough? Are you sure?" I said, after handing him the check.

"Yeah, that's perfect," he said. "Thanks."

"Well, thanks for bringing it, and for coming," I said.

"No problem."

We were silent for a second. I was holding a pen that had taken me a few minutes to find. For a moment, because I had been so used to holding a thin wineglass stem, I almost forgot what it was and started to bring it to my mouth. But I stopped myself just in time.

I had to give Morgan some credit for sticking around the longest of all the invited guests. But there was something desperately unanswered in our rapport. He had his jacket in hand, ready to leave, and there was a strangely vapid, phony smile on his face right then, as if to say, "Okey-doke."

I wanted to ask him, in that brief pause, just what exactly was going on. What was he doing here? Why was he standing in my bedroom, exchanging checks for wines that he'd offered to bring—and why did he contact me in the first place? We barely knew each other. What was the meaning of this?

"Well, good night," he said.

"Yep."

I walked him to the door. We said good night once again at the door, and nothing else.

I closed it shut and turned to the threesome of Jordan, Karol, and Matt.

"You know what?" I said, after giving the door a good tug. "Who cares?"

"Turn that stereo up this minute!" Matt yelled. I gladly obliged.

"He's really not that cool," Jordan told me seriously. "You're so much better than him."

Karol was sprawled out on the couch but nodded without pause.

I realized then that in my eagerness to cook up the best, swoon-worthy meal, I let myself dismiss the goal of finding just the right person to swoon over.

We stayed up until well past four in the morning, dancing, drinking the last bottle of wine, but mostly talking about why the four of us, creative, fairly attractive, and fun-loving twenty-somethings, couldn't seem to find a decent date in this big city of ours. For the first time that night (perhaps for the first time in the past few weeks since SOS planning got under way), I felt completely relaxed. We poured ourselves small glasses of the amaretto liqueur I'd used for the ice cream. We scraped up the last remaining scoops of ice cream from the carton in the freezer, and I single-handedly polished off the so-so amaretti cookies that were left behind. We got too tired from dancing and drinking to stand and found ourselves sprawled out on our backs on the hardwood floor.

"You made such good food," Jordan mumbled.

"Yeah, too much, though. I think I'd throw up if I tried to sleep with anyone tonight," Matt said.

"Do you want us to help with the dishes?" Karol asked, glancing at the stacks of plates on the counter and in the sink.

"Nah. It can wait until tomorrow."

I didn't want to think about doing the dishes, or about throwing another supper club ever again. Not right then. Yet, despite all the work and mess it produced, and it being an utter failure in terms of inducing romance, SOS was still probably the most fun I'd had all year. SOS, indeed, I thought. Sorry Old Suckers for romance.

"You know what a better name for this night might have been?"

I said, looking up at the plastered ceiling. My friends grunted in response.

"Appetite for Destruction."

~~~~~~

Asparagus, Avocado, and Watercress Salad

I've made this salad with many types of vegetables when asparagus isn't in season, like broccoli, and sometimes swap in sautéed portobello strips instead of the avocado. The crisp, blanched asparagus contrasts in texture with the rest and makes for a light, refreshing salad.   (SERVES 4–6)

> 1 bunch (about 10 thin stalks) fresh asparagus, tough ends trimmed and discarded, and chopped to 1-inch pieces on a diagonal
> 1 avocado, cubed
> 1 bunch watercress, roughly chopped
> 1 scallion, thinly sliced on a diagonal
> 1 tablespoon fresh lemon juice
> 1–2 tablespoons extra-virgin olive oil
> Salt and pepper to taste

Bring a wide, shallow pan of water to a boil. Set up an ice bath in a large bowl. Place asparagus in boiling water and cook for about 2 minutes. Remove asparagus with tongs and immediately transfer to ice bath. Let cool about 1 minute; then drain and pat dry.

Toss the rest of the ingredients with the asparagus in a large bowl. Can be covered and chilled up to 2 hours before serving.

~~~~~~

Pomegranate-Braised Beef Cheeks with Butternut Squash Puree

(SERVES 4–6)

5 pounds beef cheeks, trimmed of excess fat and cut to
    equal-sized pieces (depending on how many you're
    serving)
Salt and pepper
½ cup flour
2–4 tablespoons vegetable oil
1 medium onion, chopped
1 carrot, chopped
1 celery stalk, chopped
2 cups Chianti or other dry red wine
2 cups pomegranate juice
1 large butternut squash
1 tablespoon butter
½ cup heavy cream
Fresh pomegranate seeds for garnish

Pat beef cheek pieces dry. Season with salt and pepper on
all sides and dredge in a light coating of flour. Heat the oil in
a large, oven-safe pot or Dutch oven over high heat until oil
begins to pop. Shake off excess flour and place beef cheeks in
a single layer on the bottom of the pot (working in batches if
necessary). Brown on each side until lightly golden. Remove
beef cheeks with tongs and set aside in a bowl.

Preheat oven to 325 degrees. Add the onion, carrot, and
celery to the pan (adding additional oil if bottom is very dry),
and sweat over low heat until softened, about 6 minutes.
Season with salt and pepper and scrape up any browned bits
from the bottom of the pot. Return the beef cheeks to the
pot, and add the wine and 1 cup of the pomegranate juice.
Bring just to a boil, stirring. Cover, and transfer to the oven to
braise for 3–4 hours.

Meanwhile, slice the squash in half lengthwise and scoop
out the seeds. Generously oil a baking tray and place squash
halves cut side down. Roast for about 1 hour while the beef
cheeks are braising, or until the tops are soft to the touch
and the flesh underneath is tender through. Let cool, and
scrape out the flesh from the skins with a spoon. Transfer
to a saucepan and add the butter, cream, and a couple of
pinches of salt while stirring over medium heat. Using a
hand blender, process until smooth.

Return the pot with the beef cheeks to the stove. Transfer beef to a separate dish carefully with a slotted spoon. Add the remaining cup of pomegranate juice and reduce sauce to about half, depending on how much liquid there is to begin with. Arrange beef cheeks on a plate with a scoop of the squash puree, and top with a ladle or two of the sauce. Garnish with fresh pomegranate seeds.

CHAPTER 12

Hanging Over in New York

THE MEXICAN MENUDO INCIDENT

At work one day, my coworkers and I somehow got on the subject of tripe. We were gathered in the narrow aisle that connected our six cubicles, chatting because, as had been common over the past few months, the server that enabled us to do virtually any work was down. It was a recurring technical problem, one that no doubt drove the company mad, but for us, it was a pleasant little break in the day. We'd come to expect it at least once a week.

We'd pushed our chairs to the farthest edges of our cubicles so we could sit and talk in the aisle. Across from me sat Keith, the kitchen and electrics copywriter. To my right was Mike D., a menswear copywriter, and across from him was Melissa, a freelance copywriter who came in about twice a week. Mike M., the furniture copywriter, was across from me to my left, and in the cubicle left of me was Josh, a Web technician who really had nothing to do with our creative department. He spent most of his time on long-distance conference calls, trying to find ways to reprogram the server that was constantly crashing. (Our boss, Lauren, once referred to Josh as the "Chandler" of our little section, because for a long time she had no idea what he did all day.) That day, Keith brought into the office a box of dried cricket snacks, a free sample someone had given him on the street to promote something or other, and Josh, Melissa, and I had bonded over being the only ones brave enough to try them. Everyone else in our aisle had been horrified by the sight of the dried, spindly creatures. But they all stared in awe as first Josh, then I gamely popped one in our mouths. It took Melissa about five minutes to work up the courage, egged on by the others, but she eventually put one in her mouth with her eyes shut and quickly swallowed.

Maybe that's how we got on the subject of tripe. In any case, Mike D. spoke up:

"Yeah, my wife's grandmother sometimes makes menudo, and I can never get myself to eat the tripe in it."

"What's menudo?" I asked.

"It's like, this Mexican stew. It's supposed to be good for hangovers," Mike D. answered.

"Let's look it up," Keith said, and promptly pulled up a Wikipedia entry for menudo. A spicy, chili-based soup, essentially of beef tripe and occasionally hominy, it said.

"It does say it's supposed to be good for hangovers," Keith observed, scrolling down.

"My wife and I always pick out the hominy and eat it all instead of the tripe. I just can't stand the texture . . . it's so gristly and weird."

Melissa made a face. "I've never had it before."

"I don't think I could eat tripe, either," said Keith.

"Sara's grandmother always makes it with much more hominy these days than tripe," said Mike D. Our conversation was interrupted when he had to take a phone call.

A few minutes later, I sent an instant message to Mike D.

"Does the tripe in it look like this?" I copied and pasted a link to a photo of whitish, prickly-surfaced rumen tripe in a bowl with a thin, clear sauce.

"No," he typed. "That actually looks more appetizing than the kind she makes it with."

I brought up another image of braised honeycomb tripe with

turnips, another Chinese dim sum specialty. The honeycomb tripe had much larger welts on its surface, hence its namesake, and a floppier, softer texture.

"Yeah, that's what it looks like," he wrote back.

I asked Mike if he might be able to get his grandmother-in-law's recipe for me so that I could make it myself. I joked that I'd have to plan on getting really wasted the night before and then try it out.

"Sure," he wrote. "But I can't vouch for its healing powers since I never eat the actual tripe."

By the end of the day, he'd sent me a Word document with the simple recipe, passed on from his wife. (On days when the server was down for hours, things moved very slowly.)

"Sara's Super-Secret Menudo," the recipe was titled. I looked it over. It seemed awfully easy to prepare. I printed it out and began thinking of how and to whom I was going to serve up this rare treat.

I would throw a brunch, of course. And I'd invite a few gung-ho friends to spend the night before getting soused with.

My friend Aaron immediately came to mind as someone to bring into this experiment. Aaron and I had gone to college together, and over a semester in Europe we had both seen what the other was capable of eating—which was pretty limitless. We had also traveled to Thailand with two other friends, on a separate trip after graduation. On the streets of Bangkok, Aaron had eaten a scorpion from a vendor. Its spiky exoskeleton looked like it had been baked (or simply dried, perhaps?) to a polished mahogany, and just before handing it over to him, the girl attending the cart sprayed it with some kind of sauce from a plastic spray bottle. As Aaron held the scorpion to his mouth, a few other Westerners passing by stopped to gawk at him and got to witness the earth-shattering crunch when he popped it into his mouth whole and bit down.

"Oh, my god!" a girl had shrieked in a British accent. As if hypnotized, the bystanders stood there a minute longer, twisting their faces in horror as Aaron chewed noisily.

"Tastes like burned chicken," he declared.

By now Aaron was married; he had met his wife, Mai, during the two years he spent teaching English in Japan. Jordan and I had gone to Cincinnati for their casual weekend-long wedding about a year ago. Now he and Mai were living in New York, but we rarely found the time to hang out due to our different schedules; Aaron was in his first year of law school. We still found time to catch up on the phone and by e-mail, though, and I fired off a rambling e-mail to him explaining my menudo mission.

Aaron replied immediately with enthusiasm.

"That is perhaps the greatest idea I have heard in a long time," he wrote. "I am totally intrigued by this ancient Mexican hangover cure. We should get completely wasted, and I'm thinking maybe a sleepover should be in store, just so it won't be so much trouble for us to get to someone else's place the next day."

He even went so far as to say that he and Mai were experts at bunking on people's floors. I wasn't sure this was necessary but was excited that my idea had garnered solid interest. I requested Jordan's attendance next. It was no surprise to me, after the time we'd spent together in Morocco eating local delicacies that included sheep's brain, that she was game.

A couple of weeks flew by, and then Aaron told me he and Mai were planning to celebrate Mai's birthday at their place on a Saturday. He suggested that we make this our designated "get wasted" night and have brunch the following day at my apartment. Aaron said it was the perfect occasion since chances were good we would all be getting trashed together anyway. We agreed.

Literally the lining of an animal's stomach, tripe is one of those cuts categorized as offal. These include kidney, heart, liver, brain, ears—the entrails and organs from a butchered animal aside from the fleshy, meaty cuts. These are generally considered less delectable than meat, although for any one of these cuts, you're bound to find aficionados for it in some part of the world, or some beloved dish that features it. Offal has traditionally been reserved for the poor; hence, it is cheap, but people have been finding ways to make it more palatable across the world, in some cases turning them into delicacies, such as headcheese (made from simmering a pig's head and coagulating the pieces into a sliceable block), foie gras (the fattened liver of a goose), fried sweetbreads (the thymus gland), or braised chicken feet, another one of my dim sum favorites. The offerings go on. Tripe is usually chopped, then simmered, stewed, or steamed until it becomes very tender and has soaked in plenty of flavor, as its rubbery-textured though fairly tasteless character is hard to swallow for many.

My experience with tripe before this had been limited to Chinese food; either served cold and gently seasoned, or in a warm five-spice stew, it was usually on the table at dim sum brunches I attended when I was growing up. I knew that tripe was almost unheard-of in American cooking, and I would learn over the years that its texture was particularly off-putting to my peers. It's true that its blubbery mouthfeel and rippling, weblike surface are uniquely weird, especially at the first sight or taste.

Most meat purchased by Americans today has been stripped of any traces of the animal it once was—reduced to trimmed, boned, and often skinned cuts of white meat, or ground meat patties. It often comes to grocery stores as chunks of ready-to-cook stew meat or stir-fry strips, no slicing necessary. I've found that many people are horrified or offended by the sight of raw meat with telltale signs of the animal it came from, such as a quail with its feet still attached that I once cooked for friends, or a whole fish cooked and served with its head still intact. As a culture, we've strayed pretty far from having to acknowledge what meat actually looks like before it's prepared, so their shock is understandable.

I personally share the opinion of many advocates who say that if an individual chooses to eat animals, he or she should be willing to confront their death face-to-face by taking part in their slaughter, if only once—just so that we're more mindful of what it takes to put meat on a plate. Well, I hadn't witnessed an animal slaughter (unless you counted boiling those lobsters, cooking live shellfish, such as clams, or just catching fish). But I agree with the premise of facing what you're going to eat, even at the unpleasant necessary stages of rawness. I'll further that by arguing that if an individual enjoys eating tripe, headcheese, or another type of offal, he or she should be willing to cook it—and that often means encountering meat at its unsightliest.

The next day, after confirming Aaron, Mai, and Jordan for the menudo brunch, I called my parents to ask them how to say *tripe* in Chinese. Sensing that Chinatown was the easiest place to find a butcher to purchase the cut from, I thought it would be helpful to know. On the phone, my mom got distracted and started asking me life questions. By the end of our conversation, I still had no idea how to say *tripe* in Chinese, as she insisted she had forgotten. She must have told my dad about my tripe-cooking plans, though, because I got an e-mail from him the next day.

"*Nyo dza,*" he wrote. "I think that's the name of the beef tripe at dim sum with the turnips and Chinese spices. Or else the other, smaller kind of tripe that mom likes, but I don't." Then, thinking that I was planning on making one of these delicacies, he offered to look up recipes in some of his old Chinese cookbooks.

"I think there's one in Pei Mei's," he wrote, referring to the brightly colored, circa-1960s cookbook with the prim woman in a traditional high-collar dress smiling on the back flap.

I wrote back, explaining the menudo dish and the recipe from Mike's grandmother-in-law, tactfully leaving out the part about the controlled hangover experiment. My dad replied with a by-the-way warning: "Once or twice, I have eaten tripe that tasted yucky. I do not know if this has to do with the stomach acid from the inside of the animal left over. You will want to wash it thoroughly, and probably, it needs to be soaked in a chemical opposite of acid for a period of time before it can be used, but I don't know what."

Great. I would have to keep this in mind, though throughout my own, fewer years of eating tripe, I had never experienced an off taste.

I crashed my bike the week before the menudo brunch. I was riding home from a dinner party at Kara's, and it began to rain as soon as I got on my bike. When I was only a few blocks from home, I got too close to a curb and scraped my front wheel against it. In a combination of the slippery conditions and my carelessness, I toppled sideways onto the sidewalk, kissing the pavement pretty hard. While the bike and my right hand caught most of the fall, I busted up the inside of my lip pretty badly and sprouted a nasty purple bruise on my chin the next morning that lasted a week and a half.

Matt injured himself that week as well. While apartment sitting for his friend (who was in the hospital with a broken ankle after a driver had clipped her on her bike), Matt was attacked by her cat. The cat's deep claw puncture struck a vein in his wrist, which became infected and swelled up to the point where he could barely walk without the slight movements of his arm causing him pain.

That Friday night, before Mai's birthday party, I went to Matt's after work to make him dinner since it pained him to cook. I brought some salad greens, apple, gorgonzola cheese, and a crusty baguette for a light dinner on his rooftop. I tossed up the salad, and we sat and watched the sun drop and the sky fill with a dusty purplish hue, set off by the Manhattan skyline. A short while later, Jordan, Karol, and a few other friends joined us, and together we spent a long night celebrating no particular occasion.

The next day, both Jordan and I were hungover and moving at an excessively slow pace. It started raining that afternoon, and by the time I got out of the subway that evening to go to Mai's party, there was a furious rainstorm. I got lost trying to find the building and ended up soaking wet even though I'd been holding an umbrella the whole time. The rain was so fierce, and coming at me from all directions, that I took every chance to duck into an alcove or underneath an awning, shivering in my thin long-sleeved shirt. When I finally arrived at the party, my clothes were dripping, my hair was matted to my face, my glasses were fogged from the stuffiness indoors, my chin was yellowish purple, and I had a preexisting hangover.

"Hey, are you ready to get hammered?" Aaron greeted me from across the room.

I couldn't actually step over to him to say hi, as it was too cramped in the small apartment to get by. I smiled wanly. On a round table, an array of sushi-stuffing ingredients was set beside a bowl of sushi rice and squares of nori seaweed wrappers for make-it-yourself *maki* rolls. On the kitchen counter a couple of bottles of hard alcohol accompanied some juices, soda, and a blender half filled with orangish slush. Just what I needed for a second hangover, I thought.

As it turned out, cocktails were just what I needed to lift my body from the hard knocks it had taken. There's something to be said for the old hair-of-the-dog hangover remedy that stipulated a bit of alcohol the day after drinking. This either reversed the effects of the hangover or temporarily prolonged it—I wasn't sure which. But I got my hair of the dog, in the form of a mango-and-pineapple-juice mixed drink, and went on to seconds with beer. I devoured plenty of sushi hand rolls, too, taking sheets of nori and wrapping rice, cucumbers, smoked salmon, tuna salad, and other tidbits in them.

"That's what I'm going to do for my next party," Jordan said, pointing at the sushi-making spread as she chomped down on a roll.

"Yeah, what a good idea," I told Mai.

She shrugged modestly. "It's not a lot of very special ingredients, just basic."

Aaron came by and gave Mai a little squeeze.

"So, are we ready for tomorrow?" he asked me. "I can't wait to try out this spicy Mexican legend."

"Yeah . . . it should be interesting," I said.

Earlier that day, I'd managed to make a trip to Chinatown to pick up the honeycomb beef tripe. It was next door to the seafood market where I'd picked up the lobsters, and once again I found myself toting a very strange object with me on the subway ride back to Brooklyn. This time, even though nothing was live and kicking, it felt about ten times weirder. Never had I seen honeycomb tripe in its raw, unprepared state before. I knew I'd be able to point it out the moment I saw it at a butcher shop. That flabby, honeycomblike texture was impossible to miss. So when I strolled to the end of the case of meats on display at the shop, I immediately spotted my prey. Whitish in color, somewhat translucent in parts, the floppy, baggy, deeply scored intestinal sacks were heaped one on top of another, like deflated monster-truck tires. On the meat shelf, the honeycomb pattern was a tight-knit lattice. But once the butcher lifted one up to take it out of the case, the rubbery flesh stretched out to reveal a gaping three-dimensional surface and a balloonlike shape with a wide O-shaped opening at one end. The intestines needed to be sold whole; unlike the neat cuts of flank steak or the individual trotters in the meat case, there was no trimming them down to certain weights. One had to eyeball these pieces for size and choose accordingly. I needed just one pound of tripe for the recipe Mike gave me, but looking at the bloated, watery texture of the offal, I had no idea what kind of weight it might carry. I got the butcher's attention and ordered what looked to be the smallest of the tripe pieces.

He had given me a curious grin when I pointed to the tripe. He'd pointed to it with a smile as if to ask, "You really want this?" He seemed amused all the while as he wrapped and weighed the product. The meter read that it weighed approximately 1.6 pounds. At $1.69 per pound, this was an overhaul I could afford. Plus, I wanted to make plenty of menudo for my brunch guests, enough for seconds.

As I told the story of purchasing the tripe to Aaron, trying to describe the actual, physical appearance of the stuff, an uneasy feeling crept into my stomach.

"So, wait, tripe is actually a cow's stomach? Did I hear that right?" Aaron said.

"Yeah. There's lots of different stomachs in a cow—seven to be exact. So that's just one of the kinds, with the honeycomb texture," I said.

"Huh," he said. "For some reason, I just thought tripe was a type of fish."

"What?" I said.

"Oh, no," said Jordan.

"No, I mean—I'll eat it," Aaron quickly responded. "I don't know what made me think that, though. Weird."

"Maybe you were thinking of . . . trout?" Jordan offered.

"I have no idea." Aaron shook his head. "Okay, so, yeah, hooray for tripe! Let's all get wasted and eat it tomorrow." We shared a toast.

"Did you cook it yet?" Mai asked.

"Partially," I told her. I had cut the tripe into one- to two-inch squares and brought them to a boil with the onion and chili powder, following the recipe. I was planning to cook it the hour or so more it needed the next day, then would add the hominy, so that it would be piping hot and ready to serve when my friends arrived. (By then, of course, we'd decided against having a sleepover at someone's place the night before.)

At the party, we met a few of Mai and Aaron's other friends. Once my social powers were somewhat restored from the drinks, we even decided to tackle a board game. Board games, card games, and any type of game in general were a signature of Aaron's from as far back as I could remember. In his closet there was a game called Guesstures. The concept of the game was similar to that of charades; each player drew a card and acted out the meaning of the word on it without saying a word.

"It's like charades in a box." Aaron shrugged. "It's like paying for it instead of not."

It turned out to be the perfect game for our group; out of the guests Mai had invited, several of them had limited English-speaking skills, and we were having trouble making conversation with them. But they all readily understood written English.

Jordan, myself, and two of Mai's friends named Nao and Ho ended up playing for hours. The rounds were quick and simple, and it was funny to see the way people struggled and eventually interpreted ordinary words. I was on the floor laughing when Nao did his impression of *hail*, as I was also, when I tried to mime *slug*. After a few rounds, it was clear that Jordan and I were tuned into each other's way of thinking and body language a lot more than either of us had expected. We nailed more correct answers than anyone else, one of us usually shouting out the word correctly within a few seconds of the other performing it. But Nao and Ho were pretty good at "Guessturing" too, and we didn't stop until most of the other guests had filtered out of the party.

"We know each other so well," I sobbed after nabbing a word Jordan was miming that had us all stumped for a few minutes.

At some point after midnight, Mai put out a wedge of Brie and crackers that she had forgotten about earlier. I naturally gorged myself on this as the night continued.

The next morning, I found myself with a classic hangover. Remembering the Brie and all those nori seaweed wrappers mixing in my stomach gave me a bad taste in my mouth and a want-to-wretch dread in the pit of my stomach. Plus, with all the different drinks around, I had forgotten to obey the golden rule of hangover prevention: Drink lots of water before sleeping. Now only the menudo could save me.

I pulled myself out of bed at ten in the morning, groggy and nauseous. I was grateful I didn't have to touch or chop the tripe as I removed the covered stockpot from my fridge. I made the mistake of opening the lid right then and peeking inside, though. All the fat, which was stained bright orange from the chili powder, had entirely sealed the surface of the concoction, and after prodding it with a spoon in an attempt to skim some of it off, I realized that the soup's liquid had turned into jelly.

I'd picked up another funky ingredient on my Chinatown trip. At the butcher shop, I'd decided that the soup base in the menudo could benefit from some pork bones, to mingle with the vegetables for a richly flavored broth (and to flavor the tripe as much as possible). But I didn't see any bones in the cases, so without giving it much thought, I'd asked for a trotter—essentially the foot of the pig—instead. Once home, I took all my ingredients out and put them on the counter. The light pink, thick-skinned trotter definitely looked like the same limb that a living pig would stand on, except that roughly half a foot above the hoof, it had been sliced clean through the calf bone, revealing a circle of pink, red, and white swirls of bone and tissue at one end. I'd sunk the trotter into the center of the stockpot. The menudo squares, vegetables, garlic, chili powder, and cumin were already bubbling away. The trotter was too tall to be fully submerged, so I gave it a turn upside down, so that the hooved end was sticking a bit outside of the soup.

I would later discover that what I'd really made that morning was a spicy, tripe-studded aspic. A key ingredient in headcheese and other chunky terrines, aspic is a clear jelly that's made from the natural gelatins in meat when it's boiled and flavored with other ingredients. Pig's trotters were a particularly common ingredient for making this substance, since the cartilage turns stock into jelly once they're melted down and then chilled.

I let the mixture warm up again on the stove, hoping that it wouldn't taste as bad as it looked. In the meantime, I preheated a Dutch oven for a loaf of no-knead bread that I'd let sit out the night before. Once the menudo was heated through again, I was glad that the jelly texture had broken, and the clear, reddish liquid was now bubbling. I lowered the heat to a low simmer and hopped in the shower to ready myself for my guests.

The kitchen had taken on a deeply savory aroma by the time I got out. It was marked by piquant and spicy red chili powder, which I'd bought at a specialty Mexican grocery, since the recipe called for pouring in a whole cupful. It didn't smell recognizably like pork, or trotter, or tripe. But it smelled pretty good. For the first time, I was actually looking forward to tasting the crazy combination of substances I had thrown into that pot. Over the next hour, I watched the stove as I baked a loaf of no-knead bread to go with the brunch, chopped fresh cilantro, and added hominy to the stew when it was almost done.

By twelve thirty, my three guests had arrived. Jordan was nearly unresponsive, she was so hungover. It didn't help matters much that it was unbearably hot that morning. I brought my single fan into the living room and tried to air out the room, but between baking the bread and simmering the stew for an hour and a half, plus the sunlight streaming in through the windows, the heat was scorching.

I'd turned the heat off under the pot of menudo about a half hour earlier, once I'd tasted the stuff. While doing so, I noticed that the squares of tripe had not only shrunken to about half their size, but were the texture of soft jelly rather than rubber and were becoming softer the longer they cooked. They had also turned from off-white to deep brown, thanks to the burgundy broth they were simmered in. The hominy, since it had been added so much later, added some nice contrast in that it was still white. I'd had cold salsas that had hominy in them before, but I'd never had it in a soup or stew. The pale pellets of preserved corn tasted a lot like fresh tortillas and were a welcome, neutral addition to the stew.

It was a humid morning, and a short-lived downpour had added to the moisture the steaming stockpot had already brought to the room. We sat down at the small table in the middle of the room. Just as I'd predicted, Aaron looked the worst off. His eyes were bleary and half-open, his throat scratchy sounding when he spoke. Jordan had probably suffered the worst of her hangovers for the weekend the morning before that one, but she still was definitely not at 100 percent. Mai didn't look too bad, nor did she say she felt so bad herself. I was strangely awake, and very hungry. Everyone dove for the bread first.

We had a round of coffee before my guests tiptoed over to the pot of menudo on the stove. I'd made sure to remove the trotter before they came. Aaron stared into the pot.

"So that's tripe, huh?" he said.

It looked a lot more appealing now that it had been cooked than the strange white stuff I'd chopped the day before. The tripe squares were so light, they came floating to the surface of the stew easily with the stir of a spoon. I scooped out portions into individual bowls for everyone and garnished the tops with sprigs of cilantro. Brunch was served.

"Mm," Mai said, taking a slurp of the broth alone. "What did you do to make the soup?"

I told her about the extraneous pork bone, leaving out the fact that it had actually been a foot, rather than just a bone.

Jordan coughed on her next sip. She cleared her throat. "This is spicy," she said, her eyes reddening.

"Yeah, but it's kind of waking me up," Aaron said. "I can see how something with a really good kick would do that, for a hangover. Actually, that's a pretty good metaphor. It has kick."

We all nodded. Even though the tripe was very tender by then, it was still a chewy, springy little piece of offal. It needed to be worked on for a while with the molars before it gave way and broke into separate chunks. I didn't find the texture unappealing, though; this need to chew, while savoring the flavor that it had been steeped in, was a trait I'd always loved about dim sum braised tripe before. I dipped my piece of bread into the reddish, spicy broth. Everyone soon followed suit.

"I can't believe I'm eating this," Jordan said after a brief silence.

"Mm, the soup is really good," Mai said.

"I'm actually liking the tripe a bit, and the hominy? Is that what these things are?" Aaron asked, holding up his spoon.

"Yep. They eat a lot of hominy in Mexico, apparently," I explained. "But for some reason, not so much here. It's a good way of preserving corn."

"I see."

We continued to slurp until, miraculously, all our plates were empty. I hadn't been sure if my friends would take to the dish— probably because I had been the one who had seen and worked with the strange ingredients, in all their raw glory. I had expected a little more hesitation and perhaps a couple of dislikes. I didn't think anyone was making an extra effort to be polite, either. I knew for a fact that Jordan would put down her spoon and be quite content not eating something if she found that it was not to her liking. But her plate was cleared just as well as anyone else's.

The thing about tripe is that it doesn't really have a particular taste. It's all texture—weird, blubbery texture—but tastewise, it is completely benign. So traditionally whenever it's cooked, it's stewed for long hours with savory broths and spices, so it soaks up that flavor. What we were eating basically tasted like red chili pork broth–soaked sponges. Which was actually quite nice, especially for a hangover.

"I'm actually starting to feel a bit better now," Jordan said.

"It worked?" Aaron asked her. She nodded, smiling for the first time that morning.

"I'm going to go for seconds," he said.

After the four of us had seconds, there was no more menudo left to go around. In the end, we concluded, it was probably the rich, savory spiciness plus the warm soupiness of the dish that had eased our hangovers the most. I wasn't sure the tripe itself was integral to this. We could have been eating spicy chicken soup or any other type of meat prepared in the same way.

I felt a great pride in my friends right then for doing what Mike D. and even his wife never dared to—eating the actual tripe. It wasn't so bad, really, once you got used to the new texture. It was completely different from any other texture in the world, sure, but that was what was so great about food anyway, that it could vary so endlessly.

After we'd filled our stomachs with menudo and bread and had another round of coffees, the four of us tried to retrace our steps from the previous night. It was fun to recall the fuzzy details we'd nearly forgotten, like rubbing clear a fogged window and catching new glimpses with each swipe. Why had we thought coconut rum and vodka would go well together? Why was I talking about the stage adaptation of John Waters's *Cry-Baby* with someone—and who was that with, anyway? Slowly, we began to fill in the blanks. There had even been a little skirmish with the police at one point, when a guest stepped outside onto the front stoop and got ticketed for holding a bottle of beer outside.

This was a classic hangover, healed. I was convinced then that I had discovered the best way to remedy that old morning-after affliction, and I would follow it as much as possible—if not with tripe, then at least with something spicy and soothing. The key was to also spend the day with friends, filling our stomachs with something—anything. And, perhaps, to experience new foods, or new cuts of an animal, and breaking down those cuts from a raw state yourself. Well, this last part was probably best saved for a clear, nonhungover state of mind.

~~~~~~

Sarah's Super-Secret Menudo

This recipe is actually improvised from the one that my coworker gave me, written by his wife, Sarah. I added one pork trotter to the broth to give it extra flavor; for the faint of heart, a few pork soup bones can be used instead.

(MAKES ABOUT 4–6 SERVINGS)

2 tablespoons vegetable oil
1 large onion, finely chopped
5–6 cloves garlic, minced
Salt and pepper to taste
1 pork trotter (or substitute 3–4 pork bones)
½ cup red chili powder*
1 teaspoon oregano
1 teaspoon cumin
1 bunch cilantro, chopped
1½ pounds honeycomb beef tripe, cut into 1–2 inch squares (they'll shrink)
2 cans hominy, drained and rinsed

In a large pot, heat the oil and sweat the onion over medium-low heat until translucent, about 6 minutes. Add the garlic and a few pinches of salt and pepper. Add the trotter or pork bones and cook, stirring, another minute. Stir in the chili powder, oregano, cumin, and half the chopped cilantro. Add the tripe and enough water to cover. Bring to a boil, then reduce to a simmer; cover and cook for 1 hour. Add the hominy and continue cooking 20–30 minutes. Taste for seasoning, adding extra salt or spices as desired. Serve in bowls with the reserved cilantro for garnish.

---

*It's best to use pure, unseasoned red chili powder, which can be found in Latin American or specialty spice stores. Most seasonings called "chili powder" have a mixture of other spices, such as cumin, and a lot of salt. You'll want to adjust the salt accordingly if using one of these.

~~~~~~

Blood Orange and Bacon Hangover Salad

The various and unusual mixture of textures and bright, punch-in-the-face flavors is bound to wake one up in the morning after a rough night out. This salad combines spicy radishes, tart blood oranges, savory bacon, and a crumble of roasted pistachios in a salad that's as visually stunning as it is wake-worthy.

(SERVES ABOUT 3–4)

½ cup shelled pistachios
1 tablespoon red wine vinegar
Salt and freshly ground pepper to taste
1 teaspoon Dijon mustard
3 tablespoons olive oil
1 head Boston lettuce (or another leafy green lettuce, such as green leaf or red leaf)
1 large or 2 small blood oranges, peel removed and slices cut out without the pith (membrane that separates the slices)
3 strips bacon, cooked to crispy
2–3 small radishes, quartered to wedges

In a small bowl, combine the red wine vinegar, mustard, and a couple of pinches of salt and pepper. Drizzle in the olive oil while whisking rapidly until mixture is emulsified. Gently tear lettuce into bite-sized pieces. Toss in a large bowl with the dressing and remaining ingredients. Serve immediately.

CHAPTER 13

Cooking Up a Storm

COMPETITIVE COOKING AND

COLLABORATIONS

I lay on my back in a shady patch of grass in Prospect Park alongside Karol, staring up at the sky. It was clear blue, with just a few wispy clouds like tautly pulled lambs wool. I could think of no better way to spend the warm June day than like this: surrounded by friends sitting on a pastiche of blankets in a clearing of trees, nibbling at homemade cookies and sipping on iced caipirinhas. It was a warm but breezy eighty degrees in the sun. There was a fountain bursting with a tall spray of water in the center of the large lawn where we'd staked our picnic, creating a constant tinkling noise behind the chatter. I could smell the sweet clover from a small patch in the grass beside me. Occasional shouts could be heard from friends who were playing Frisbee down the mead—did I just say "mead"? I think I did. Basically, it was pure heaven in Brooklyn.

As I closed my eyes, Karol yawning at my side, I conjured images of an outdoor picnic in the English countryside. Victorian straw hats, girls fluttering fans before their coyly pressed lips as male suitors stretched on the grass, peeling slices of apple away from their cores and presenting them to the damsels. I imagined spreads of fruit from the Dutch masters' paintings, or Manet's *Luncheon on the Grass* with its lone nude female seated front and center. Only we were fully clothed. Well, all but one. A tiny elderly woman had stepped into the park a short while ago, and promptly into the fountain. She began to strip to her underpants and a long button-down shirt, then continued to stand there in the sprinkling pool for a few minutes, absent-looking and utterly silent.

But aside from that interlude (she soon took off, ambling back through the bushes), it was a picture-perfect summer day. Not counting the woman with no pants, and a couple who came by with their dog at one point, there was no one on that particular stretch of lawn in Prospect Park but my friends and me.

The section of the park was called the Rose Garden, named so long ago, because there were no longer any rosebushes. Yet looking at old photos online, I saw that the Rose Garden had been lined with rose trellises in the 1800s, when the park was built, and had looked to be a very elegant knoll. The space was vaguely separated into three conjoined lawns, the middle one with the fountain in its center; the lower one, where Frisbee was being played, rested alongside a thick brush of forest; and the one opposite had just the faintest fringe of tall trees surrounding it, so that our picnic food could be set in the half shade. Matt and I had come across the location on my second foraging walk of Prospect Park with Steve Brill, earlier that spring. I found the setting oddly private, for Brooklyn at least. It was just obscure enough—to get there, one had to follow a small, shady trail—that not too many people seemed to know of it. Back in the spring on the foraging tour, the fountains had been sucked dry to circular ditches of concrete, and one's voice echoed when one was standing in the middle of it. I thought the Rose Garden would be a perfect place to hold an early summer picnic, so I invited a horde of friends by e-mail and wisely chose a warm Saturday, and my dream was realized.

I asked each picnic guest to bring a potluck dish and decided that chicken salad would be the theme. Why chicken salad? Erin and I were sipping wine one night, and for some reason she began to talk about how wonderful it would be to eat cold chicken in a park. Inspired, I encouraged people to bring their own unique takes on chicken salad in my invitation, and I'd provide the bread. I also asked that no one bring disposable plates or cutlery, just a serving spoon for their salad. One of the reasons I thought sandwiches were the ideal picnic food was because they could be eaten by hand, so no wasteful paper plates or forks would be needed.

Adam brought a tremendous chicken salad with portobellos and roasted red peppers. Scott brought one with smoked paprika and radishes. Pauline brought one with walnuts and grapes. David and Shana brought a seitan vegetarian "chicken" salad with fresh dill. I brought one with nectarines and basil, and another one laced with Scotch bonnets and Caribbean jerk seasonings, plus some loaves of no-knead bread. Karol made deviled eggs, someone else made brownies, and Jordan and Ben brought peaches and nectarines. The Greenmarket at Grand Army Plaza, at the tip of the park, was open that day, and some people came toting fresh fruit and vegetables directly from there. Zoya brought a bag of fresh sugar snap peas, and we invented a delightful appetizer by removing the peas and filling the empty, crisp green pods with chicken salad. Konrad arrived victoriously toting a heavy cooler filled with fresh limeade, a bag of ice, and a bottle of Cachaça rum for making the Brazilian cocktail caipirinhas. Aaron brought a Frisbee. Nick brought juggling pins and was teaching others to use them; someone had brought a harmonica and was buzzing away on it. Trevor brought a picnic suitcase, filled with essentials like plates, flatware, and napkins.

This day should never end, I thought to myself as I closed my eyes and soaked in the sun through my thin cotton dress. True, I felt like a full tank by then because I had eaten so much. But who cared? Not I.

Have I mentioned that summer is the best time of the year for not eating out? And it wasn't just because of "parknics." Cooking and eating together with friends and family may have relatively peaceful moments, like these. But more often than not, they're filled with frenzy. Looking back on all the barbecues, Thanksgivings, Friendsgivings, supper-club dinners, and other communal cooking events brings back memories of how intense the heat of the moment can get. How a kitchen acts as a stadium for a team sport, fighting against time and utter cooking failure. How smoky and sweaty it gets with four burners and the oven on, how many cooking utensils and half-prepared ingredients are juggled at a time, how much bodily contact there is with your collaborators, who are frequently in your way while concentrating on their tasks. And of course, the reward: how satisfying it is to share a meal together when all is done. It's the greatest sport in the world, if you ask me.

That summer, 2008, would turn out to be the hottest, sweatiest, and most collision-worthy season of communal cooking for me yet. First, there were tons of cook-offs to attend. Over the last year, Karol and I had become pretty regular participants in local amateur cook-offs. Karol's obsession preceded mine, and our friends David and Shana had been bitten by the cook-off bug, too. Any type of cook-off, and anywhere in the city: a pie bake-off on Governor's Island, a chili cook-off in a bar we'd never heard of, you named it. Just what was an amateur cook-off in New York City like? In a nutshell, they were infrequent special events where anyone could enter their homemade dish to win cash, bar prizes, and bragging rights. They were usually held in bars, organized by someone who worked there, or an outside host who'd gotten the bar's permission. The rules were simple: Cook up a batch of X, in the biggest pot you owned, haul it to the cook-off venue by whatever means possible, talk about how you made it as you serve it up, while other contestants serve up their versions, sample everyone else's food until you are stuffed silly, and await judgment time, when it was announced whose X was the best. Prizes might be given out, or for smaller cook-offs the winner might receive just a bar tab. The winner was often determined by audience vote: Anyone in attendance could write the name of their favorite on a slip of paper and submit it. But many cook-offs had a panel of judges, pulled together by various affiliations with the host and having some pedigree in the professional food world.

One of the main reasons cook-offs appealed to me was that they offered a unique mode of interaction over food—competition— and only the home-cooked kind. Because the food wasn't made by professionals for a profit, I didn't count filling up on an assortment of homemade chili as "eating out," even if the event was held inside a bar or restaurant. I appreciated the social atmosphere of these events, hungry as I was for that now that I was living alone. Plus, everyone I met at cook-offs definitely had one thing in common: a love of home cooking. Karol and I began entering cook-offs, determined each time to invent the most mind-blowingly delicious, creative version of X at first. I'd like to think that each time we did, too. We didn't make the food just to impress others, but to contemplate, experiment, and come up with our best effort, for ourselves— usually spending weeks mulling over our recipes, and at least a whole day preparing them. Karol made a sweet potato chili with all kinds of fresh peppers and chipotle, and once achieved her dream of pulling off a checkerboard pattern out of pumpkin and cheese-cake pie filling on a winning pie of hers. I made a salsa that riffed on the Bloody Mary once, with horseradish, celery, and olives, just for the heck of it, and succeeded in concocting a creamy, fresh watermelon juice pie that was more or less watermelon panna cotta with a graham cracker crust, and chocolate chips as the "seeds." It didn't matter whether we won or not after a while. We'd become friendly with a bunch of like-minded home cooks who'd enter the events often, too. I enjoyed getting to know their cooking styles, and it was always fun seeing what someone did to outdo themselves since the last cook-off—and maybe to outdo the person who'd won that one the last time. I found it fascinating to see how other nonprofessional chef-foodies like me liked to cook. How did they achieve this or that effect? How long did it take them? Some people like to spy or "people watch"; I like to watch how other average people cook.

I had gone to a couple of cook-offs that year hosted by an actor and sometime stand-up comedian named Matt Timms. The "Takedown" series, as it was called, began with just Chili Takedowns, and several rounds later, the classic cook-off spawned other competitions based on fondue, cookies, or key ingredients, such as bacon. Though we'd go to all of them, it seemed like there just weren't enough Takedowns and other local cook-offs for us. One night as Karol and I were having drinks, we found ourselves discussing what type of food *we* would choose if we were hosting our own cook-off. Then we nabbed it: risotto. The creamy-textured rice dish, we decided, was easily adaptable to so many flavors and ingredients that it would make a perfect cook-off food. We looked at each other and each raised an eyebrow: Why not just organize it ourselves?

The Risotto Challenge, as we called it, took place in early April that year, in a crowded bar in Brooklyn. Eighteen amateur risotto chefs entered, inventing risottos that were more creative than I could have ever conceived: One had blueberries, another kimchee; one had white peaches and pancetta; others, artichoke or loads of herbs, and they were all uniquely tasty. As much fun as it was, the event required a hefty amount of organizational work for Karol and me, and because we didn't want to charge anything at the door or ask contestants to pay for anything but their homemade risottos, we each lost a bit of money on incidental expenses. But a good time was had by all, and from our success, I could sense a growing fervor for the amateur cook-off in New York City.

One of the annual cook-offs in the city was actually hosted by Kara from Ted and Amy's Supper Club. It was called the Great Hot Dog Cook-Off, and in its past two years Kara had run it as a fund-raiser for a pet shelter in Brooklyn. This year, she asked me to join her in hosting the event in her backyard in July. I eagerly jumped on board. This time, though, in response to the growing prices of food and shortages of food donations across the city, we made it a benefit for the Food Bank of NYC, a hunger nonprofit. Again, the creativity from the amateur chefs was impressive, the event a huge success despite a lot of organizational work on our part, and through ticket sales from attendees, we raised our goal of $1,000 for the charity. I was amazed by the support. By doing something that we would have already loved to do in any case, we'd somehow managed to make money appear for the Food Bank. I vowed that any cook-off I hosted from that point on would be a fund-raiser for a nonprofit organization.

Cooking competitions are hardly a thing spawned on New York City soil. Home-cooking pride has inspired cook-offs throughout the world, from humble potluck-like affairs to more organized competitions with venerable judging panels and often a charity fund-raising cause. There are some that are hosted by major food corporations, such as the Pillsbury Bake-Off, while others remain grassroots traditions like the innumerable chili and barbecue brawls of the South. The Chili Appreciation Society International moderates more than 550 cook-offs around the world annually, which raise more than $1 million for charity. Every October since 1967, another chili cook-off organization, the International Chili Society, has hosted the World's Championship Chili Cook-Off in different locations throughout the States. It is the world's largest cook-off event.

It seemed that New York was only beginning to take part in a culinary phenomenon that had been captivating home cooks for half a century. That summer, I was beginning to see a community of us newbie fanatics forming. I'd invited many of the contestants from the Risotto Challenge to compete in the Great Hot Dog Cook-Off, and many of them entered. At the Chili Takedowns, there was a familiar batch of regular cooks, myself and Karol notwithstanding, and once word caught on about other cook-offs, the factions began to blend. There were occasional cook-offs held by the Brooklyn Kitchen, and my friend and fellow food writer Emily Farris had hosted three annual Casserole Party cook-offs in the fall in Brooklyn. Other bars and restaurants, like the popular Williamsburg drinking hole Barcade, had their own annual chili cook-offs, too. There was nothing formal or restaurantlike about these events, but they brought in bigger and bigger crowds of avid eaters as well as competing home cooks as time went by.

When I was growing up, the church my family went to held annual potluck dinners. Part of the fun of the night was a blind ballot: Everyone got to vote on their favorite dish. My dad made his signature pepperoni lasagna each time; some years he won with it, others he lost to more novel entries. But he brought the same dish each year; people at the church had grown to expect it, and my dad was happy to oblige.

Perhaps it pleased him most of all to know that other people enjoyed his food enough to vote for it in a competitive arena. This is the draw for the cook-off fanatic. After attending, competing in, hosting, and judging so many, I've learned that recognition and admiration are often unfulfilled needs in the home-cooking sector. It's not always so much about cooking what one wants to eat but impressing a large number of people, or the judges, enough to win. For instance, strangely enough, my dad never really made his pepperoni lasagna just for us to eat at home.

A Chili Takedown had been scheduled for that August, after a couple of months' hiatus. Matt Timms had chosen to move the event to a popular bar in Brooklyn called Union Pool and had teamed up with our mutual friend Scott Gold to host the competition. They asked me to be one of their "esteemed" judges, along with a couple of local food luminaries, including chef Camille Becerra and butcher Tom Mylan. I was looking forward to seeing whether all the cook-off excitement I'd seen building recently would amount to something big.

But before that, I had another cooking task to tackle. My friends Darin and Greg, twin brothers who deejayed by the name Finger on the Pulse, introduced a series of parties with barbecue food at a club in Brooklyn called Studio B. They were calling the parties Studio BBQ. For each party, they pulled together a different group of chefs to serve their food to the masses, for a cheap $5 a plate. I went to the first one in June, which had garnered so much hype that it was nearly impossible to move through the outdoor patio where the party was held, let alone dance, and the line for food snaked around the entire place. Fortunately, the space cleared up by the late night, and my friends and I lingered, dancing and for a brief while splashing around in the patio's decorative wading pools. I think Matt and I were two of the last people to leave.

For their next Studio BBQ at the end of July, Darin and Greg decided to round up a team of "underground" chefs. Despite my behavior at the last barbecue, they asked me to be one of them and got Mark from Whisk and Ladle and our friend Michael from A Razor, A Shiny Knife on the case, too. I had cooked at Michael's supper club a couple of times by then, and so had Mark, so the three of us knew one another and had cooked together before. This would be our biggest undertaking as a team, though. Instead of making a dinner for twenty to thirty people at a supper club, or even cooking enough chili for one hundred cook-off attendees, Darin and Greg asked us to prepare enough food for four hundred prospective attendees at the next Studio BBQ. The menu was up to us to figure out. Somehow, all of it would be prepared at our homes and brought to the space merely to reheat and serve.

We had a lot of work ahead of us. But something happened shortly into our planning that knocked me off my food-obsessed course for a while, if only in spirit. On the Fourth of July, I went to a backyard barbecue at David and Shana's place with all of my best friends. We moved on to another friend's rooftop nearby to catch a clear view of the fireworks just across the East River. At the third party we'd migrated to, our group began to dissolve. We were down to just Jordan and her friend Dan by the time I took off. As I strapped on my bike helmet to ride home, I can remember Dan asking me, firmly, at least twice, whether I was sure I'd be all right biking home.

"Psshhh." I'd shrugged him off. "Of course I'll be fine."

I was completely fine, as it turned out. Dan and Jordan, however, were not. They'd gone to another bar in the area a little while after I left and were hit by a car when crossing the street on their way home. According to witnesses they were both tossed from the impact almost halfway down the block.

Jordan broke her pelvis in three places and spent the next month recovering at her parents' home outside Philadelphia. Dan fared slightly better, with a leg injury and lots of bumps and bruises. My first reaction to the news, after talking to Jordan on the phone, was to bake something tasty and send it to her. Fresh blueberries were in season, so with a little improvisation, I managed to mold pastry into four heart-shaped tarts and filled the centers with blueberries. When they were baked and ready to eat, I packaged up the tarts in a box and shipped them out to her parents' house the same day.

The rest of my friends were naturally just as shocked as I was by the accident. We decided to do something more for Jordan. Her hip and the bruises across her entire body were slowly healing, according to her doctors. She was expected to make a full recovery, but it would be several weeks, maybe even months, before she could walk again. In the meantime, despite the everyday obstacles of using a wheelchair and coping with the pain, Jordan was extremely bored. What's more, while she was in the emergency room in Brooklyn, her wallet, cell phone, and iPod had all been stolen.

Karol suggested we all go in on a new iPod for Jordan. Over e-mail the first week of the accident, we rounded up a number of Jordan's friends who were happy to pitch in for the cause. We decided to get the iPod engraved, and deliberated over just the right message to put on the back of the device. It should be something lighthearted but sincere. Miraculously, Jordan was keeping her chin up and was dying to get better fast so she come could back to New York and continue her life as soon as possible. DJ finally nailed the inscription: "Takes a lickin', but keeps on tickin'." The newly engraved iPod was in Jordan's hands in a few days.

These things were all we could do to feel a little bit better about the situation, shower our friend with gifts. But the accident disconcerted me more, long afterward. Maybe it had to do with the fact that I had been with Jordan and Dan shortly before it happened—it could just as easily have been me, riding my bike through the busy streets of Williamsburg, getting pummeled by a car. I thought about all the things I'd focused my summer on, the food events, cook-offs, and cooking in general that I'd been obsessing over. It all seemed a little bit silly, suddenly, and indulgent.

But there were still commitments to honor and meals to make. No sooner had the hot dog cook-off ended than I found myself in the midst of preparations for Studio BBQ. Michael, Mark, and I debated the menu, and how many dishes to serve. We decided on three barbecued main-course options: brisket, pulled pork, and braised duck. For sides, we would serve everyone two of the following four options: black-eyed pea succotash, coleslaw, braised collard greens, and a cold sesame noodle salad. Finally, everyone would get the same dessert, a slice of coconut banana cornbread with peach compote. We didn't want to serve anything that had to be cooked on location, like the hamburgers at the last Studio BBQ, which created waits and long lines. Plus, Mark and Michael didn't want grilling to be confused with barbecue. In the traditional sense of the word, barbecue was slow-cooked meat, like beef brisket or pulled pork butt. So all of our courses would be premade and scooped out of chafing dishes at the club. The only thing that would be grilled was the vegetarian main course option, a grilled peach half stuffed with spiced goat cheese and caramelized shallots.

Because Mark lived closest to the venue, we decided to do most of the cooking at his apartment. Between the two of these guys, I couldn't have had more interesting cooking partners. Over the past month, I'd gotten to know them fairly well. Mark, originally from upstate New York, was a math and English tutor when not planning supper-club dinners. Tall and athletic, he was a fervent runner and health-food fanatic. Michael was a consultant for luxury real estate deals on Long Island, and in part to impress his well-to-do clients, he sported a thick black mustache and had a straight-shooting sort of attitude that drew him comparisons to the title character of the 1970s gangster film *Serpico*. But his real passion was for food—sensational, delicious food—and for making it by innovative means. One of the first things I helped cook at a dinner by A Razor, A Shiny Knife was smoked avocado slices in Michael's backyard smoker, to go inside a crabmeat ravioli filling for beet-stained pasta sheets; there was always an immersion circulator holding a vacuum-packed bag of meat going for a slow, moisture-sealed cook, or perhaps speckled quail eggs bobbing about as they poached.

Michael's culinary heroes included Ferran Adrià, Grant Achatz, and Wylie Dufresne, all chefs who used "molecular gastronomy" heavily in their cooking. In fact, all of us were curious about these novel cooking techniques; a couple of weeks before the Studio BBQ, Michael, Mark, a couple of other friends, and I took a six-hour food-science class taught by a fellow gastronomical geek, Alex Talbot, who writes a blog called "Ideas in Food." I left with several pages of scribbled notes on chemical additives like methocellulose, hydrocolloids, ratios, and temperatures, and a bellyful of pectin-glued, vacuum-compressed fruit, among other oddities. I wasn't really sure how much food science was going to measure into my own home cooking—I'd gone along just for fun. But Michael and the rest of the guys were soaking up every word, eager to try out the procedures with new ingredients at home.

At nine o'clock the morning of the barbecue, I arrived at Mark's apartment to start cooking. There was only one oven, and we'd need to somehow bake enough trays of cornbread for three hundred servings. I was completely making up the recipe for the coconut and banana cornbread that morning. Neither of the guys enjoyed baking much, nor claimed to know anything about it. But we all agreed the dish sounded simple enough to wing on the fly. I got started on a small dish that would be my test batch, mashing up one banana and mixing it with a cup of coconut milk and some eggs. The cornbread that came out of the oven, about thirty minutes later, was soft, dense, and sweet, with its note of tropical flavors. It was perfect, I thought. Plus, we planned to top the finished squares of cornbread with a warm peach compote, to compliment the fruitiness. I set myself on re-creating the exact same proportions from my cornbread test batch, baking tray after baking tray.

I was also in charge of the sesame noodle salad. Again, it would be a classic dish with a twist. For a more colorful, crisp salad, I wanted to add shredded red cabbage, cucumbers, and plenty of fresh scallions to the cold noodles in a sesame-based sauce. I'd made cold sesame noodles countless times throughout my life; it was one of the staple backyard barbecue sides in my household when I was growing up. In recent years, I'd noticed the dish was becoming more popular with the American mainstream—I'd read stories about it in newspapers and on websites. I thought that it would be a hit with the young folks at the barbecue, and Darin and Greg had agreed. I filled the largest pot I could find in Mark's kitchen with water and brought it to a boil. I'd never dropped four pounds of spaghetti into a bubbling, cavernous pot before then. It was pretty fun. I began stirring it immediately, to prevent the strands from sticking together, and dumped all the contents into a colander just as soon as the noodles turned al dente. I looked at the counter. There were ten boxes left to cook. Then I needed to make all the sesame sauce, shred all the vegetables, and somehow— somehow—fold it into all those noodles.

I was up to my elbows in noodles, squatting over a large, industrial-sized plastic tub, when Mark came back from an appointment. He'd had to work that day, so he'd done the brunt of his cooking the night before, roasting the pulled pork and simmering the collard greens. He hadn't slept a wink. In one corner of the kitchen, I'd created a Jengalike stack of aluminum trays with fully baked banana-coconut cornbread. I had a system down, filling one greased tray and shoving it into the oven just as soon as one of the trays was ready to take out. I was half machine by then, fueled only by my sample batch of cornbread; nothing could stop me.

Meanwhile, Michael was preparing the brisket, duck, and succotash from his home in Greenpoint. He'd called both of us several times since ten o'clock that morning, checking in on our progress, asking about any extra ingredients we might need. He made a last-minute run to the supermarket, picking up some cans of coconut milk for me. He came by Mark's at around three, plopping boxes of groceries on the crowded floor of Mark's apartment, his eyes darting around the kitchen.

"How are we doing on the cornbread?"

"Under control," I said. I offered a taste of the sample batch.

"What have we still got left?" Michael asked.

"The coleslaw," Mark said. "That can be done last though, so it'll be fresh."

"Better start that now," Michael said.

"Yeah, I know—that's what I'm about to do."

"What else are we missing?"

"The peaches. We've gotta do those peaches," I said, pointing to two bushels of fresh, fuzzy peaches lying on the floor in cardboard boxes.

"Right—the vegetarian entree." Michael snapped his fingers.

"And the compote," Mark added.

"Hey, man—you busy?" Michael asked Nick, who was seated at a table in the living room (aka the Whisk and Ladle cocktail lounge). Nick was putting together a turkey sandwich and shrugged.

"Nah—what can I do?" he replied.

"Once you're finished with lunch, wanna help peel and core all these peaches?" Michael asked him, pointing to a stack of cardboard boxes filled with fruit.

"Sure," Nick said. "I think I can handle that."

"Good." Michael put his hand on Mark's shoulder. "I've got an apartment full of duck grease. Gotta check on the brisket."

"See you in a few hours," Mark said.

Like Zorro, flinging a sack of onions over his shoulder instead of a cape, Michael was off.

Somehow, we all managed to remain focused and stick with our individual tasks until everything was complete. I even relaxed a little, enjoying chatting with Mark and Nick as we worked. But by crunch time, six thirty, we were still stirring an enormous pot of bubbling peaches, trying to cook it down to something saucelike for the compote.

"It's so hot; how are we going to bring it there?" Mark asked.

"I don't think we have enough. Is that the only pot you have left?" I asked. The dented metal pot held about ten or twelve quarts, and I worried whether it was enough for the four hundred servings.

"We'll make it work," Mark said. We were still throwing peaches into the pot after they were peeled and sliced by the ever-helpful Nick.

"I know what; let's add these bananas," I said, pointing to an extra bunch of bananas left over from the cornbread.

"Let's do it," said Mark.

Half an hour later, we piled all the pots, vats, and trays of cornbread into Mark's car. It took two trips with two cars—Mark's and Michael's—to cart all our food to the venue. I was just glad we'd no longer have to carry it upstairs to the rooftop at Studio B. A week before the event was scheduled to take place, the rooftop patio at Studio B was shut down by the health department. Darin and Greg had scrambled to find another space to host the party in, and luckily nailed a nearby Williamsburg bar called Hope Lounge. It boasted a large backyard with a working grill station, just what we would need.

Once at the venue, we arranged all the courses in chafing dishes and platters along a serving table. The only thing that needed to be done now was grilling the peach halves. While the guys got to work on this, I carefully cut each cornbread tray into equal squares. The crowd was beginning to filter into the backyard, and people came over to the grill station, eyeing the offerings. The music started to play. Darin and Greg had created an organized system so people could line up for food. As I was waiting to begin service, I saw an extra bunch of scallions lying around and decided to add them to the sesame noodles. While chopping the bunch with one of Michael's razor-sharp knives, I sliced off the tip of my thumb along with a sliver of the nail. I lurched for paper towels while blood rushed down my wrist.

"Are you okay?" Michael asked, in the midst of slicing brisket. I nodded, as it didn't hurt terribly. But the blood was quickly leaking through the thin towel. I went to the bathroom in the bar's basement and twisted a sturdy paper towel knot around my thumb. But by the time I got back upstairs, it was soaked through, and we'd just begun serving the anxious line of customers. I grabbed another paper towel and stood by the chafing dishes, ready to scoop collards or succotash onto plates. One of the first people who came to my station was Matt.

"What's wrong with your finger? Do you need a Band-Aid?" he asked. I nodded, wincing. The pain wasn't horrible, but it also wouldn't cease. The harder I squeezed on my finger to stop the bleeding, the more piercing it felt. Matt returned a few minutes later with a Band-Aid, some paper towels, and something that looked like it was made of rubber.

"Here; the bar gave me this finger condom. You put it on over the Band-Aid," he explained. I'd never seen or worn a finger condom in my life, but after wearing it for the rest of the night, I can say that it's effective against the spread of blood in the food you're serving up. Over the next dizzying hour, we managed to serve most of the people who'd shown up to the party. The line slowed down afterward, and the three of us chefs, plus Darin, Greg, and a couple of friends of theirs who had been helping to serve, could get a drink and relax. The compliments we'd received on the food had all been positive:

"Insane."

"Ridiculous."

"Freaking delicious."

Greg chomped into his third or fourth slice of brisket, looking to the heavens in thanks. My friend Chrysanthe, a vegetarian, gave a thumbs-up on the grilled peach half, and I snuck an extra one onto her plate. The cornbread dessert had turned out to be a big hit, too, to my relief.

But the best part of the meal was yet to come. A hearty lump of beef tenderloin had been bobbing about in the immersion circulator that Michael brought to the venue and snuck beside the grill. This would be for the staff or "family meal," in restaurant terminology, which we would all enjoy after service. We had all eaten our share of the barbecue food by the time the tenderloin was ready to come out of the bath, but as soon as Michael peeled away the air-suctioned plastic the meat had been wrapped in, a whiff of perfectly seasoned beef and rosemary filled the cooking station. He tossed it onto the hot grill for a quick char. After it had been browned, he sliced the tenderloin into pieces, revealing a juicy, pink, perfectly medium-rare complexion. I could barely put down three bites of that tender steak, though I wanted to eat much more. There was also potato salad Michael had somehow found time to prepare, served alongside it.

"This is the real stuff here," Michael said, waving at the rest of the barbecue food we'd labored over for the past day or two.

Darin, Greg, and their friends eagerly filled up on the family meal. I couldn't decide which food was better—that or the barbecue meal. They were both some of the best foods I'd ever tasted.

"I don't think I can look at food again for a long time," Mark joked.

I shook my head. "I'll never look at cooking the same way again."

I eventually took off my apron and left the grill station to hang out with friends. Everyone was there—Karol, Matt, Maia, Scott. Well, almost everyone. Jordan was still away.

I managed to forget about the cut on my thumb for the rest of the night; the pain had mostly subsided after the finger condom went on, and I didn't have to see the bloody mess that was the tip of my finger and its missing slice of nail for the rest of the night. But blood had welled up inside the rubber sheath, gluing it to my finger. I tried to peel it off my finger when I got home later, but when a new spurt of blood erupted, I quickly put it back on for the night. In the morning, I examined both my hands and found many more cuts, blisters, and burns than I could have imagined. They were with me for the rest of the week, tokens of the great undertaking my friends and I had managed.

At one point during the barbecue, Greg introduced me to his friend Josh. Josh was helping to organize another barbecue later that summer, hosted by *New York* magazine. There would be a cook-off component to the event, and Greg thought I'd be a perfect judge. The next week, I got an e-mail from Josh to confirm my interest in serving as one of the judges of the cook-off. The event was called the Highbrow Barbecue, to be held at a waterfront venue in Manhattan and hosted by former *Top Chef* contestant C. J. Jacobson. This event was clearly not going to be an "underground" party or cook-off. It was also on the pricey side for attendees, at $25 a ticket for an all-you-can-eat barbecue meal prepared by the celebrity chef and a live musical performance by the band the Islands. From lowbrow to highbrow, I thought, shaking my head. Why not?

But before the Highbrow Barbecue came the next Chili Takedown. As promised, I was on the judging committee. Matt Timms and Scott had pulled together a very Brooklyn foodie-based group of judges. There would be Tom Mylan, a butcher for three restaurants in Brooklyn, and Camille Becerra, the chef-owner of the Brooklyn restaurant Paloma and another former *Top Chef* contestant. I had met Tom Mylan a few times before, but I was a little nervous about chatting with Camille. She was a first-time restaurant owner, after all; what would she make of my anti–eating out blog?

It was a rainy, muggy day in Brooklyn when I arrived at the bar where the Takedown was being held. The crowd of eager chili eaters was so large that they couldn't fit inside the venue and spilled out into the crowded backyard patio. What's more, the number of contestants blew away those who had taken part in any previous takedown. Whereas previous competitions had averaged maybe ten contestants, twenty-five amateur chefs had made chili for this one. Long tables with twenty-five homemade chilis lined two walls of the bar's back room. The diversity among these chilis was over-whelming, too—there were some made with pulled pork, some with brisket, some with beer, tequila, and wine. I recognized sev-eral of the contestants from previous cook-offs, but from talking to some of the others, I learned that many were first-timers to the cook-off scene.

That it had become a bona fide "scene" by now was evident. When the other judges and I had finished our powwow and de-cided on a winner, we walked up to the bar's stage. I looked out at the wriggling, clamoring audience below me. Everyone had eaten their fill of the free chili, and they were eager to hear the results. There must have been close to two hundred people packed into that bar, snapping flash photos or weaving their way to get closer to the stage. After introducing himself, Scott handed me the microphone.

"Uhh," I said. "I'm Cathy, and I write a blog called 'Not Eating Out in New York.'"

A cheer erupted from the crowd, probably from a handful of friends. I tried to think of what to say next. In the crowd that night, I'd run into several fellow food bloggers and writers whom I'd become friends with over time, and other acquaintances who were avid home cooks and foodies. I'd also made new friends with readers of my blog who'd come out to compete in the fa-mous chili cook-offs that I wrote about so much. While I still loved the spirit of competing in them, in the past year and a half I'd grown from mere avid participant to promoter of amateur cook-offs.

"I started writing about cooking at home, or cooking some-thing at home and bringing it to events like this," I went on, cor-recting myself quickly. "And now that's what I do pretty much all the time."

Everyone cheered again. I turned to Scott. He nodded at me as if to say, *Well said*. And then I passed the microphone off to Tom on my left.

*   *   *

A few weeks later, I was perched on a rock at the Manhattan waterfront venue Solar One. It was one of the warmest days of the late summer, without a cloud in the sky. Beneath a white, flapping tent at one edge of the yard, C. J. Jacobson and his team were doling out plates of grilled ribs, corn, and other sides as the party's barbecue feast. On the stage, Greg was providing beats as the DJ. Along one end of park, hibachi grills were set up as the seven Highbrow Barbecue cook-off contestants prepared their stations. Among them were two contestants who had won different awards at the Great Hot Dog Cook-Off, the winner of the last Chili Takedown, and Serpico himself, Michael Cirino. I'd just come back from chatting with them and some of my fellow cook-off judges and a few other foodie friends who were looking on.

The cook-off was a little less streamlined than I would have liked. There was a long wait before the chefs were given the cue to begin cooking, so since we were all sort of standing around and waiting, I had returned to my earlier post at the rock, beside Jordan. There wasn't much seating in the outdoor space, so we'd claimed a tall rock facing the deep blue East River.

In the past month, Jordan had surprised her doctors with her progress. She was determined to recover and reclaim her normal life in Brooklyn much faster than their initial predictions, and miraculously, she had succeeded. After the last checkup, she decided it was time to come back home to her one-bedroom apartment, all by herself. She'd need to heave herself up the four flights of stairs to her apartment on crutches, but this was apparently a feat of endurance that she was happy to challenge herself with. I'd offered to let her stay at my place or to stay with her at hers and help out, but she was willful—and optimistic. She'd see how things went. "Takes a lickin', keeps on tickin'"—the engraving on her new iPod—couldn't have been a more fitting statement.

Jordan's crutches were leaning against the side of the rock. I could tell that she was frustrated and exhausted from having to carry her entire weight around by her armpits. She complained of sweating a lot, and of course it didn't help that it was the hottest month of summer, and just sitting down in the sun was causing beads of sweat to pour down her pale forehead. She'd been indoors most of the summer, so the sun was also probably doing a number on Jordan's fair skin and turning her blond hair even lighter. Still, she had been excited to hang out with friends again and to come along to this barbecue. I was speechlessly grateful that she'd hobbled all the way out here to support another one of my crazy food adventures.

Unlike so many of my new friends, Jordan has never been a "foodie." She didn't have a penchant for cooking, and once admitted, laughingly, that she still hadn't turned on the stove in the apartment she'd been living in for six months: "Not even to heat anything up," she'd cracked.

Our friendship was obviously never based around food or cooking together.

As the sun blazed down on our backs and a gust of wind threatened to topple Jordan's crutches from their post, I was humbly reminded of how friendships—and life—did not revolve just around food.

~~~~~~

Corn and Black-Eyed Pea Succotash

This was one of the crowd-favorite sides at the barbecue I co-chefed at Hope Lounge with Mark and Michael. It works great in late summer, when fresh corn is in season, or in the fall, as a Thanksgiving side.   (MAKES 4–6 SIDE SERVINGS)

> 1 pound dry black-eyed peas, soaked overnight
> 4 tablespoons butter
> 1 large or 2 small red onions, roughly chopped
> Salt and pepper to taste
> 1 large sweet red pepper, chopped
> About 2 cups fresh corn kernels
> 1 tablespoon chives, chopped (optional)

Drain the peas and return to a pot with enough water to cover about 2 inches above the top. Bring to a boil and reduce to a simmer. Cover and cook about 40 minutes, or until beans are tender and liquid has almost all reduced to the surface level of the beans (add more water if liquid drops below). Drain.

Melt 2 tablespoons of the butter in a large saucepan over medium-high heat. Add the black-eyed peas and cook, stirring, until just beginning to brown slightly on their surfaces, about 2 minutes. Transfer peas to a bowl and return pan to the heat. Reduce to medium-low and add the onions and a few pinches of salt. Cook, stirring occasionally, until translucent and slightly caramelized, 4–5 minutes. Add the bell pepper and cook another minute or two, stirring occasionally. Toss in the corn and another 2 tablespoons of the butter. Cook, stirring occasionally, until tender, about 3–4 minutes. Return the peas to the pan. Toss with salt and pepper to taste. Add chives with the last toss and serve.

Grilled Peaches with Spiced Goat Cheese and Caramelized Shallots

This was the vegetarian option at the same barbecue, which all the vegetarians in attendance seemed to love. I've given this recipe a couple of extra touches, like the lemon zest, but any way you spice the goat cheese, it's really a hands-down crowd pleaser.

(MAKES 8 GRILLED PEACH HALVES)

2 tablespoons butter
15–20 shallots, thinly sliced
8 ounces goat cheese
¼ teaspoon cumin
¼ teaspoon coriander
1 teaspoon finely grated lemon zest
Oil for the grill
4 ripe peaches, halved and cored

Heat a sauté pan with the butter over low heat. Add the shallots and cook over very low heat, stirring occasionally, 15–20 minutes, until caramelized. Reduce heat if edges are beginning to crisp, or add more butter if pan becomes dry. Remove from heat and let cool. In a mixing bowl, whisk the goat cheese with the cumin, coriander, and lemon zest.

Preheat a grill over a high flame. (Alternately, heat a cast-iron griddle with grill marks.) Add vegetable oil to the grill to prevent sticking. Place peaches cut side down on the grill and cook about 5–8 minutes, or until just charred and lightly softened. Transfer to a platter. Stuff the middle of each peach half with a scoop of the goat cheese and top with a pinch of the caramelized shallots.

CHAPTER 14

The End of an Era

"Cath," my mother squawked through the telephone receiver. "I'm coming into the city today. Going to meet with Jo-Jo for lunch, maybe see a movie."

"Okay," I said. I was sitting at my desk at work, tweaking the last sentence of copy that I'd just written for a flatware collection. I hit SAVE.

"I'm meeting him at twelve thirty outside Macy," she said, referring to Macy's Herald Square store, just a few blocks south of my office building. "Then we're going to that Korea street for lunch. You know."

I did know. Koreatown, or K-town, as it was often called, was a stretch of Korean restaurants, clothing shops, hair salons, karaoke clubs, and other businesses that took up a block of Thirty-second Street. In my eating-out days in New York City, I loved going to restaurants there for a bowl of spicy noodle soup, sizzling Korean barbecue, and all those little trays of cold appetizers that came to your table as soon as you were seated.

"That's nice," I said.

"You wanna come? Just for the lunch?" my mom asked.

"What? No," I retorted. What was she thinking? I thought. Only during visits to New Jersey, across state lines, did I allow myself to go to restaurants with my family. Okay, so there were a small handful of occurrences when I'd broken my streak and eaten in a New York restaurant, notably when I was hired at my new job and when I left my old job, and my current and former bosses took me out for lunches. But aside from the night of the drunken pizza slice, these exceptions were all work related, which was in accordance with the guidelines I'd set forth at the beginning of the mission. Going to K-town that day would be a clear violation of the Law. Besides, I had brought my lunch with me that day, some shell pasta with sautéed zucchini, garlic, parsley, and chives that was sitting in a container in the communal office refrigerator.

"Well. I don't know," my mom said. "Maybe you can take a break. You can't?"

"No, no breaks. What? Of course not," I said.

"Oh. Okay," she said glumly.

"What movie are you seeing?" I changed the subject.

"Well, just think about it. I'm meeting him at twelve thirty. Just come along," she said.

"But I already brought my lunch—," I began to say, right before my mom got another call and quickly got off the line.

Shaking my head, I turned back to my product copy.

It was August. The next month, I would hit the two-year anniversary of my blog and of not eating out. I had no idea how to celebrate this milestone. Many of my friends had been asking me lately if I would keep on not eating out, like I had proudly said a year before. I never liked the thought of scrapping my strict diet on an exact date, though. I thought it might end more gradually somehow, or else spontaneously, with an earth-shattering circumstance, or an epiphany. I guess I just didn't want to know in advance or think about how I would end it.

But two years was a long time. Long enough that I had adapted to the daily demands of not eating out without thinking of them as extra work, or unusual in any way. Hey, people didn't eat out many centuries ago, and even though my days were busy, for a New Yorker at least, when push came to shove, I'd become pretty agile at feeding myself without the help of restaurant workers. Today, for instance, I'd brought an oatmeal bar that I'd made two days earlier, with some dried cherries that I'd bought for a salad a few weeks back. Along with the zucchini pasta for lunch, I'd provided myself with a roasted beet, wrapped in foil, for afternoon snack cravings I knew I would have. Then, as an extra guard, I'd brought a couple of unpeeled carrots, fresh from the Greenmarket. The way I was living now, making dinners for myself at home on most nights, eating the leftovers for lunch, and cobbling together snacks from this and that in my fridge, was so routine that I knew I could keep at it indefinitely. It truly could go on forever.

My mom of course knew better than to suggest lunch in a restaurant in the city, something that I would so routinely object to. Maybe you can take a break, she had said. As I continued to work throughout the morning, my mind was spinning with a dizzying storm of rationales for either going to meet my mom and uncle for lunch or not. I could . . . meet up with them at the restaurant, sit and talk, but not eat? I had done this before with friends, and it was not fun. I could bring my lunch out to a park and suggest they get takeout and sit at an outdoor table with me instead? Too much trouble for my relatives, I concluded. Plus, they would hate being outside on a hot day like this. Or I could, as usual, just not meet them at all.

I sighed loudly. I remembered the first day I began to work at my current job, my two bosses had taken me out to lunch. It was something they did for all new employees, an icebreaker, a kind gesture, and I appreciated the offer. I couldn't say no. The lunch was hardly comfortable, though. We'd gone to an Italian restaurant around the block, a popular business lunch spot, it seemed. I had a salad with a huge mound of greasy, undercooked, and underseasoned salmon on it, and I'd pecked hopelessly at the leaves of baby spinach underneath it while trying to make simple conversation. That had been my last midtown Manhattan restaurant experience, and it didn't make me hungry for more. Why, then, was I so naggingly tempted to meet up with Mom and Jo-Jo for lunch today? It struck me then as somewhat unfair; I had eaten out with my bosses but wouldn't make an exception for my mother and uncle?

A couple of hours later, I stood by the rotating door of Macy's. It was the middle of the week, late summer, not exactly any particular season for shopping, but the entrance to the store was flooded with traffic as usual. The dollar had been in decline all year long, and in recent months I'd heard that hordes of Western European tourists were coming to New York, traveling in flocks through Times Square, or shopping in midtown to take advantage of the weak dollar. As I stood by Macy's, it sounded like everyone around me was speaking with a British accent.

"Hi, Cath!" my mother called from a few paces away on the street corner. Beside her, Jo-Jo was waving his arms like slow wind-shield wipers. I squeezed past a small crowd to meet them.

"Okay, let's eat," my mother said, turning to Jo-Jo. "Which place should we go to?"

"Any. It doesn't matter," he said. We walked two blocks down to Thirty-second Street, turning at the start of K-town. We chitchatted along the way, my mom asking her usual questions about pieces of my wardrobe that she had never seen before ("When did you get that?"), as if I was supposed to tell her every time I bought some clothing. The topic of why I had spontaneously decided to join them for lunch was oddly, or perhaps purposely, not raised.

We stopped at the door of one of the first restaurants we passed. My mom took a look at the menu on the window.

"This is the good one, I think," she said.

"Okay," Jo-Jo agreed.

We filed into the narrow lobby. It was the middle of lunch ser-vice, and the tables were filled with customers. Luckily, we were quickly seated at a table just as a party was leaving. A waiter brought a metal teapot to our table as soon as we sat down, and another waiter came by moments later with a half dozen trays of cold appetizers.

"Okay . . . great," my mother said, taking in the sights.

The kimchee was closest to me. Now, this was something I hadn't eaten in quite some time. Nor had I thought to try my hand at making it myself. I'd learned how to make several types of pickles, tinkering around with cauliflower and Brussels sprouts at different times, and unusual spice combinations for the brines. But the fermented and chili-soaked cabbage that was so essential to Korean cuisine had evaded my DIY home-cooking attempts and my taste buds for the past two years. I was ready to dig in. Only, I had no chopsticks. In all their speediness to serve us the appetizers, our waiters had forgotten to place utensils at our table.

My mother signaled to a waitress, who nodded and came to our table. She said something indecipherable in Korean.

"Uh . . . don't speak Korean," my mother said.

"Oh, sorry," the waitress responded in English. We asked her for chopsticks and she nodded and left.

"I guess we look Korean," Jo-Jo said, grinning. My mom shrugged. In the past, I'd seen my mom confused for Japanese at restaurants with Japanese-speaking staff. More commonly, at Chinese restaurants she would have to revert to English when a waiter began speaking Cantonese, and not her native Mandarin. This never happened to me, since my Mandarin is elementary at best and my appearance more Caucasian than anything else. But just from years of being around my mother and uncle, I knew about the advantages of the native-language exchange with restaurant workers. For instance, at Chinese restaurants my parents frequently had dishes that were not on the menu, or they might receive more authentic menus printed only in Chinese. Usually, there was some dialogue with the waiter about what was best to order, or to clarify what was available. Sometimes dishes were specially made at my parents' request. This was the way my parents always ordered at Chinese restaurants—with a back-and-forth exchange and at least one off-the-menu course. But alas, it was not to be for this Korean lunch.

The waitress returned shortly afterward with the chopsticks. I appreciated the fact that they were reusable plastic chopsticks, unlike the wrapped, wooden disposable types that were served at so many restaurants. Really, what was the point in using these at a sit-down restaurant, where everything else on the table was washed and reused? The only reason I could think of was laziness.

"What is this?" my mom asked nonchalantly, poking her chopsticks at some pickled turnips. They crunched loudly as she bit into one, and nodded to indicate that whatever it was, it was good. Jo-Jo went for some seaweed first. I got my satisfying taste of kimchee—a little crunchy, a little wilted, and completely saturated in a spicy, acrid brine. We nibbled through the rest of the offerings. Our favorite was the salty preserved whitefish, with tiny bones that one needed to be wary of. Jo-Jo left my mom and me to decide what to order for lunch. First, a seafood pancake was in order. Korean pancakes are an appetizer that no one can resist ordering again and again. Crispy, savory, and often the size of a dinner plate, the pancakes are grilled in a pan with big strips of vegetables and meat in the batter. My mom chose a spicy tofu and seafood casserole next, and clear mung bean noodles stir-fried with beef and vegetables.

"We have too much food. As usual," Jo-Jo said.

"It's okay," my mom said. I remained silent, salivating at the thought of eating everything we had just ordered. I'd skipped breakfast that day, so my stomach was gurgling. I refilled my cup of tea for the third time since sitting down a few minutes before, even though it was sweltering hot outside. The restaurant's air-conditioning didn't seem to be keeping up, and the place was filled to the brim with customers.

"So warm," Jo-Jo said, fanning himself with a folded napkin.

Our pancakes came to the table first. They were as hot as the smoking griddle they must have just been flipped from. Chopped tentacles of tender octopus and scallions studded each one in about equal parts to the batter. We dipped our slices into a thin soy-and-vinegar-based sauce.

"So this movie, Jo-Jo says is supposed to be very good," my mom said in between bites.

"What is it?" I asked.

"This English movie, from a novel by this English woman writer," she said.

"Oh, Jane Austen?"

"No, not that one. Evelyn something," she said.

"Wor," my uncle filled in.

"Oh, Evelyn Waugh. That's a man, actually," I said.

"No. Ev-el-yn," my mother said, sounding out the syllables.

"Yeah, it used to be a man's name, too," I said.

"Evelyn is a man?" my mother asked, incredulous.

"Can be." I shrugged.

"That's weird," she proclaimed. My uncle heaved with laughter behind his napkin.

The rest of our food came shortly after the pancakes. We were each given a bowl of short-grain rice, cooked with small dark-purple pebbles of black beans throughout. I helped myself to the soupy tofu casserole first. There was always something different to be found in a ladle of its red, chili-based broth. A clam or whole shrimp came up with every other scoop. I spooned a knife-scored piece of squid into my mother's rice bowl since I knew it was her favorite. I picked up a piece of shrimp and a hearty wedge of tofu. The tofu was the best part of the meal—it was silky smooth but held its shape. It also held up its mild, nutty flavor against the soaked-in chili broth.

"We did pick the right one," my mom said, pointing to the casserole. "This is so good." Jo-Jo nodded, scooping up some more tofu. So far, everything I'd eaten was completely unlike anything I'd had in the last two years. Tofu stew—now, that was an idea I could find time to play around with, I thought. But it would never taste as good as this plentiful seafood-studded version. That is, unless I went through the laborious task of collecting all these various small amounts of seafood to add to it myself. No, this dish, and especially its broth, was made with an abundance of ingredients, like fish heads and other scraps found in the restaurant kitchen. I didn't have any seafood hanging around that I'd need to do that with very often, like a restaurant's kitchen might.

The glass noodle stir-fry was less impressive than the other dishes, but I still ate more than my share of it. It came to our table on a cast-iron plate, its gingery brown sauce bubbling at the edges. I was still pecking away, far past being full. With all the food still available in front of me, it was impossible to resist.

"Aren't you afraid somebody's going to see you eating here?" my uncle joked. He stifled a snort of laughter.

Actually, I had been a little afraid of this possibility. Had we been eating at another, more popular restaurant, I might have been even more fearful. What if a fellow food blogger, wielding a camera, happened to come to this restaurant and see me? I had reached the stage where strangers began to recognize me and come up to me to ask if I was that not-eating-out girl. What if I ended up on *Gawker* the next day, with the headline NOT EATING OUT: A TOTAL HOAX!

But I pushed the ridiculous thoughts aside. I definitely wasn't that newsworthy. And I was pretty convinced we'd be concealed from the mainstream media juggernaut tucked inside the nothing-special, nothing-new Koreatown restaurant. What was bothering me, though, was a constant feeling of guilt. It seemed to multiply with every bite I took, adding another layer of confusion to the dilemma about my experiment that was brewing inside.

Why was it okay to host elaborate supper-club dinners in someone's home where patrons paid a price comparable to the cost of a restaurant meal? Why was it okay that we nonprofessional chefs made the food for that Hope Lounge barbecue, if it was going to be served at a commercial bar where customers paid $5 a plate? Or what about the hot-dog cook-off benefit where attendees had to pay a donation for admission? What if a professional chef were cooking for an event that also had an amateur-cooking element, like the Highbrow Barbecue where I served as a judge? Would his or her food count as not eating out then?

I knew when I began the blog that not eating out was never going to be a cut-and-dried equation. From the start, there had been a number of moments for pause: If a fresh-baked loaf of bread from a bakery is considered not eating out, then are baked goods from coffee-and-bagel carts, too? What about a handful of bar snacks from your friend's plate that he or she didn't want to finish? There was also the dilemma of the particular bar in Brooklyn that served a free individual-sized pizza with every pint of beer one purchased.

Then, how could I be so staunchly supportive of specialty food-related businesses, like small artisanal food makers, or the family-owned stores that sponsored my risotto cook-off, but not a friendly, independent restaurant that shared many of the same community-driven values? What if a friend who happened to be a professional chef cooked a meal for me? What if a friend happened to open a restaurant in New York? By now, I had a small handful of good friends who worked in the restaurant industry in some capacity. Some were people who shared a lot of the same ideals I did about food, particularly seasonal, local food, and wanted to push the movement further into restaurant kitchens. Would I not support them? To put my strict not-eating-out diet into perspective, it was beginning to seem a petty tirade compared to these more relevant, pressing, food-related issues.

All these thoughts clouded my mind as I ate my Korean restaurant lunch, reluctantly enjoying every bite. I slurped up the last drop of seafood soup from the bowl.

"Are you dating anyone now?" my mom asked.

"No," I said. It was half true. Over the summer, I'd had a spotty and mostly short-lived string of relationships. But by the end of August, things had pretty much fizzled out by all accounts. I was in the habit of biking down to Brooklyn's Brighton Beach by myself on free afternoons and was loving the peace and solitude. Jo-Jo commented on how dark my skin had gotten from the sun.

Earlier that month, I had also switched to freelancing for the same company where I worked, instead of being a full-time employee. This meant that I had a flexible schedule—I worked usually three days a week instead of five. Taking long bike rides and walks in the park, reading and sunning in the afternoons, and swimming or just lying in the sand had become my favorite things to do, besides spending a whole day on a particular cooking project, or participating in cooking events. Between these solo activities and running errands around Brooklyn, like going to the library, grocery store, or Laundromat when the crowds were mostly in their offices, the end of the summer had become a very tranquil time for me. It's said that sometimes you need to get out of a crowded situation to hear yourself. I heard myself thinking a lot around this time.

"Boys don't know what to do with you," my mom said. "I told you so."

I shrugged. But I detected a hint of pride in her voice, instead of sympathy.

We lingered for a while after the plates had been cleared from our table. The cluster of the business lunch-hour crowd had wound down a bit, and tables were beginning to empty. I had to get back to my office, though, so I said good-bye to my mom and uncle and headed off. My mom, as usual, took care of the check.

I slipped quietly back to my cubicle after the long lunch break. I nudged my mouse across the pad to light up the screen. A large, retouched photo of another flatware collection appeared, reminding me of the words I had been dredging up to describe it an hour before.

Being with Jo-Jo that afternoon reminded me of something he'd said a few months before. It was on Easter, and we'd both gone to my parents' house in New Jersey for a home-cooked feast of rack of lamb. Jo-Jo and I rode the train back to the city together afterward. It was Sunday, and we both had to get up for work the next day. We'd talked about my blog and eating experiment for a while, sitting across from each other on the vinyl seats. It was always nice to have some one-on-one time with my uncle.

My uncle and I actually have a long history of being on trains together, and having alone time. When I was little, my uncle loved to take me to museums and galleries in New York. We'd roam around the Metropolitan Museum of Art or Soho, and along the way he'd tell me stories about my parents from before I was born, or from his and my mother's childhoods in Taiwan. Once I got a little bit older, he'd take me shopping in the East Village. There we'd rummage through secondhand boutiques, my uncle picking choice finds for me to try on, and taking hats off the racks and mannequins to place on my head. Jo-Jo was a men's clothing designer. So when I developed a fondness for vintage clothing and ramshackle costume jewelry as a teenager, he was the only one in my family who actually shared some interest in it with me.

Every now and then, my uncle would offer some sort of prophesying wisdom that would really stick with me and make me think. One Thanksgiving or Christmas, when I was in college studying creative writing, we were sitting on the couch talking when he told me that some people are only truly creative for a certain period of their lives. Some people just lose their creativity after this spell. Inspiration is fleeting, or even fickle, is what I took from that conversation. Since then, I've always tried to seize the moment whenever creativity struck. It's what happened when I became so obsessive about cooking, living in that apartment with Erin. So I started a food blog. I also took away the sense that only really meaningful work springs from honest, unstoppable creativity. In other words, only write something, only do something, only create something, if you're really passionate about it. Don't force something out or beat a dead horse.

My uncle himself had experienced periods of drought in his passion for design. He'd gone on a hiatus from his career once, when I was young, and retreated to a Buddhist camp in California for a few months. He took off to Taiwan and China a number of years later, and rekindled his interest in photography, taking remarkable photos of classical Chinese subjects. Most recently, he'd dropped everything in his life to take care of my ailing grandfather for almost one year. Over lunch in Koreatown, my mother kept voicing her concern over when Jo-Jo would return to work now that Gong-Gong was gone. His previous employer had welcomed his return initially, but they now found themselves with no position to offer him. Jo-Jo didn't seem very concerned about this. He'd find something, he assured her. He might not return to fashion at all, he'd said. Jo-Jo always had something new up his sleeve he wanted to explore.

In any case, that Easter, when Jo-Jo and I were riding back from

New Jersey, he had asked me whether it was time for me to move on. We had just eaten a meal of rack of lamb, which I had meticulously roasted with fresh rosemary and served with a red-wine reduction sauce.

"How long are you going to continue this?" he asked, referring to "Not Eating Out in New York"—the blog, the strict diet, or both. I wasn't sure. This question had been put to me so frequently in the past year or so by others that it almost reverberated in my ears without having an impact.

I shrugged. Jo-Jo nodded slowly, keeping his gaze leveled at my eyes as if searching for clues.

"How do you know when it will be time?" he asked.

I was tempted to give another shrug, as I would have done if he were anyone else. But I thought for a moment.

"I think I will know. I just don't think it's done yet; there's more stuff I want to do," I'd told him. "I don't think it's run its course yet."

"Okay . . . okay," he said. He kept staring for a long while, and I thought he was about to say something the whole time, and he probably thought the same of me.

He suddenly broke the silence. "But you have to explore, right? Don't you want to try new food and explore it? You're going like this, holding in." Jo-Jo hugged his arms around his shoulders and folded his torso into a ball.

I couldn't stay this way forever, I thought. In no way would that be comfortable. Not eating out in New York . . . it was a lot of fun, and a good exercise for me personally in saving money and learning how to make a lot of different foods. But I sensed I was beginning to grow out of its shoes.

The same flatware image glared from the monitor in my cubicle. I opened up a Word document and started to take notes on its features. Now, it may sound nuts to some, but I had a real fondness for my work, for creating memorable sentences about fine dinnerware that would drive a reader to hit the button and purchase what was on the screen. I also had a huge passion for cooking and for writing about it. Yet as I sat there at my computer screen, staring at the photo, I just wanted to crumple over on my desk and disappear. It wasn't because I couldn't force myself to write something pretty about the flatware set—no, I quickly straightened and let my hands amble across the keyboard, typing up some prose about their luminous stainless steel and stamped pattern. I could do it in my sleep.

Perhaps that was just it: I could do it in my sleep. This was the way I operated in my day-to-day eating routine, too. Sure, there were bursts of creativity, when cooking with new ingredients, or creating an elaborate original recipe for a pie cook-off, perhaps. But for the daily grind, eating in had become something I had once so despised about food—monotonous, ritual, with little thought or care. Jo-Jo had instilled in me a sense that if I was going to do anything, it should be with genuine, uncontrollable verve. I was running out of this type of steam for the concept of not eating out, I began to sense. And I had been genuinely, uncontrollably compelled to eat at the Korean restaurant with my mom and uncle that day.

That week, I did a lot of thinking about the future of my blog and of my eating habits. On the one hand, my readership had been steadily increasing all summer. How would it look to both new readers as well as loyal followers if I were to announce I was *not* not eating out anymore? Above all, this was the most difficult question in my head. My blog meant everything to me by then—it had turned into my "real" career, as opposed to my copywriting day job. The last thing on earth I wanted to do was to stop writing it. On the other hand, if I was going to continue writing about food, I'd have to keep learning new things all the time. And that might mean opening some new doors. I smiled, remembering the tucked-up pose my uncle had made on the train that night, illustrating my closed-off approach to certain foods. As mentioned, I always dreamed that my blog might end abruptly, as if by some divine intervention. It occurred to me: Jo-Jo *is* my divine spirit.

Several months later, after I had begun eating in restaurants again, I would have dinner with my mom and uncle in Chinatown one night. Over our meal, I suddenly thought to ask them a question that for some reason I had never thought of before.

"Did you guys eat in restaurants growing up?"

My mom and uncle looked at each other. "Yes," my mom said, nonchalantly. "Only on the weekends, usually. We would go for dumplings."

"With Gong-Gong?" I asked.

"Yes," my mom said. "Especially on days when he got paid. He would want to spend the money by going out with us to eat." The whole family would pile into a rickshaw, my mom and uncle went on to explain. They had a few favorite dumpling places, which required the ride.

"Always it was dumplings, for some reason," my mom said, turning to Jo-Jo, who nodded in agreement.

"See, dumplings are northerners' food," my mom said, referring to people from northern China. "We're southerners, so we don't eat many dumplings at home. So it's something special."

"I see," I said.

I decided that I liked that way of treating a restaurant meal: as something special. A special occasion, or a special dish you couldn't easily make at home. Something to savor, a rare treat. Not the normal, de facto eating routine. I had a feeling that many New Yorkers had it the other way around—cooking at home was the special occasion.

On one of the first weekend nights in September, just before my blog and eating adventure would turn two years old, I told Jordan and Dan over beers about my decision to stop not eating out. Oddly enough, we were at an outdoor beer garden in Brooklyn again, though not the same one where I'd sat two summers ago with Erin and her friend Sergio. This place had recently opened in Crown Heights and quickly became one of my favorite local watering holes. We sat at a small square table on a blacktop patio. It was nighttime, and there was a votive candle on the table that made the last few sips in my pint glass glow amber. Jordan had her leg propped up on a spare chair next to mine. Her crutches were resting against the table. Since the accident, she and Dan had become a steady couple, and I couldn't have been happier for them.

"Guys," I said, "I think I'm going to stop not eating out."

Jordan's eyes widened. "Really?" she said.

"Are you going to keep writing the blog?" Dan asked.

"Yup," I said, nodding. "It'll still focus on recipes, home cooking, cook-offs, and whatever. But I just won't be not eating out all the time."

"Wow," Dan said. "What made you decide on that?"

"I don't know," I said. "I guess a lot of little things."

Jordan looked thoughtful for a moment. "You've been doing it for such a long time," she said. "I'll bet half the people who read your blog don't even realize that it's this strict diet thing anyway."

I agreed. Many people, I'd come to learn from their comments and e-mails, simply read my site for the recipes and "food porn." But still others were actively engaged in my unconventional fast. Those were the people whom I still felt nauseatingly nervous about making this announcement to.

"I think that's a smart decision," Jordan said after I explained a little bit about the doubts I'd been mulling over lately. "I think it's a good time for you to do this," she said.

"So . . . what are you going to do for your first restaurant meal?" Dan asked.

I grinned widely. During my decision making over the last week, I'd hatched another plan. That, I couldn't wait to tell them and the rest of my friends about.

"Oh—me first!" Karol cried the next day when I told her I was going to need some restaurant dates.

"Oh, my God, there are so many places you have to go to," Matt said, and immediately began creating a short list of the places I'd have to hit.

It was simple. For my first straight week of not eating out in September, I'd do the reverse of what I'd been doing the past two years: I would eat out for every single meal, every snack, every day. It would be "opposite week."

~~~~~~

Fresh Corn and Zucchini Scallion Pancakes

This is another East-meets-West hybrid of Korean-style scallion pancakes with fresh summer corn and zucchini. They're dipped in a lightly sweetened soy and vinegar sauce, and once you've tasted them, you may never want to eat corn without soy sauce again.

(MAKES 3–4 SERVINGS)

1 cup all-purpose flour
1 egg
1¼ cups carbonated water (seltzer)
½ teaspoon salt
Dash of white pepper
4 large scallions, thinly sliced
½ cup fresh corn kernels
½ cup grated zucchini
3–4 tablespoons vegetable oil
1 tablespoon soy sauce
1 teaspoon honey
2 teaspoons rice or white vinegar
1 tablespoon water

Sift the flour into a large bowl. Whisk in the egg and seltzer until there are no lumps. Add the salt, pepper, and the vegetables and stir.

Heat a large pan with enough oil to fully coat the bottom over medium-high heat. Ladle a scoop of the batter on the pan at a time, working in batches (probably of two). Check underneath the pancake after a couple of minutes, and flip before the pancake batter on the top begins to cook (it should still be liquid by the time you flip—just like cooking regular pancakes). Cook another couple of minutes on the other side. Remove from pan, add more oil to coat, and repeat with the rest of the batter.

Whisk the soy sauce, honey, vinegar, and water in a small bowl. Serve as a dipping sauce.

~~~~~~

Stir-Fried Noodles with Cabbage and Shiitake Mushrooms

This is the kind of dish I'd make repeatedly, and often make ahead for lunches. I usually give it a spicy kick by adding plenty of chili garlic sauce (bright red in color, found in most Asian groceries), but this can be left out if desired.

(MAKES 3–4 SERVINGS)

½ pound dried Asian wheat noodles
2 tablespoons vegetable oil
3 eggs
About 2 cups shredded cabbage
1 cup fresh bean sprouts (optional)
1 cup sliced fresh shiitake mushrooms
About 2 teaspoons soy sauce
1–2 teaspoons chili garlic sauce
Dash white pepper
2 scallions, thinly sliced

Bring a medium saucepan of water to a boil. Cook noodles according to package instructions and drain.

In a large nonstick pan, heat 1 tablespoon of the oil. Crack eggs into a bowl and scramble lightly. Once oil is hot, add eggs and scramble until cooked. Remove and set aside in a separate bowl.

Heat the other tablespoon of oil and cook the cabbage, stirring, for about 2 minutes. Add the bean sprouts and shiitake mushrooms and cook another 2 minutes. Season mixture with a few sprinkles of the soy sauce, chili garlic sauce, and a pinch of white pepper. Add the noodles and the scrambled egg to the pan and toss. Add more soy sauce and chili garlic sauce to taste. Add a little more oil to the bottom of the pan if anything is beginning to brown. Finally, add the scallions and toss once more before serving.

CHAPTER 15

The Opposite-Week Experiment

PART I

"NORMAL WEEK"

I checked the last sentence one more time and squeezed my eyes shut as I clicked PUBLISH. It was my twenty-fourth "Reason for Not Eating Out" blog post. It was September, roughly two years since I'd posted my first reason of the month for not eating out. This time, I announced not only that it was the two-year anniversary of the blog, but also my plans to bring the not-eating-out experiment to a close.

I reached for my glass of water and gulped it down. It was past one o'clock in the morning, according to the numbers at the bottom right-hand corner of my computer screen, pretty typical for the time of night I tended to hit the PUBLISH button on my blog.

I went to the bathroom and began to brush my teeth. I had to get up for work the next morning, as usual. I would sit down at my desk, open up my e-mail account, and sift through the early comments, if there were any yet, on my latest post. Tomorrow would be just like any other day, I told myself, even though I had posted the most unthinkable, abnormal news I could think of in the past two years. Or so it seemed to me.

To my relief, when comments started flowing in the next day from readers, they were all congratulatory and positive. Comments continued to trickle in through the day, and no hard feelings about my decision were expressed. I was immensely grateful. The uneasiness that I'd tossed and turned about all night long was quickly draining off. Readers even asked about where I was planning to eat out first, as I had mentioned I was doing "opposite week" sometime this month to end my streak.

There were many different angles I could give to my week of only eating out. I pondered over how to best set up the week's meals. Should I try to score tables at the latest, greatest hot spots in the city like a true restaurant zealot? A few of my friends suggested this, a whirlwind tour of the city's most awesome eating-out delights. Or should I play it more by ear? In the end, I decided to combine a couple of carefully chosen restaurant outings with an eating-out regime that seemed typical for the young professional. This would be more or less the way I used to eat two years ago, and the way many of my peers still did. This might include breakfast sandwiches from the deli, Thai takeout weeknight dinners, and a couple of meals at hot new restaurants with friends. I had no set goals or expectations for opposite week beyond these. I figured I'd just enjoy it and see what happened.

I looked at my calendar and chose a week that didn't have too much going on: There were two back-to-back weekends where I was cooking dinners with A Razor, A Shiny Knife. I decided to begin my opposite week the Sunday following the second one. The only caveat was that the following Saturday, I was supposed to compete in a special, small-scale Chili Takedown being held as part of an annual chili pepper festival at the Brooklyn Botanic Garden. It would be the last day of my supposed "opposite week," and it would require me to cook, since I had already promised Matt Timms that I would participate. We would also be celebrating Jordan's birthday later on that Saturday night, and she planned to throw the party in her apartment and serve homemade hors d'oeuvres. These events were both not-eating-out adventures in my book. I sighed and settled on that week anyway (the following ones had cooking events, too). It had become more difficult for me to avoid cooking than to avoid eating in restaurants by now.

"Normal week" officially began on a Sunday in mid-September. After eating a leisurely oatmeal breakfast, I arrived at Michael's apartment in Greenpoint, Brooklyn, to start prep for the supper-club dinner we were hosting that night. Daniel and Gene, two other cooks who collaborated with the group, were there already. Previous all-afternoon-and-evening supper-club preparations had taught me how easy it is to forget to eat real meals while we were busy cooking. So I came armed with six chocolate-chip muffins that I'd pulled out of the oven that morning, to share.

"What's that you've got in the pan?" I asked Gene. It was chicken livers, he explained, for the pâté. I hadn't seen mention of pâté on the menu for the night when I'd checked it. The pâté, he explained, would eventually be spread on top of the braised short ribs and torched individually to create a brûlée effect.

"Do you like pâté?" Gene asked.

"Yeah, I love it," I said.

"Would you want to take over with it? I'm not really a huge fan," he said.

"Sure," I said. I'd made pâté from chicken liver before, so I had a pretty good idea of what needed to be done. Using Michael's food processor, I slowly ground the simmered livers and onions with their reduced wine sauce with some butter, cream, and fresh thyme.

The rest of the afternoon's preparations went fairly smoothly. But when the diners began to stream in at around six or seven o'clock, the kitchen was in full swing and utterly packed. There were a lot of things that needed to be cooked just before serving. We'd planned to make a dessert and had nearly forgotten about it in the midst of preparing the other courses. We had our guests join in and help pipe the ladyfinger batter into neat ovals on a cookie sheet. I found myself stationed at the deep fryer for a while, carefully frying up batches of chickpeas and shaking them in a bowl with cumin, salt, pepper, and a squeeze of lemon once they were cooked. I was sweating in the late-summer, cramped-kitchen heat, and collecting tiny splatters of hot fryer oil as I worked. A guest came up to me and offered to help. I demonstrated a batch for him, showing him how to slowly lower the basket of chickpeas into the oil and lift it out when they were done. A little later I'd be dipping prawns into a black-squid-ink-dyed batter and carefully dropping them into that fryer, too. It was tricky work, since we'd de-headed the prawns to extract the flavorful "juice" from them for another course, a seafood étouffée, and the prawn heads had to be fitted back together with their bodies and carefully dipped into the batter, then lowered into the deep fryer.

I took a brief rest in the backyard before dinner was served. I put my beer to my forehead. For some reason, every time I cooked at these dinners it ended up being one of the hottest nights of the summer.

The next morning, I slept in. I'd biked home late the night before in the heat, on a full belly, and was completely exhausted by the time I got home. I was glad to have the day off from the office. I usually worked three days a week, and this week I was off Monday and Tuesday. I put a pot of rolled oats on the stove and stepped into the shower while it simmered over a low flame. After an oatmeal breakfast and writing a blog entry, I packed a towel, some fruit, and a thawed Jamaican veggie patty that I'd made a few weeks before and headed down to the beach.

Tuesday was another warm, sunny day. But I had a cooking project to take care of. I'd been invited to a "cupcake meet-up" happy hour hosted by the writers of the food blog "Cupcakes Take the Cake." Earlier that week, I'd made a spur-of-the-moment batch of homemade cookies as a midnight snack. Spooning up the remaining slicks of dough from the mixing bowl while they baked, I'd wondered whether raw cookie dough wouldn't make a great alternative to cake frosting. I wanted to recapture this binge and make a batch of cupcakes to bring to the event with chocolate-chip cookie dough on top, and no frosting. I'd never seen it done before, but how hard could it be? That afternoon, I beat together a basic vanilla cake batter and filled lined muffin tins with it. While they baked, I made the same chocolate-chip cookie dough I'd made a few nights before, using chunks of dark chocolate from a bar instead of chips. Once the cakes were baked and cooled, I took a spatula and tried smearing some cookie dough on top. The cake crumbled. That wouldn't work; the dough was much stiffer than frosting. I took a small scoop of cookie dough and formed it into a ball with my hands. I smushed it into a round disc about the size of a chocolate-chip cookie and pressed it on top of the cupcake. Perfect! I carefully packed my finished cupcakes away in a container and stored them in the fridge for the next night.

I'd signed up for a pig butchering class at the Brooklyn Kitchen that Tuesday night. The popular classes were taught by Tom Mylan, the local butcher and one of the judges from the last Chili Takedown. His butchering classes had become a big hit among curious foodies in Brooklyn, eager to zero in on what was for most a previously unexplored side of cooking: butchering. They tended to sell out fast, and I had grabbed the last seat at this class.

I arrived at the Brooklyn Kitchen a few minutes late for class. Tom was talking about the heritage Berkshire pig breed to a group of about twelve pupils standing before a large side of the specimen. The next two hours of class were filled with fascinating facts. Aside from learning about the parts of the pig that constituted certain cuts, like the chop or the tenderloin, I was able to grasp how far the art of butchering had dwindled in the last few decades of industrialized agriculture. Nowadays, butchery was generally done with large saws, and shipped to groceries rather than by skilled, in-house butchers. During the class, Tom also explained how he had become a butcher only a few years before. Training under the guidance of Joshua Applestone from Fleisher's, the upstate New York distributor of small farm meats, Tom had learned to appreciate the differences in free-range and humanely raised animals. This Berkshire hog, for instance, had unique DNA and was not genetically altered, as was 99 percent of the commercial pork available. What's more, pastured animals raised by conscientious farmers, like that pig in front of us, are granted longer, fuller lives before they are slaughtered, and benefited from a natural, healthy diet. He pointed to a slightly off-hue patch of flesh next to the rib.

"See, that might look kind of weird since it's sort of yellowish, but that's actually a good sign. It's because of the beta-carotene, from the grass," he said.

At the end of the class, all the students took their turns picking cuts of the pork that Tom had demonstrated on to take home. I'd chosen a hunk of pork shoulder, a piece of loin, and a small strip of spare ribs. I planned to braise the shoulder into a chili for my upcoming Chili Takedown the next week. With about ten pounds of meat in a bag, I had the perplexing dilemma of how I was going to bring it home that night. I'd planned to meet friends at a CD-release party for Matt's band at a nearby bar in Brooklyn right after class. There was no way I'd be able to carry all that meat on my bike, then put it down at the crowded bar for the duration of the party. I asked Taylor and Harry if they had room in the store's refrigerator, and they kindly accepted the meat. I'd have to pick it up the next day, though, I was warned—since they were planning on filling the fridge space with a shipment of something or other on Thursday.

After a late night at Matt's show, I got up bright and early for work the following morning. I brought my container of chocolate-chip-cookie-dough-topped cupcakes to the office with me, and another frozen veggie patty for lunch. I left the patty on my desk to thaw a little during the morning and, at lunchtime, reheated it in the microwave. By midafternoon, I was craving a snack and headed guiltily toward the office vending machines for a bag of chips. It seemed no matter how healthfully I strived to eat, I'd go through junk-food phases like these from time to time.

That afternoon, my friend and fellow food blogger Winnie sent me an e-mail, asking if I was attending the *Edible Manhattan* magazine launch that night. I was a fan of *Edible Brooklyn*, and the new Manhattan-based food magazine was throwing a launch party at the South Street Seaport. I told her I'd try to swing by, right after the cupcake meet-up.

The cupcake event turned out to be a lot of fun—I got a chance to chat with Rachel and Nichelle, two of the three bloggers behind "Cupcakes Take the Cake." I was also duly rewarded for my cupcake innovation. As soon as I revealed what I'd topped my cupcakes with, jaws dropped all around me. Somehow, in this crowd of cupcake enthusiasts, I had done something they'd never seen. The first few people who tried one let out moans of guilty pleasure. My cupcakes were finished off before any other batch at the party. Before leaving, I grabbed a chocolate cupcake for the road. It had been a special request from my friend Chrysanthe, whom I planned to meet up with after the *Edible Manhattan* launch party. She'd asked me to come along to the opening-night party for a new music venue in Brooklyn called the Bell House. She also loved chocolate cupcakes.

I'd had a suspicion there would be free food at the *Edible Manhattan* party, but I had no idea what this would entail. The party was stretched along two or three blocks at the southern tip of Manhattan. Some of the shops had been transformed into venues for various food merchants, like wineries, cheese makers, and fish and oyster specialists, all small businesses hailing from the borough of Manhattan. The party was exceptionally well put-together, and teeming with familiar faces from the foodie world, bloggers, writers, and local artisanal food producers. It also had excellent food.

Throughout all the schmoozing and tasting of various delectables, I was once again faced with the question of what constituted not eating out. Did this count? A bunch of small, local food purveyors gathered for a celebration of food on the South Street Seaport, sharing and boasting of their wares, for free?

I had no idea anymore. There were too many events like these lately, anyway. I'd walk into a party, or a foodie meet-up, and there'd be samples of catered food, or something else that was borderline restaurant fare. I went to a tasting night at the Grand Central Market, which really is a market in the sense that it sells fresh produce, meats and cheese, and fresh-baked bread, but so much of the food that night was fully prepared hors d'oeuvres. There were just too many loopholes in not eating out. I shook my head as I thought about it.

The next morning, I put together a quick lunch to bring to work. Earlier that week, I'd boiled a half dozen or so small baby red potatoes, some of the first newly harvested ones of the season at the markets. In another bag in my fridge, I had some fresh zucchini and summer squash, also from the Greenmarket. I heated some oil on the stove and smashed a clove of garlic. I chopped up two of the squashes—one green, and one small yellow one—with my knife and added the slices to the pan along with the garlic. After seasoning them with salt and pepper and flipping them twice until just a little caramelized, I took the squash out of the pan and put it into a plastic container alongside two of the potatoes. With the addition of roasted beet—I'd roasted a bunch of beets over the weekend, too—I popped the lid on the container and took it to work.

I liked this easy lunch so much, I brought more or less the same thing with me to work the next day, Friday. By suppertime that night, I decided I was tired of eating potatoes, zucchini, and beets. I found a bag of yellow cornmeal in my pantry and made a quick polenta to go with some vegetables instead. There was a bag of green beans in my crisper that had been hanging out perhaps one too many days, and I sautéed them with some garlic and a sliced half onion also lingering in the fridge. I added a bit of butter and some grated Parmesan to the polenta before topping it with the brownish pan juices from the sautéed green beans and onions. It was a good dinner, if simple. Afterward, I spent a relatively quiet night at a bar with Jordan, Dan, and a handful of other friends. I knew I was in for a crazy day of cooking another supper-club dinner with A Razor, A Shiny Knife starting the following morning.

The dinner we'd served at Michael's apartment that Sunday was actually a preparation for a larger, more elaborate supper-club dinner. Michael had teamed up with a local dramatist who went by the name of Jonny Cigar for an event he called "Dinner Theatre." Theatrical interludes would be performed by the actors in between the six courses of the meal. The idea was to match the presentation of the food with the drama that was being acted before the diners. Therefore, every course would be as elaborately staged and whimsical as the underground theater group's performance style.

Sporting a bowler and a three-piece suit, Jonny was a character, and great fun to be around. He and his fellow actors rehearsed while the rest of us prepared the meal all day. Instead of at Michael's, this dinner was held at the large loft of a friend, and small round tables covered with white tablecloths were placed around the room to create a cocktail-party feel. As usual, guests were encouraged to arrive in the afternoon to participate in the cooking process and watch demonstrations by the chefs.

I arrived at the loft shortly before noon and spent the next twelve hours cooking, eating, teaching, and serving. The menu, like the performers, was filled with interesting quirks. We used hydrocolloids to turn out distinct textures, like soft blocks of green curry custard to serve underneath the black-squid-ink-battered shrimp dish. Michael was also determined to create perfect cubes of "square sausage" to serve with a Creole-style étouffée. I tasted and nibbled through all the food, by the end scooping up hunks of the braised short ribs with my bare hands. I also ate more than my share of tobacco-laced ladyfingers. We'd revised the dessert from the previous dinner slightly, perfecting the cigarlike shape of the ladyfingers and sandwiching a layer of coffee-flavored buttercream frosting between two of them (a riff on "coffee and cigarettes"). Jonny had walked around the tables filling shot glasses with whiskey for guests to sip with their dessert or to use as a dipping sauce.

As we were cleaning up, I got a text from Scott, wondering if I wanted to grab a drink. Since we happened to be in the same neighborhood, we decided to meet up for a nightcap at a nearby bar. Scott had recently begun working as a bartender at a newly opened restaurant in Brooklyn and was enjoying a night off. We talked about the restaurant and his new gig, and I made plans to have dinner there during "restaurant week" when Scott was working behind the bar, on Monday.

"Are you sure you're okay to ride home?" Scott asked, standing outside the bar after we'd finished our nightcap.

"Yep! I'm an old pro," I said as I strapped on my helmet to begin my long ride home to Crown Heights.

PART II

"OPPOSITE WEEK"

On Sunday, I woke with a terrible hangover. But I had a full day's worth of eating out in New York to begin. There was no time for sleeping in.

A couple of weeks before, Mark had e-mailed me with a question: "Do you know Grace Piper? She's a producer/blogger for a food website with cooking videos and interviews called 'Fearless Cooking.'"

In fact, I did. I'd met Grace about a year ago to discuss some possible video projects, but we didn't immediately come up with anything and gradually fell out of touch. The reason Mark asked me this was because he was trying to hunt down a coauthor of a 1985 book called *The Brooklyn Cookbook* by the name of Lynn Stallworth. The cookbook was all about historically Brooklyn-based food, like the famous blackout cake created by Ebinger's Bakery, or the pierogis and kielbasas of Greenpoint, Brooklyn's Polish community. Mark wanted to create a Brooklyn-themed menu at an upcoming Whisk and Ladle dinner and desperately wanted to meet her and invite her to come. He'd seen a photo of Lynn on Grace's website with a caption and figured they must know each other. Mark connected with Grace, who connected him with Lynn, and he proposed a casual brunch with everyone. He invited me to come along, and that brunch fell on the first day of opposite week.

Lynn had chosen to meet at a restaurant close to her home in Park Slope, Brooklyn. It was an elegant, New American restaurant called Stone Park Café, a popular destination for brunchers, situated along a classy strip of restaurants and shops in the neighborhood. I had never been to the restaurant before my not-eating-out days but had eagerly scoped out its website days before the brunch. Such was my fascination with every place I was to eat at this week.

I arrived at the restaurant on time, hangover and all, and spotted Mark and Grace standing by the bar. Grace introduced me to her boyfriend, James, and the four of us chatted for a while as we waited for a table. Lynn arrived not too long after I did. With her petite frame and frail, shaky step, I never would have expected the vivacity in her voice as we greeted one another. Lynn was as chipper as any woman could be, her pale eyes glowing as she was introduced to Mark and me.

"Why don't they have a table for us yet? Let's just go ahead!" she suggested.

Fortunately, we were escorted to a table almost immediately after Lynn arrived. We were seated at a comfortably sized round table and handed menus.

"I'll have a Bloody Mary, please. On the rocks," Lynn told the waiter before he could leave.

I glanced at the menu. I'd already seen it online a few days before and had eyed the crab cake. But my hangover had changed my appetite from adventurous to simply ravenous. It was too bad there was no menudo on the menu.

"We always order the same thing," Grace said, for herself and James. "The Hangtown Fry. Except we get ours with a side salad instead of the potatoes. The waiters all know us here; we come just about every Saturday." She and James smiled.

"So Mark, as I was saying a bit before, has a supper club that he runs in his apartment," Grace said to Lynn. "And there are four or five who do this with you?"

Mark jumped in to explain Whisk and Ladle to Lynn, adding that they had recently begun a series of dinners that were being shot for an upcoming online show.

"Oh, why, that's terrific," Lynn said. She took the straw out of her Bloody Mary and sipped heartily.

We chatted for a few minutes about the supper club, alternating with conversation about who in our group liked Bloody Marys and who didn't. As a non-liker, Mark was persuaded by Lynn to try a sip of one. He still didn't like it.

"Actually, I'm not terribly in the mood for one. I think I'd prefer a glass of white wine next," Lynn said.

"Are we ready to order?" asked Grace. The waiter had stopped by our table. Grace and James ordered their standard, while Mark and Lynn decided to try the pulled pork hash. I opted for the Stone Park Omelette, with tomatoes, spinach, Swiss cheese, and the house-cured sausage. I planned to eat every piece of the toast that came on the side. While the rest of the table ordered white wines, I declined and ordered a cup of coffee instead, explaining that I'd had a long night. Mark, too, had been up late for a Whisk and Ladle dinner, and in between talking with Lynn and Grace, we shared snippets about our respective feasts from the night before.

Our meals came to our table after a short wait. I was happy to find that my omelette had been prepared in the classic French fashion—quickly beaten in the pan and rolled into a uniformly textured, pale yellow log. I enjoyed the house-cured breakfast sausage, which was spiced with basic breakfast-sausage seasonings. I was surprised by the tomatoes in the omelet—I was pretty sure they were canned Italian plum, chopped roughly. The intense, bright color and equally strong flavor made them an interesting choice, though not, I deemed, an unpleasant one.

But the real highlight of the meal was the conversation. Grace was an effusive talker, and we discovered we'd both recently written about similar topics on our blogs. We talked with Lynn about *The Brooklyn Cookbook* for a while, as Mark tried to gather ideas for his dinner menu. Lynn was a whip, sharing stories about her short-lived theater career long ago, and offering strong opinions on everything from Brussels sprouts to bagels. She reminded me of Ruth Gordon's character in *Harold and Maude*, the feisty old woman who falls in love with a teenager and looks death in the eye with a twinkle. Somehow, the topic of James Beard came up.

"I knew Jim from way back," Lynn explained, wrinkling her nose as if the late food connoisseur were a childhood pest. "He was a real fruit, you know." She gossiped about the penthouse he'd owned on Park Avenue, adding that Beard used to shower before a clear window facing the public. She finished her wine and began to ask the waiter for another. Grace suggested ordering a bottle for the table, since the four of them were up for another glass.

While the waiter was pouring, I asked Lynn if she was originally from Brooklyn.

"No, we're from Pittsburgh," she said. "My parents were in the iron and steel business. She ironed, and he stole."

"Can I steal her?" I whispered to Mark as our table laughed.

"So you're part of a different supper club now?" Lynn asked me.

I nodded and told her about A Razor, A Shiny Knife.

"So you cook a lot, too, then?" she went on.

"Yes, and my blog is about just cooking, instead of eating at restaurants. This is actually the first time I've had brunch in a restaurant in two years."

The other faces around the table froze.

Mark clanged his fork down. "That's right! I forgot about your restaurant week."

"Your what?"

I briefly explained my current weeklong experiment and the concept of my blog to the rest of the table. Once the confusion cleared away, Grace remarked, "Wow, I can't believe you really didn't eat out for two years! I didn't realize that."

"Well, with some exceptions," I said.

Lynn smiled. "That's incredible."

"How's that going so far, by the way?" Mark asked.

"You're looking at it," I said, tearing into a piece of buttered toast.

We spent a long time talking after our plates were taken away. Everyone else was finishing up the bottle of wine, and I was on my third or fourth cup of coffee. Our waiter approached our table and asked us if everything was okay.

"I feel bad; there are so many people waiting for our table," Grace said once he walked away. "But we come here all the time."

We received our check a few minutes later, and our party decided it was time to get going. We passed the check around the table. My brunch with coffee cost $14, and I added another $4 for the tip. We decided we'd better leave a good tip, for lingering so long.

It was a beautiful day. The morning fog had cleared away, and a vibrant farmers' market across the street from the restaurant was teeming with shoppers.

"How'd a cookie get so thin?" Lynn said, eyeing me up and down. "Because you're a cookie," she said with an affirmative nod. "That's what you are."

I didn't really know what this old-fashioned nickname meant, but I smiled and took it as a compliment. We bid Lynn farewell as she headed across the street to her home with a wave. Mark and I chatted with Grace and her boyfriend for a while in front of the restaurant. The brunch meeting had gone well: Mark had succeeded in convincing Lynn to come to his dinner, and he invited Grace as well. We'd been at the restaurant for almost two hours, and it was getting close to the time when I'd have to take off for my next eating-out appointment.

"What are your plans for the rest of the day?" Mark asked as we walked toward my locked-up bike.

"I have to meet my brother in the city pretty soon. Then we're going to Flushing, Queens, to eat in Chinatown," I said.

A few months ago, my mom had read an article in *The New York Times* about the incredible, authentic Chinese food throughout Flushing, Queens. She had been desperate to try it all summer long but never got around to it. It was a perfect destination for my opposite week, though, so she and my dad were driving into the city that day, to meet up with me, Jo-Jo, and my brother, Chris, who happened to be in town with his band that weekend. But before dinner, Jo-Jo was taking Chris and me around Flushing for a mini-tour in the afternoon.

"That's brilliant," Mark said. "Have a good time."

I got home to park my bike and grab some things to read on the subway. Once there, I suddenly remembered one part of opposite week that I'd previously forgotten. I had to get a scale.

Now, it may sound like a far-fetched idea that my weight would change over the course of just one week. I certainly wasn't intending on gorging myself on excess food, and I experienced very little fluctuation in my weight in general. But I couldn't help but be a little bit curious about this possibility. What if it did change drastically due to a restaurant-only diet? I didn't own a scale and hadn't remembered to buy one in time to weigh myself before the day began. I hurried to a pharmacy a few blocks down and roamed the aisles in search of one. While I was there, my mom called—what time should she and my dad plan to meet us in Flushing? she asked. While I was on the phone with her, I got an idea.

"Mom, can you bring your bathroom scale with you?"

"Why?" she retorted.

"Because I'm trying to weigh myself before and after the week," I said, "and I can't find one at Walgreens."

My mom pulled her Honda up to a corner in downtown Flushing, where Jo-Jo, Chris, and I were standing. My brother and I were each holding plastic cups of bubble tea, with wide, neon green straws sticking out of them to allow the marble-sized, chewy tapioca pearls at the bottom of the tea to come through. Before my parents arrived, Jo-Jo had taken us to a couple of bakeries in the neighborhood and bought a package of high-end moon cakes. At another one, he got a bag of beautiful, individually wrapped pineapple cakes, or *feng li su*, a specialty of Taiwan. These had been my absolute favorite treat in Taiwan while I was there, and unlike bubble tea (which could be found throughout New York City), I had never seen the real thing outside the island before. We also strolled through a shopping mall and eyed the Chinese food court's hand-pulled-noodle shop. Again, I hadn't seen a chef pull fresh dough into noodles with his hands since the street-food stands of Taipei—although I knew that handmade Chinese noodles existed elsewhere in New York City. For a predinner snack, we'd stopped at a small window to a restaurant on a busy block with a line of customers crowded around it, a good indication that this restaurant had the goods. At the window, I bought a freshly steamed pork and leek bun for $1 and shared it with the others. The moment I took the first bite into its soft, foamy crust, the juices from the filling dribbled down my wrist.

"Okay, we decided on two options," Jo-Jo said to my parents once they emerged from the car. "There's a very good Taiwanese place, up the street. Then there's that Szechuan place you read about. In the article."

"Ooh. Hm," my mom said. I took the bathroom scale she was holding out of her hands as my parents thought about this for a minute. I placed it on the sidewalk and stepped on it.

"What are you doing?" my brother asked.

"Never mind," I said, taking mental note of my weight. I picked the scale back up and stuffed it into my tote. Chris shrugged.

"The Szechuan place looks nice. It might be a little more formal than the other," Jo-Jo offered.

"Is it crowded?" my mom asked. We walked down to the end of the block and craned our necks through the glass storefront windows. "It does look pretty good," she said, eyeing the trays of prepared appetizers at a cook's workstation, which were all dyed a rich red hue, a signature of Szechuan cuisine because of its heavy use of chili oil. It might not have been the only authentic Szechuan restaurant in the city, but according to *The New York Times* article, it was certainly one of the best. It was called Spicy and Tasty—which was an understatement, considering the bold flavors of Szechuan food.

"Why don't we go here?" my dad suggested. We all agreed.

We filed into the restaurant and settled at a large round table that was really meant for about twelve people. It was the only available table in the restaurant. As platters drifted by us balanced on waiters' palms, we stopped to gaze at them all. "Wow, what's that? I want to get that," my mom would say as each one went by.

To be sure, this was exotic food to all of us at the table. My mom and Jo-Jo grew up in Taiwan, and their parents hailed from Hunan Province in China. We had never tasted anything like the pungent, spicy dishes of Szechuan until a trip to China a few years back. Soon after that, my parents discovered a gold mine of authentic Szechuan food at a restaurant in New Jersey. Since then they'd been developing an ecstatic, burgeoning love of the spicy, salty, and yes, tasty food.

When we left the restaurant, I was beyond full, and my spicy taste buds were well satisfied. Later that night, even though I was still fairly full, I found myself alone in my apartment with one of the pineapple cakes that Jo-Jo had bought, and three of his moon cakes. I ate one of each. The moon cake was really exceptional. It was dense and moist, its molded cakelike crust gleaming with egg wash and tasting faintly of dried fruits, or molasses. On the inside, it was filled with a sweet black sesame seed paste. "The best," Jo-Jo had said to me in the car, pointing to the black sesame one. I fell asleep that night as soon as my head hit the pillow.

The next day I had the day off from work. I skipped breakfast, not having a glimmer of hunger in my belly until about noon. That morning I strapped on my helmet and pedaled off to the library and a few other spots in Brooklyn, running errands. As I was heading back home, I sped by a sushi restaurant that I recognized. It was a place that my brother had gone to often while he was living in New York, a few years back. I retraced my path, then walked inside and picked up a laminated menu. The small, quaint restaurant was sparsely decorated with a few Japanese motifs, like koi fish. I placed an order for a *chirashi* sashimi bowl to go, and paid the waitress at the counter. As I was waiting for my order, I watched the sushi chef behind the raw bar take a slip of paper from the waitress and begin to work on my order. He took out a few bundles of plastic wrap and from one of them removed a block-sized portion of sushi rice. He placed this in a flat, even bed on the bottom of a round plastic takeout container, and topped it with a hairlike mass of extra-thin radish ribbons. One by one, he placed uniformly shaped slices of raw fish on top of the rice and radish. His eyes darted about quickly as he checked for ingredients, but his hands moved ever so delicately with the food. I had never seen such focus and concentration. He must have made this same dish a thousand times. Consistency, I remembered, was one of the keys to a successful restaurant.

I biked home with the takeout lunch hung from a plastic bag around my handlebar. The meal had cost me $9, or $10 with tax. It looked so pretty when I opened the takeout container at home that I felt I had to take a picture of it to do it justice.

That night, I planned to meet Karol for dinner at Char No. 4, where Scott was working. I also knew Char No. 4's executive chef, Matt Greco, whose class on charcuterie basics at the Brooklyn Kitchen I'd attended a few months back. I'd had a great time learning from him and had kept in touch. I knew that he was planning to open the new restaurant, and its launch fell just a couple of weeks before my opposite week, so it seemed like a perfect idea to check it out.

Karol was sitting at the bar when I arrived. Scott and one other bartender were shuffling behind the bar, and another couple was seated a few stools over.

"This place is really nice," Karol said, admiring the sleek, cylindrical light fixtures against the neutral-toned room. We ordered cocktails, and Scott made me one of his new signature drinks—

Bourbon laced with ginger ale and lime. The menu, as I'd heard about previously from the chef, was a refined take on Southern-style classics. We decided to order two appetizers: bacon- and corn-topped baked oysters, and fried cheese curds with smoked-pepper dip. After discussing some of the options with Scott, we decided to split the pulled pork sandwich and ordered the side of eggplant stew.

As we waited for our food, Karol and I gossiped. We were in desperate need of a girl-talk session. About a week ago, after Matt's show, I'd met up with a guy I'd been sort of seeing that summer. Instead of hanging out, we got into an argument and parted ways less than ten minutes later. He'd decided to break things off with me because he couldn't see a long-term future for us. It was a mutual feeling, but it still stung to hear, and I made my long ride home through the familiar darkened streets afterward crying, for the first time on a bike. We hadn't spoken since. As for Karol, she had recently been told by her love interest that he was "not ready" to be in a relationship.

"Well, I'm glad that you've had this experience," Karol concluded after we agreed that our sort-of breakups were for the best.

"Yeah, me, too. For you, too," I said.

Scott, who had been bending over to get something behind the bar, popped up and raised an eyebrow.

"Hey, how's it going?" I said.

"Not too bad," he said. "It's not too busy here tonight. Can I make you two another drink?" he asked. We nodded.

Our appetizers came out. Karol and I shared bites of each other's—my deep-fried cheese curds were luscious and crisp on the outside. Made from the extra-mild, rubbery curds of cheddar before they're aged and actually become cheese, they reminded me of mozzarella sticks, only much better. Our entree was even more delicious. Served on a soft brioche bun, the shredded pork was tender and had a good kick of vinegar in the sauce. We liked the stewed eggplant, too, which had a mild tomato-based sauce and minimal, savory spices. When we were about halfway through dinner, Matt Greco poked my shoulder from behind.

"Thanks for coming, guys," he said. In his arms were two extra plates. He placed them on the table before us. One had a home-made lamb pastrami and pickled onion appetizer, and another, smoked almonds. We chatted for a while about the restaurant and business so far. From all indications, the restaurant was off to a good start. He politely excused himself and got back to the kitchen after a few minutes.

"Matt works really hard," Scott said. "He is almost never outside of the kitchen."

Karol and I made a good dent in the extra food and had one more round of drinks. Everything about our dinner date—the food, the drinks, and especially the friendly service—was delightful. We split the check between us, which came to a little over $60 total. Matt had thrown in the extra appetizers, and Scott had given us each a drink on the house. We left them a good tip.

The next day I went to work. I'd felt funny the night before not preparing myself something to bring in for lunch. As I got dressed and ready that morning, I kept having the nagging feeling that I was forgetting something. When lunchtime rolled around, at about twelve thirty (once again I'd skipped breakfast), I was ready to eat.

Lunching from midtown restaurants and delis was one of the main reasons I had begun my not-eating-out-in–New York quest. But here I was, two years later, strangely ecstatic about all the choices at my disposal. A twisted sense of excitement had been building up to this moment for weeks: my reunion with the typical New York working-class lunch. So, what would it be today?

I'd noticed a few coworkers coming in with bags from a Japanese sushi and noodle place down the street. I decided that something different like udon noodles sounded like a good way to start. When I got to the noodle place, I found myself in the back of a long line. As I waited, I looked over the options written on a board. There was udon with chicken, beef, vegetables, tofu, or kimchee. I set my mind on kimchee. When it was my turn to order, I paid the cashier for the kimchee udon first. With tax, it cost $6.47. Then I stood in a shorter line and watched as a cook behind a glass window took a block of squashed udon noodles out of a package and dropped it into a vat of water that had a small draining rack inside it. He lifted another draining rack beside it and dumped the cooked udon noodles that were inside it into a polystyrene foam cylindrical bowl. To the bowl he added a few ladles of broth from a large pot, and next he picked up a small handful of chicken from a small container with his gloved hands. He topped the dish with a handful of chopped scallions, put a lid on the bowl, and wrapped it up in a bag for the customer. A moment later, he lifted the other portion of boiling noodles from the water and dumped it into another polystyrene foam bowl. He added broth and a scoop of kimchee from another container behind the glass. That one was my order.

Once I got back to my desk, I cleared away my papers and set the bowl down in front of me. A set of disposable wooden chopsticks had been thrown into my bag faster than my eyes could really make out, so I took them out of their wrapper and snapped them apart. I tasted the broth with a plastic spoon first. There was nothing special about it. Next I tried the udon. My first bite actually tasted like fresh plywood. I'd forgotten the way these chopsticks spread their delightful flavor into each bite. I wondered whether I could also taste polystyrene foam in the soup, and it was right then that I remembered that fact about hot foods causing styrene to leach from polystyrene foam the most. I started to freak out, and the feeling grew with every bite. After about twenty more seconds, I couldn't stand it anymore. I went to the kitchen and opened the cabinet doors, trying to find a stray ceramic bowl. No luck. There was, however a small stack of plastic disposable cereal bowls. I grabbed one and dumped the contents of my polystyrene foam bucket into it. I was able to get about three-quarters of the contents in before the rim overflowed with soup. It wasn't big enough. I thought about grabbing another white plastic bowl, then remembered my coffee cup sitting on my desk. I dumped out my coffee, rinsed the cup out, then filled it with the rest of the udon and soup. This saved me from wasting three disposable vessels for the udon alone, instead of two. What a feat.

I had numerous options for dinner that evening. Matt had gone on tour with his band that week but left me with a list of highly recommended restaurants. My friend Nick was going on a trip in a few days and suggested we check out one of his favorite Indian places. Chrysanthe had been raving about the food at a restaurant that just opened in Williamsburg. Scott, too, had offered several high-end restaurant suggestions. But that night, Tuesday, I decided to dine alone. On whatever was closest to my vicinity. I got home and looked at the empty sink and kitchen counter. I usually relaxed and unwound when I got home from work by doing the previous night's dishes. Instead I pulled open a drawer underneath my TV and sifted through the many takeout menus that had been slipped under my apartment door over the months. Most of them were Chinese takeout places, a few Japanese. I put my jacket on, deciding to see what was in the neighborhood. There were a number of hole-in-the-wall Caribbean restaurants in my immediate neighborhood, since it was populated largely with people from the West Indies. There was one right around the corner from my building. I decided to check it out.

I walked into the brightly lit, small restaurant. There were about six square tables. All were empty except for one, where a sole customer sat. I took a look at the trays of food behind a glass window. The lady behind it greeted me and offered me a menu.

"Can I try the jerk chicken, please?" I asked a few moments later.

"Sorry, tonight is curry chicken and barbecue," she said. She pointed to the word *Tuesday* on the menu. "Each night we have these," she explained, drawing my attention to the list of days of the week and the corresponding entrees that were served on each one.

"Oh, I see," I said. So tonight's offerings were barbecue chicken or curry chicken.

"But we have all the same sides, too," she went on. Trays full of stewed greens, macaroni and cheese, and other sides were steaming behind the counter. I took a look at them and another look at the menu.

"I'll have the curry chicken," I said decisively. The lady smiled and began to fill a round aluminum takeout tray. "Do you want it with plain rice, or rice with pigeon peas?" she asked. "It's a Jamaican specialty," she said, referring to the rice with pigeon peas.

"I'll have the pigeon peas, please." She ladled the curry chicken stew on top of the rice and filled up the last third of the tray with a scoop of soft-cooked cabbage. I paid for the meal, which cost just $7. She gave me a curious smile when I asked for no bag, and placed a few napkins on top of the takeout tray. I smiled and thanked her. The tray was heavy and warm, and I realized that the napkins were handy for holding it without burning my hands. I turned the corner and walked back to my building.

I turned on the television to a news show but found myself

watching only the food as I ate. The tray was filled to the brim. The chicken was so tender that it fell off the bone at the slightest touch. Its warm, spicy mix of ginger, cumin, and other Jamaican spices was soothing and had steeped into the meat well; my nose began to run, and my glasses fogged up, but I couldn't stop scooping up forkfuls of the stuff. The pigeon peas bled color into the soft, short-grain rice, and the mild, lightly seasoned cabbage was a welcome retreat from the other strong flavors. It was comforting and delicious. It also seemed more like a homemade meal than anything I had eaten so far that week. It reminded me of my mother's soy sauce chicken stew; the chicken was braised with spices until falling off the bone and also served over rice. I finished the entire dish.

I wasn't sure what my dinner plans the next night would be. There was a music show I wanted to check out in Brooklyn. It wouldn't start until eleven, and this seemed like a good reason to go out for dinner beforehand. I had been exchanging a few e-mails with a new acquaintance I'd met a few weeks before at a party. Keith was a restaurant critic for a local news website, and we'd joked about him being on the opposite team. In his last note, he had offered to be my guide to the local Brooklyn restaurant scene during my opposite week, if I should want one. The show I wanted to see was at a venue close to a new Williamsburg restaurant that Chrysanthe tipped me off to. Called Walter Foods, it had all the makings of a hot restaurant: a chef who'd left his recent post at a renowned Manhattan restaurant, a hip location, and positive hype. I sent off an e-mail to Keith suggesting we check it out that night. A couple of hours later, I received a positive response: It was on. Here I was, going on a dinner date with a restaurant critic, to a highly anticipated restaurant's first week. The epitome of opposite week.

I couldn't decide what to eat for lunch that day. I walked around in a circle through a giant deli below my office building. The number of choices was overwhelming—there were soups, sandwiches, wraps, paninis, and grilled hamburgers. There was an udon and soba noodle station (which I had no appetite for due to yesterday's cafeterialike affair), sushi, pizza, and pastas and salads with any number of choose-your-own ingredients. There was a hot bar and a cold bar, each with a dizzying assortment of entrees and salads. There were specials of the day. After I made a full round, I found myself back at the front door and walked out. I walked into Pax Wholesome Foods next. This was a nationwide chain, so it had a uniform color scheme and printed labels for every offering behind its glass counters. I eyed the sandwiches over and over and finally settled on a balsamic grilled chicken "Zesto." It was just a sandwich, actually, on focaccia. But like any good chain's sandwiches, it had been given a distinctive name. I wasn't too pleased with this lunch. At almost $9 with tax, the sandwich was dry, the chicken especially, and though the balsamic flavor was fine, the way the sandwich had been sliced in half to reveal its padding of greens and roasted red pepper was a little misleading—all the fresh stuff seemed to be clumped in the center. Still, I finished the last bite and was full for the rest of the day.

We decided to meet at the restaurant at nine. It was mid-September, and the air was beginning to get chilly. I put on a heavy knit sweater and boots and rode over to the restaurant, arriving a few minutes late. The restaurant was handsome. It had a well-worn air despite being freshly renovated. A mahogany divider with a brass railing ran along an elevated section, separating it from the bar area. The waiters were dressed in bow ties and black and white. Keith was at the bar when I arrived. We were seated immediately, and I ordered a glass of red.

"Well, this must be an interesting week for you," Keith said.

"Yeah." I nodded. "It's been fun." I told him a little about my recent eating-out adventures, in Queens and then at Char No. 4. I asked Keith whether he would be writing up Walter Foods for the website, and he nodded.

"How does that work, anyhow? Don't you need to put on a disguise sometimes? Go incognito, so they don't treat you overly well?" I asked.

"Not really. I'm not much of a food critic. We actually don't write very long reviews nowadays; everything's short snippets, facts . . . ," he explained.

"Oh," I said.

"Sometimes I don't even have to go to the places to write about them."

"Is that how it works?" I asked.

"Not all the time." Keith shrugged.

"That's sneaky." We laughed. "Sometimes I wish I didn't have to eat the things I cook for my blog when they turn out bad or are really fattening."

We glanced at our menus as we chatted.

"What should we start with?" I asked.

"I heard the warm beet salad is good, and the blackened shrimp," said Keith.

We decided to go for the blackened shrimp. Our waiter came to our table to tell us the specials. After he described the last one, seared sea scallops with haricots verts, I was sold. It had sounded simple but wasn't something I would normally cook at home; sea scallops were a luxury I rarely felt like indulging in just for myself. Keith ordered the apple-glazed pork chop. Our appetizer arrived a few minutes later. Four fat shrimp were speared with a wooden skewer, looking juicy and crisp on the outside. A lemon half on the side of the plate had a funny-looking cheesecloth fitted around it with an elasticized edge.

"It looks like it's wearing a little hairnet," I said as I squeezed the juice through the cloth onto the shrimp. "I guess that's for keeping the seeds away."

The shrimp was hot and perfectly seasoned with blackened Cajun spices. It was not innovative or very fussy, but the shrimp itself was deliciously fresh.

"Wow, that's really good," I said. "Totally classic. I can appreciate that."

Keith agreed. As we slowly finished the appetizer, we kept a conversation going, first about movies, then about authors that we found we both liked. We had both recently gone to see films at the same noir retrospective at the Film Forum.

It soon became clear to me that I was on a classic first date—the restaurant type. Everything about the affair was very reserved and polite. I couldn't remember the last time I ate with friends when I didn't throw a piece of food at Matt or didn't eat with my hands. "Are you going on a date?" Chrysanthe had written over instant messaging earlier that day, when I described my dinner plans. I scrunched my nose. "No, it's more like a weird opposite-week challenge," I had insisted. Whatever.

As I sat across from Keith, though, talking in between slicing through buttery lumps of scallops, I did have to admit that I was having a nice time. And that I did think he was pretty cute. Halfway through my entree and well into my second glass of wine, I wasn't eating out of hunger, just enjoying the unique sensations of the food on my plate. I took my time with it, savoring the delicate spindles of haricots verts, which were pleasantly lemony and resilient to the bite. The restaurant was busy for its first week of service, but it seemed that the noise level never rose above a soft murmur. We finished dinner off with another drink—Bourbon on the rocks. It was another thing we found we both liked. When our glasses came to the table, they were filled to the brim.

"Gosh, they really don't skimp on portions here," Keith said.

Our waiter never made us feel as if we should rush, but I ended up drinking that Bourbon pretty quickly. Keith was game for checking out the music show afterward, and I didn't want to miss the act. When our check came to the table, Keith snatched it up.

"Wait, let me get half," I said, pulling out a credit card.

"No, it's fine," Keith said, hovering over the check protectively.

"No, really! It was my idea!" I pried, trying to angle my card into the billfold. But he was having none of it. The waiter came by and took the check from Keith's hands with a nod. I had no idea what the total bill was, but I guessed it was well over $100, with six drinks, two entrees, and an appetizer between us.

"I can expense some of it." Keith shrugged. I was defeated.

We walked outside to get our bikes, since we had both ridden to the restaurant. I strapped my chain lock around my waist and strolled up to his bike.

"Shall I lead the way?" I asked.

"Go ahead."

We arrived at the small, dark venue before the show. It had taken us a while to find the place even though we'd both been there before on separate occasions; it had an unassuming exterior and was located on a stretch of blank street facing the East River, overlooking Manhattan. It didn't occur to me that I was fairly drunk until we ordered our second beers there, and I stumbled into the seedy, unmarked bathroom. It was also later than I'd predicted, well past midnight. The act I'd wanted to see—a singer whom I'd met recently at a party—had just gotten on stage after the opening bands. We stayed around for half of his set until I decided I was too droopy to stay any longer. As Keith and I unlocked our bikes outside, he looked at me strangely.

"Are you sure you're going to be okay riding all the way back to Crown Heights?" he asked. I laughed, as if it were the last question in the world that needed answering.

"You don't understand. I own this road," I said. We said good-bye, and I took off on my twenty-minute journey back to my sanctuary.

The next morning, I was in need of breakfast. The dinner the night before had been plentiful, but even more so had been the drinks. For the second time that week, I wished menudo had been a more popular New York menu item. I walked straight into a deli after getting out of the subway and ordered a toasted bagel with egg and cheese. I sat at my desk, blankly staring at the computer screen in front of me as I gobbled it up. Instantly, I felt much better.

For dinner that night, I'd planned long beforehand to meet up with Michael "Serpico" Cirino at Momofuku Noodle Bar. Michael was one of the people who, on hearing about my opposite week, was full of restaurant suggestions. He was a passionate fan of the country's most innovative chefs. David Chang, chef of the wildly celebrated Momofuku restaurant empire, was one of his heroes. Chang's rise to fame had happened suddenly and had taken the entire food world by surprise. It had also all happened over the last two years, meaning while I'd been eating in. I'd read much about Momofuku Noodle Bar and its sister restaurants, Momofuku Ssäm Bar and Momofuku Ko, and was well aware of Chang's reputation as a culture-crossing culinary genius.

"We're going to the one that started it all," Michael had responded when I asked him which Momofuku he intended to take me to. The noodle bar: Chang's once humble and now classic take on the Japanese ramen noodle shop.

Chang was also both celebrated and criticized for his insatiable love of fatty cuts of meat, like pork belly. Knowing that this lay ahead of me, I thought I'd go easy on lunch that day. As it neared lunchtime, I started talking with a coworker about places to get soup. She suggested a place not too far away, on the southern block of Bryant Park. The place was packed when I got there. The line for the cash register ran the length of the restaurant, and alongside it were two separate counters of food options. I spotted the soup section and eyed the day's specials. Out of the four choices, two were cream based, which I wasn't feeling up for. Then there was a minestrone and a yellow split pea. I went with the yellow split pea. With no bag.

"How is it?" my coworker asked as I ate the soup with a tiny slice of French bread that had come with it.

"Pretty good," I said. And it was. Although comprised of only vegetables and no meat stock, the soup was thick and hearty, if a bit on the salty side.

"It smells pretty good," she said.

It was also a good deal cheaper than my previous day's lunch, at just $5.45 with tax for a large cup. Later in the day, I was feeling like a snack again and hit up the vending machines down the hall for a bag of chips.

I got an e-mail from my friend Saha that day. Knowing that I was on my restaurant-only week, he excitedly offered up a suggestion.

"Have you ever been to the Doughnut Plant? If not, I think you need to go. Let's check it out sometime this week. I'm free today and tomorrow."

He provided a link to Doughnut Plant's website, and I clicked on it. Instantly, my screen was filled with a computer-animated logo with highlighted doughnuts as tabs. I clicked on the "History" tab and read a little animated timeline about the famous doughnut shop. It sounded like a real New York legend of a place. I agreed that I had to check it out.

"How about tomorrow morning, for breakfast?" I suggested. I was off work the next day, a Friday, and I knew that Saha had a pretty flexible schedule, too.

"Okay," he wrote back. "How about bright and early? I'm actually going to the office tomorrow, so I can pick up a bunch to bring to folks there."

We agreed to meet at nine o'clock. I continued to click away at Doughnut Plant's website infrequently throughout the day, building up an appetite for the sweet dessert I had normally thought so little of. It seemed like Doughnut Plant was the very height of doughnut sophistication in the city—with different specialties for every day, all-natural, homemade jellies and curious combinations, and their signature square shape. I read an article about the store's founder, Mark Isreal. "Well, we had to be different," he was quoted as saying, explaining why they had gone with a square shape for their jelly-filled doughnuts. What a niche food to get sophisticated about: the once scrappy, proletarian, police force breakfast.

After work, I hopped on the subway and got out in the East Village. I found Momofuku Noodle Bar quickly and, since it was raining, ducked inside even though I was five minutes early. The hostess greeted me with a smile. I told her I was waiting for my friend and asked if I could sit at the bar.

"We don't actually seat people until their whole party is here, and the bar's another seating area. But you could hang out here and order a drink if you'd like," she explained, gesturing to the space within five feet or so of her and a small wooden bench beside a wait station with a computer. She handed me a menu and moved aside a small pile of them on the bench. I put my coat and bag down and settled on the bench. Five minutes later, after I'd ordered a beer, Michael arrived.

"Hola," he said as we exchanged hugs. Our waitress led us to the end of a long table that was taken up with other parties. We sat across from each other.

"Where's Kathryn?" I asked, referring to Michael's girlfriend, whom I adored.

"She's in Ethiopia right now." Kathryn worked for a nonprofit hunger organization and occasionally traveled to Africa. We talked for a moment about Ethiopian food.

"When I told her about your restaurant week, Kathryn predicted there was going to be a huge line of guys wanting to take you out on dates," he said, grinning.

I laughed and denied any such line.

"How *did* you go on dates all this time?" he asked, echoing a question I'd heard plenty times over the last two years.

"Well, for the first year I had a boyfriend," I began.

"Uh-huh," he said, listening attentively.

"And then, I don't know. . . . I guess it's been weird."

We laughed.

"This place is a lot less busy than I thought it would be. I'm surprised we got seats right away," Michael observed. I looked around us. It felt chaotic and busy, and I felt squished into a corner of the table, on a backless wooden stool. The long tables were all completely packed, and people were constantly getting up and sitting back down. Behind a separator along one side of the room, the cooks scurried around one another as they worked.

"So what should we get?" I asked.

"Start with a couple of appetizers, and definitely get the Momofuku ramen," Michael said. The menu was heavy on meat, especially pork. The only criticism I'd heard about the place was that there was only one vegetarian entree on the menu, a rather boring ginger and scallion noodle soup.

"I'd say definitely get the pork buns if you haven't tried them; they're what everyone comes here for," said Michael.

"Okay . . . and what else?" I thought aloud, my eyes scrolling through the menu. "Have you tried the pig's tails?"

"No, I've never had that one."

We decided to get it. Our waitress came by for the second time—she had already nudged in a couple of minutes ago, before we had even glanced at our menus. We ordered the two appetizers and decided to share the ramen noodles. As we waited for our food, Michael and I kept up a rapid conversation about upcoming A Razor, A Shiny Knife dinners. He told me about a plan he was devising to re-create, dish for dish, a menu created by one of his favorite chefs, Thomas Keller of the French Laundry. It sounded like an elaborate challenge, but I knew well by then that when Michael had a vision and a mission to complete, not even a meteor crash could stop him.

"So what else do you do or think about? I feel like we always talk about food," he said suddenly at one point. For once, I was stuck for a response. I stammered, searching for an accurate answer.

"I don't know. I guess I'm just trying to learn as much about food and cooking as possible," I told him.

"Fair enough."

Our appetizers came quickly. The pork buns surprised me at first sight. I had expected to see a traditional Cantonese-style steamed bun that completely encapsulated a reddish, barbecued shredded pork center, but these buns opened up like thick, puffy tacos. Tucked in their creases was a filling of thick slabs of pork belly coated in dark sauce and garnished with cilantro.

I gulped down the last bite of one of them and sat in wonder.

"That was amazing. It's like an open-faced pork bun. Who'd have thought of that?" I said.

"They're good, right?" Michael said, working on his.

"They kind of have a little more sauce than I would have expected . . . ," I began to say.

"But it keeps it moist, right? I hate it when they're too dry."

I had to admit, he did have a point. David Chang's pork bun might have been an improvement on the age-old classic in this regard. Or perhaps, I thought again, the unorthodox ensemble more closely resembled a heavily dressed sandwich and so was more appetizing to the Western palate. The pig's tails, however, were quite the opposite. Instead of curlicue tails, they were walnut-sized chunks of bone surrounded by strings of tender meat, like a turkey's neck, or oxtail, only they had been glazed heavily in a deep brown, hoisin-based sauce. Michael didn't seem to be much of a fan. I enjoyed working the pieces of meat off the bone with my teeth and found the flavor pleasant. Although, novelty factor aside, I wasn't sure how great the meat of pig's tails really was. Perhaps these could have been cooked a little more.

The steaming bowl of ramen came to our table two minutes later. Floating on top of the noodle soup was a delicately arranged selection of different cuts of pork, a fish cake or two, some spinach, and a poached egg. We asked our waiter for a small bowl, and I made a separate portion for myself.

"This is the best part," Michael said, lifting up a chopstick pinch of some braised shredded pork. He also marveled at the perfect poaching of the egg.

"I bet you that's seventy-one degrees Celsius," he said.

"What?"

"The egg. It's poached to seventy-one degrees. That's the perfect temperature. It gets the white fully cooked, but the yolk stays liquid. Watch," he said, and delicately punctured the middle of the egg with a chopstick. The creamy orange liquid spilled into the soup.

When we had finished our noodles and the waitress came by to take our plates, Michael stopped her as she was leaving.

"Could you tell me what temperature the egg was poached at?"

The waitress looked confused. "I don't know. But I could ask one of the cooks," she offered.

"That would be terrific, if you could. Thanks so much," Michael said.

She came back a few minutes later, reporting that it had been poached to seventy-one degrees Celsius. Michael snapped his fingers and thanked her. The waitress handed us our check as she took our plates.

"I've got this one," Michael said, hastily snatching away the check.

"What? No! Let me get half," I insisted.

"No, really. I owe you for all the times you've cooked for dinners," he said.

I sighed. I never imagined that during opposite week, I might end up spending *less* than I spent during normal week. If I got treated to any more meals, this could throw off the whole experiment.

"Thank you," I said to Michael.

Michael had driven his car into Manhattan, so he offered to give me a ride home. On the way to the bridge, we passed a small side street and Michael suddenly hit the steering wheel.

"I forgot to ask Wylie Dufresne about the vacuum chamber," he said.

"The what?"

"Hold on; do you mind if we make a little detour?" he asked. I shrugged and said it was fine. A few minutes later we stepped gingerly into the quiet, well-groomed lobby of the restaurant wd-50. It was late in the dinner service, and only a couple of tables that could be seen from the front of the room were filled. A host looked up at us expectantly.

"Good evening, sir," Michael said to the host, and began to explain that he was a friend of Alex Talbot's from "Ideas in Food," who was a good friend of Wylie Dufresne's, the owner of wd-50 and a renowned experimental chef. Alex had referred him to Wylie to ask about a particular brand of vacuum-compress chambers. The host apologized that Wylie was not present at the moment but took down Michael's information to pass on the message.

On the car ride back, Michael told me about how Alex had purchased a less-than-great vacuum chamber, a large and extremely expensive device used by high-tech-minded chefs to essentially suck the air out of foods. Always lamenting his poor investment, he had urged Michael to speak with Wylie first about whatever kind of vacuum he owned.

"How much are these things again?" I asked Michael.

"It's ridiculous. Like four thousand dollars. Totally nuts. But I need to have one," he said. I knew he did, too. That was the way Michael progressed with his cooking—by constantly expanding. It was also where we fell on different sides of the track: I wanted to make cooking at home more approachable and thus simpler, and he wanted to make it as extravagant as could be. I still appreciated and was fascinated by his approach.

The next morning, I woke early to meet Saha at Doughnut Plant. It was still raining since the night before, and I put on my rain boots and took the train into Chinatown. I was running about five minutes late when I got out of the subway, so I gave him a call.

"Don't worry about it. I'm here now, sitting with the guy at the counter, who gave me a chai," he said. When I got to the bakery five minutes later, Saha was indeed sitting by the register, talking to the only other person in the store, with a cup of chai between his palms. They greeted me and went back to chatting as if they were old pals.

"So this is your friend?" The counter person asked, a few exchanges and chuckles with Saha later. His name was Luis. We nodded. "Would you guys like a doughnut now?" We nodded again. I put my umbrella down and took in the cozy atmosphere. One wall was lined with colorful doughnut-shaped tiles, and a few framed magazine features about Doughnut Plant were hung on it. Behind a large glass window, the interior of the kitchen and a couple of pastry chefs could be seen. Beside the register was a tall metal rack of fresh doughnuts on trays. The specials were written on the wall above Luis. I chose one of the special doughnuts of the day, a blackberry jam–filled, vanilla bean, glazed square doughnut. Saha ordered a coconut cream–filled glazed doughnut, also square. Luis handed them over with a sheet of waxed paper. I settled onto the bench next to Saha.

"Wow," he said, tearing into the coconut one.

"Let me try," I said. The cream spurted out as I took a bite. These doughnuts each had a hole in the middle, but the filling was stuffed all around the square of pastry. As we were eating, Mark Isreal came out from the kitchen and sat on a stool across the room. He opened up a newspaper.

"Hey, Mark, I want you to meet my new friends," Luis said.

"Hey, guys," Mark said as we waved hello back.

"Saha is a Web designer," Luis said, shooting a look back to Saha. "Right?"

"Yes," he said, mouth full of doughnut glaze crumbles.

"Really? I need to hire someone to help out with my website," Mark said. "I have a few things I need to do with it, can you?"

Saha waved his hand in apology. "I can't. But I know a lot of great designers who probably could if you asked them."

Mark Isreal's face dropped.

"I'm too busy right now," Saha quickly replied. "But seriously, if you want any of their contact info, I'm sure they'd love to do it."

Mark looked at Luis in shock and turned back to Saha. He gave him a cold glare as if to say, *How dare you not stop everything to help out with my doughnut website?* Although the look was exaggerated, I felt like he was being half serious. I was beginning to feel a bit uncomfortable.

"No, really; they'd be great," Saha went on. "I'd work on it, too, but—"

Mark gave up on the topic with a wave of his hand. He turned his attention back to Luis and began asking him a question about the daily operations.

"Yikes," I said to Saha. "How come you don't want to work for the doughnut website?" I teased. He shook his head and kept quiet. I snapped some photos of the doughnuts on the racks and of us eating doughnuts as we chatted and finished our breakfast. For a while, Saha and I had been throwing around the idea of starting up a new food newsletter, with recipes and anecdotes about the dinner-party series that we also intended to start up. We were both so busy with other projects, though, that it looked like the collaboration might have to wait.

Luis gave Saha the cup of chai on the house. We each paid for our doughnuts; mine had cost $3.25. Not a bad deal for such a tasty, carefully made work of doughnut art. But it was still a sticky, greasy, sugary, and most of all, empty calorie–filled breakfast. I was still a little bit hungry after I left. On my way back to the subway, I popped into a bakery a few doors down. It was Kossar's, a real New York legend of a place, the oldest bialy bakery in the country, opened in 1936. In fact, it was the place that had put bialys on the map in the United States. But because there was no seating and the place was strictly for takeout bialys—often by the dozen—I couldn't quite qualify it as a real eating-out experience. I ended up buying a bialy to go and brought it home with me in a bag. This I planned to eat once Sunday rolled around and my opposite week was officially over.

On Saturday, I'd need to bring a huge pot of chili over to the Brooklyn Botanic Garden for the Chili Takedown. Whether or not I ate the chili I cooked during opposite week was one thing. But I knew I'd be surrounded by the chilis of my fellow contestants at the Botanic Garden's Chile Pepper Fiesta, and probably a lot more homemade food, too. I'd also be attending Jordan's birthday party that Saturday night, and on Friday, I planned to go to my friend Nora's birthday party. Both would likely be filled with homemade treats.

So I gave up on trying to make Saturday a strictly restaurant-food-only day. It was just as well, though. I couldn't go a full normal week without encountering restaurant-made food (at the *Edible Manhattan* launch party), and I couldn't go a full opposite week without some homemade food. The two worlds had melded into my life inextricably. Once the week was done I was glad I'd made the choice to lose the not-eating-out gimmick.

I spent most of Friday making my chili. I took the pork shoulder from Tom Mylan's butchering class out of the bag of brine it had been sitting in for the last couple of days. Before leaving the class, I'd grilled Tom for some insight on how to cook it into chili, and he'd suggested brining it first. I also asked Michael for some advice and ended up borrowing from his mole-braised duck legs cooked at the Hope Lounge barbecue. After the brined pork was patted dry, I browned it in my biggest pot. I then filled the pot to the brim with a mixture of liquids—pork stock made a week before from bones from the same Berkshire pig, left over from the butchering class, the water I used to soak some dried ancho peppers, beer, and a cup of strong coffee. I tossed in onions, garlic, bacon, the soaked anchos, and a number of spices, and let the shoulder cook in the oven for about five hours. Following Michael's advice, I took the pork out of the braising liquid and let it roast on a rack above the pot for the last fifteen minutes. This created crispy, slightly caramelized shreds of meat around its surface to pull.

After pulling the meat into bite-sized shreds and reducing the braising liquid, I spent the next couple of hours rounding it out with other ingredients—tomatoes, onions, peppers of all stripes, fresh corn, more bacon, ground-up chorizo sausage, canned pumpkin, pinto beans, more beer, lots of spices. It was a long process, one that I was familiar with from entering plenty of other Chili Takedowns.

While the meat was braising, I'd grabbed some lunch. I didn't feel like spending much, after buying so many ingredients for the chili, so I opened the drawer filled with takeout menus and picked out the one for the nearest Chinese takeout restaurant. I wasn't in the mood for meat for some reason, either, so I ordered tofu with broccoli. It was tempting to ask for my order to be delivered. In my building's lobby, I frequently saw deliverymen heading upstairs with steaming bags or leaving on their battered bicycles. A lot of times, these deliverymen looked like they were past middle age. It made me sad to see them riding through the busy streets in the rain, wearing ponchos, and carefully balancing their food packages on the handlebars. I couldn't fathom someone my father's age having to do that, and for just one person's measly lunch. So I walked the three blocks to the restaurant in the rain to pick up my polystyrene foam–packed order.

It was more food than I was hungry for, but I finished it anyway. It wasn't particularly good, either. Afterward, I felt a little sick. I thought about skipping dinner and just seeing whatever food would be at Nora's party, but around six o'clock I was feeling like a snack again and headed outside to grab a slice of pizza from a local pie shop.

It was ten o'clock when I got to Nora's, and the combination of the mediocre pizza, the Chinese food, the doughnut, and the constant tastes of the chili I was cooking throughout the day had my stomach feeling more than off. Still, I tried bites of the snacks at Nora's party as I sipped wine. The theme of Nora's birthday party was 2050, the year that some scientists predicted the world would end thanks to global warming. To go with the heat theme, all the food at the party was spicy. Nora also had decked her home in streamers made from twisted plastic shopping bags, and various signs of apocalyptic doom.

I woke the next morning with half an hour to spare before I

was due at the Brooklyn Botanic Garden. It was still raining. The party had gone on until well past three in the morning, when I decided to leave. I was glad I'd finished all my chili making the day before. Since the Botanic Garden was so close to my home, I was able to carry my pot of chili and containers with extra garnish there on my own.

The Chili Takedown was just one event that was taking place at the all-day Chile Pepper Fiesta. There were at least two dozen other tastings, demonstrations, lectures, and workshops related to the chili pepper, and the highlight of this year's festival was hands down Pete Seeger's performance on the open-field stage. The legendary folk musician, now in his eighties, rarely performed anymore, and when he did it was often for nonprofit or educational events like this one. When I found out I'd be participating in the festival, I'd sent my parents an excited e-mail. My dad is a longtime fan of Pete Seeger and other folk musicians from his hippie days in the 1960s. Even so, I wasn't expecting the response I got from him, a few days later. "I may not be able to convince Mom to come along, but I'll be there," he wrote. "I've seen Pete Seeger twice— once in Berkeley in the 1960s and another time when he played in New Jersey in the 1980s. So I'll come out to your chili contest and get to see him again."

As I sat with the other chili contestants and Matt, I felt a little nervous about my dad showing up. We had never been particularly close, and I had a hard time recalling any activity we'd done together without other family members present. It was neat to discover that we both shared a huge respect for Pete Seeger— although mine was due more to his environmental achievements than his music. Of course, my dad and I had another thing in common: a passion for cooking. When he showed up, as I was in the midst of serving an enormous crowd of festival-goers, I was all too eager to step aside for a moment and walk around the room with him. We looked at other chili-themed vendors selling hot sauce and chutneys. We talked about the chili that I'd made. My dad's cooking signature may be pies, but a close runner-up just might be his chili, for which he had earned a reputation. As Matt Timms and many others have put it, chili is great communal food—it feeds the masses. It keeps well, travels well, and is open to interpretation with a number of flavors and ingredients. That's why it's such common fare, I think, for cook-offs. My memories of chili from my youth have always stemmed from my dad cooking up an enormous pot to keep eating for leftovers the entire week.

I left my dad to wander around the festival for a while as I got back to my chili-serving station. The other participants in the contest were great company. I'd seen them all at previous Takedowns but had never really had a chance to talk to any of them much. Three of them were guys in their late twenties or early thirties, and one was a middle-aged woman. Instead of being competitive, we teased, chided, chatted, and helped one another at our serving stations when it was needed. We talked to the endless flow of festival-goers, too, telling them about what we had put in our unique formulas. I got the feeling that none of us cared who won the contest at all.

I ran out of chili by the last half hour of serving. The throngs of people that came in for that time period didn't get a taste, and I knew I'd missed any chance of winning the vote. When Matt finally rounded up the contestants to announce the winners, we each took a turn at the microphone to talk about our recipes. I could see my dad in the audience smiling proudly as I explained my interpretation of the dish—which I'd named, for Pete Seeger's sake, "If I Had a Pepper." When I was awarded third place out of five, my dad proudly clapped and kept smiling, as did Nora and Andrea, her roommate, who'd showed up for the announcement ceremony that afternoon groggy from their long night of partying. I wasn't surprised at all when first place was given to the guy who'd made a smoky chili with turkey sausage, bacon, and a good ratio of vegetables.

I stuck around with friends and the chili contestants for a while afterward. By late afternoon, Pete Seeger still hadn't begun his act, and my dad was beginning to feel a little tired. To my surprise, he decided to take off early. It was drizzling anyhow, and the tarp-covered field where the music stage was set looked soggy and sort of unpleasant. No big deal, he said. I shrugged and thanked him for coming.

I made sure to take plenty of pictures of Pete Seeger while I watched him sing that afternoon. My dad had been right; it was muddy, and people were camped out on tarps underneath a huge tent that covered the field. Still, the crowd that had come out for the performance was enormous. Families, young people, and old people in wheelchairs alike were smiling, nodding, singing along, and in some cases shedding a tear of gratitude. And Pete Seeger could really sing—still. He had fire in his voice, a warmness and dearness made all the more sweet due to the fact that his backup vocalist and guitarist was his grandson, Tao Rodríguez-Seeger. The other performer, a bassist who frequently played with the duo, was Guy Davis. I didn't hear them play the song "If I Had a Hammer"— perhaps I'd missed it by the time I got to the tent—but I heard plenty of other songs that my dad must have listened to with his friends when he was about my age.

A couple of weeks later, my mom called me to tell me that my dad was attempting to make the same braised-pork-shoulder-based chili that I'd made for the cook-off.

"It's like he never knew you before or something," she said, after telling me that my dad had reported having a good time that day. She'd been slightly surprised by this.

"You know, he never really paid much attention to what you were doing," she went on. "And now he's all like, 'Whoa! This is what you can do! You can cook like this!'"

I smiled. In the last couple of years since I'd been cooking so much, my dad and I had found more things to talk about through a mutual appreciation for cooking techniques, traditional dishes, and so forth. I was touched that my chili from the cook-off that day had inspired him to make a copycat batch.

I spent the rest of the afternoon walking around the Chile Pepper Fiesta and stopping to watch Pete Seeger perform. I bumped into a couple of old friends, as well as members of the Chili Takedown gang again. I was stopped by a middle-aged couple who told me how much they liked my chili and that they had voted for it. I popped into a cooking demonstration from a family-owned artisanal chutney company and ate several of their homemade Indian specialties with the sauces. After the demonstration, I chatted with them for a few minutes about the intricacies of making chutney. They beamed as they described their process, passed down from family recipes for several generations, in between shushing their grandchildren as they scampered noisily about. I decided I wanted to try making my own chutney sometime soon. I bought two jars of theirs and thanked them for the demo.

Cooking is infectious, I thought, patting my belly. It can be passed up and down through families. It can be spread all around. It was something I wanted to keep doing, and keep learning from, for a long time yet. There was so much left to explore about food and cooking, without limiting myself to things like not eating in a New York City restaurant.

After the Chile Pepper Fiesta, I headed straight to Jordan's apartment for her birthday party. When I arrived, a small table in the living room was filled with bowls of sushi-making ingredients, just like we had seen at Aaron and Mai's apartment. I spent the rest of the night there along with several of my best friends. At some point in the night, we got to talking about dim sum. Dan, Jordan, and I made a plan to satisfy our cravings the next morning with a dim sum brunch in Sunset Park, Brooklyn. It was past midnight by then. Opposite week was officially over. So was, as a strict rule, not eating out in New York. A part of me felt bittersweet to see the journey over. But most of all, I was hungry to move on. After dim sum, who knew what would be next? I'd have to choose carefully. There were a few new local and sustainable-minded restaurants that I wanted to check out. Cuisines of the city's ethnic populations that I'd never tried. There were whisperings about underground supper clubs that I'd never been to happening all the time. There was another cook-off around the corner, organized by a new host at a bar I'd never been to. There was a local farm benefit and an amateur beer brew-off the next night in Brooklyn. There was a pig roast that I was helping to cook for. I was doing a cooking demo at the Grand Army Greenmarket in a couple of weeks, making risotto with vegetables, wine, and cheese from the market. There was the food newsletter with Saha, and we'd decided to start the project by throwing a dinner party first. My clip on the *Ask Aida* show was going to air soon, and I wanted to have friends over for lasagna to watch it with me. There was Mark's Brooklyn-themed dinner to go to. Michael's crazy mock–French Laundry menu to prepare. A new restaurant in my neighborhood. And we still hadn't held a second SOS.

But for now, I was excited about going to dim sum with Jordan and Dan the next morning. I opened my cell phone and began typing a text message to Keith, asking if he wanted to join us.

My mouth watered as I thought about all the steaming trays of bite-sized food that would soon be before us, maybe even some hangover-curing braised beef tripe. A dim sum double date, I thought to myself with a smile. That at least didn't sound too contrived or boring.

Oh, what the heck. Dating is dating, eating is eating, and if it was dull at times, then no matter. I certainly didn't plan on starting a blog about not *dating* in New York. Someday I'd have to find the courage to do that home-cooked-dinner first date, too.

My cell phone dinged with a message from Keith.

"Is it on?" Jordan asked.

I gave her and Dan a thumbs-up.

The next week, I went on a date with the chili cook-off winner.

Coffee and Cigarettes Ladyfinger Sandwiches

This was part of the dessert course at the A Razor, A Shiny Knife dinner described in the first part of this chapter. It incorporates finely ground tobacco in the cookie batter for a spicy, zesty bite, and ground coffee in the frosting.   (MAKES ABOUT 24)

> 4 egg whites
> 4 egg yolks
> ⅓ cup sugar
> ¼ teaspoon vanilla
> ¾ cup flour
> ¼ cup extra finely ground tobacco (ground in a food processor)
> 1 stick butter, softened
> About 2 cups confectioners' sugar
> ¼ cup very finely ground coffee

Preheat oven to 350 degrees. Beat the egg whites with an electric beater until stiff peaks form. Beat the yolks with the sugar and vanilla until paler in color and fluffy. Gradually add the flour until smoothly incorporated. Gently fold in the egg whites and the vanilla. Transfer batter to a piping bag (or plastic bag with a small corner snipped out) and pipe long, cigarlike fingers onto a well-greased cookie sheet. Bake for about 15 minutes or until just crisp around the edges. Transfer to a cooling rack.

Whisk the softened butter in a large bowl. Gradually whisk in the confectioners' sugar, ½ cup or so at a time, along with the coffee. Transfer to a piping bag and pipe frosting onto the back of one of the cooled tobacco ladyfingers and press together with another cookie to make a sandwich. Repeat with the rest.

~~~~~~

Four-Pepper Pulled-Pork Chili

This is a chili similar to the one I'd called "If I Had a Pepper" at the Chili Takedown in this chapter, but with fresh corn and pumpkin puree for a little more sweet to go with the spicy.   (SERVES 4–6)

> 2 tablespoons vegetable oil
> 2–3-pound piece of pork shoulder
> Pork, chicken, or vegetable broth to cover (or substitute water)
> 2 large onions, roughly chopped
> 5 cloves garlic, chopped
> About 1 teaspoon each of cumin, cayenne pepper, paprika, oregano, and chili powder
> Salt and pepper to taste
> 1 cup strong black coffee
> 1 6-ounce can chipotle peppers in adobo sauce, crushed or blended in a food processor
> 1 24-ounce can whole peeled plum tomatoes with juice
> 4 strips bacon
> 1 cup pumpkin puree
> 1 cup pinto beans
> 1 cup fresh corn kernels
> 1 Anaheim or New Mexico chili, seeds removed and diced
> 2 sweet bell or Italian peppers, preferably red, orange, or yellow, diced
> 3–4 jalapeños, seeds removed and roughly chopped

Preheat oven to 350 degrees. In a large, heavy-bottomed pot or Dutch oven, heat the vegetable oil on high for 2 minutes. Pat down pork shoulder until very dry and place in pot. Let cook on each side about 2 minutes, until most of the surface has been lightly browned. Remove from heat. Scrape bottom of pot and deglaze with pork stock. Place the pork shoulder back in the pot, and add the onions, garlic, chili pepper, jalapeños, spices, and salt and pepper. Add the coffee, chipotles, tomatoes, and enough stock to just cover the meat. Bring to a boil. Line the top of the pork shoulder with the bacon strips. Cook, covered, for at least 2 hours.

When the pork has been braising for 2 hours, remove from oven. Carefully remove the shoulder and transfer it to a roasting rack that will sit on top of the open pot, to catch any juices that drip from it. Return shoulder, now on a rack on top of the pot, to oven and roast for another 15 minutes at the same temperature. Remove everything from oven, and set shoulder aside to cool completely. Blend the braising liquid in the pot with a hand blender, or by transferring it carefully to a blender or food processor, until mixture is smooth. Add the pumpkin, pinto beans, and corn, and adjust seasoning to taste.

Pull the pork shoulder into ½-inch-thick or so shreds. Add the pulled pork to the rest of the chili mixture. Stir until thoroughly distributed. Continue cooking, reducing to a thicker consistency if necessary or seasoning to taste. Add the diced sweet peppers or sprinkle on as garnish.

Epilogue

So, what did I gain from my week of only eating out? Well, to start, I'll compare my spending for the two back-to-back weeks. During normal week, I went grocery shopping twice and spent a total of $19.54. I also bought snacks during the day, usually at work to stave off hunger (or boredom), which I've already added to that total. Then there were items that I consumed that weren't purchased in that week, like eggs, butter, flour, and a package of dried cranberries I'd polished off one night in front of the TV. With these in mind, I think it's a fair if somewhat generous estimate to put my food spending at $25 for that week.

Over the course of opposite week, I saved receipts whenever I could. So with my brunch at Stone Park Café, snacks in Flushing, Queens, kimchee noodles and dinner at Char No. 4 the next day, sushi lunch and Caribbean dinner on Tuesday plus an iced coffee along the way, the Pax Wholesome Foods lunch, bagel breakfast, pea soup lunch, a previously unmentioned snack of watermelon cubes from a deli, Doughnut Plant doughnut, Chinese takeout lunch, and slice of pizza, the grand total of my food spending was $116.51. This total does not reflect the Szechuan dinner in Flushing that my parents paid for. It also doesn't account for the expensive dinner at Walter Foods that my date paid for, or the Momofuku Noodle Bar dinner that my date, again, paid for. Finally, opposite week was really only six days instead of seven, since I didn't eat out that whole Saturday of the Chile Pepper Fiesta and Jordan's party. So the grand total was one day and three restaurant meals short.

I guess it's not so uncommon to get treated for three meals in a week for those who typically go out to eat. This skewed the final tally for my opposite week significantly, though, and I hadn't been expecting it. I'm not complaining, however. I imagine that if I had paid for my own meal, I would have spent about $15 for the family meal at the Szechuan restaurant in Flushing. Splitting the check at Walter Foods plus tip would have set me back at least $60, as a lowball estimate. And the food I'd split with Michael at Momofuku Noodle Bar plus tip probably would have cost about $30. So, adding these sums to $116.51, a more accurate estimate of what I would have spent if I'd paid my own way that week would be $221.51.

Now, in contrast, what if I, instead of my friends or parents, had been the one treating for one or two of these occasions? What if I were a guy who took dates out to dinner maybe three times a week, and wanted to foot the bill each time—you can imagine how skewed my total would be then!

I got on the scale again at the end of opposite week, too. I wouldn't have been surprised to see a slight gain. My taste buds at least were unaccustomed to encountering so many rich foods in one week, especially that doughnut. I could imagine that they did their damage on the rest of the body. But God bless the mysteries of metabolism—when I stood on the scale one week of eating out later, not a fraction of a decimal had budged from my beginning weight. The number was the exact same one the dial had read on that street corner in Flushing a week before. I'll keep that number to myself, though. It's a sensitive topic that no woman likes to share, her weight. For me, it's a little awkward because I tend to weigh what a healthy middle schooler might, even though I consume many more calories than I deserve for it. It must be in my genes; my mother's weight has remained static and she stays slim regardless of her rapacious appetite, and some of her clothes from when she was my age are much too small for me now.

But these facts aside, during opposite week I was reminded of how much I do appreciate fine dining, and the institution of restaurants as a whole. They are not "the enemy" (though this revelation might seem painfully obvious to most). As long as you don't fall hideously sick from a tainted oyster—like my friend Matt did recently—there's little harm in spending a little extra money on a special occasion for a nice meal at a restaurant. But that's the way I'd like to keep it: special. I'll treat eating out as an indulgence and a luxury. Doing it every day is just not for me—not mentally, physically, or financially. Eating out may be unavoidable for many busy people in this world, but as long as I can still squeeze my favorite hobby into my schedule, I'll be cooking happily ever after.

And what did I learn from my two years of (mostly) home-cooked food? Well, people will say that the world of restaurant food is vast. But the world of cooking and eating in far exceeds it in scope, even in a city as seemingly disinclined toward home cooking as New York. There are foragers in the parks as we speak; anarchist freegans lurking around the trash cans while you sleep; cook-offs being thrown and/or dreamed up by the second; and food bloggers eagerly tapping away at their computers with flour-coated fingers, taking in the rich smells of something wonderful cooking in their kitchens. It's a jungle out there. And unlike restaurants, there is no finite limit to the number of menu items that can be ordered and consumed within the realm of home cookery—so long as a person has a kitchen and the imagination to create something tasty all their own.

Just as there are social traditions, customs, and interactions related to eating out, there are those particular to eating in. These are the things about cooking for two years that have meant the most to me. From making brunch for hungover friends to having Christmas dinner with my family, I hope there is never a shortage of opportunities to cook and eat with people on a regular basis. Getting involved in supper clubs has proven for me a pretty good way to keep this up constantly, though running one yourself can be time-consuming and costly if you're not careful, as I humbly learned.

What had begun more or less as a simple ploy to save money actually ended up expanding my culinary scope in ways I had never imagined possible. Who knew I'd learn how to make sushi rolls, Moroccan tajines, and spicy Mexican tripe stew? There is really no limit to what can be done in the home kitchen. While not eating out I gradually mastered a slew of cooking techniques, prep skills, and entertaining savvy through practice, practice, and more practice. I cringe looking back at some of the older recipes on my blog. My experience just with handling food and seeing how it interacts with heat and other processes has sharpened my cooking skills infinitely, well beyond what just research and cookbooks can do. And that, to a foodie, is priceless.

For some reason, and I'm sure it's not entirely because of the cooking experience, the two years I spent not eating out in New York were some of the best ones of my life. Blogging is a unique modern phenomenon, one that has helped me connect with strangers and feel comfortable being open about my stories and my emotions in ways I never dreamed I'd be. I think there's something valuable in this. Whether it was because I became more used to being uncensored around people—and this is not necessarily a good thing for the other people's sakes—or because of something else, the idea of stepping away from cultural standards by doing something such as not eating out now looks much less intimidating. Going out there to Walden Pond like Thoreau, or to the Andes, as Professor Cooper did, or to the Dumpster behind a supermarket, or simply doing something a little differently from everyone else and actually enjoying it is itself a novel thrill. And as long as it's not hurting anyone, what's the harm?

The people in the examples just mentioned had a rigorous ideology, an agenda, and a principle they wanted to prove from the start. My purpose in not eating out was much more lighthearted, for fun and to save up my money. But had I not gone on with it, I might have never been turned on to wild foraging, or discovered the incredible waste situation in this country. In small ways, my quest became somewhat political. Had I not become so familiar with food over those years, I probably wouldn't be as attuned to where it was coming from, and how it was grown. I've become more mindful of what I'm eating as a result of the mission, whether it is responsibly or humanely grown, healthy, and local.

Seeing the rise in home and urban gardening in the past year or so, I know I missed a great opportunity in this book and project by not covering this very positive trend. In 2009, I briefly met Joan Gussow, who was presenting at a panel discussion after a screening of the documentary film *Fresh*. Joan is the pioneer of New York's urban gardening and farming movement, who in the 1950s transformed her backyard into an organic vegetable patch that she produced almost all of her food from—and was seen as completely crazy for at the time. Today, thanks in part to President Obama and the First Lady's organic vegetable garden, so many new people are growing plants that in 2009 there was a national seed shortage. It goes on; I have several friends now who raise chickens in their backyards, or keep bees. It's not for hobby or experimentation, either—it's utilitarian; they're eating what they grow. And they're saving lots of money and keeping healthy and environmentally aware in the process. I had at first written off the idea of doing any extensive gardening on my own during my not-eating-out years because I had no outdoor space (going to farmers' markets, joining a CSA, or foraging instead). Now there are more community gardens in New York City than ever. Why it did not occur to me to join one, or simply explore people who did live off food they had grown or raised in the city and elsewhere before September 2008, when this book ends chronologically, I am not sure. But ever since then, urban gardening, farming, and agriculture in general have certainly become a food obsession for me. And there are many more writers avidly covering these topics, too.

Any other loose ends I may have lying around here? I had fun on my dinner date with the winner of the Chile Pepper Fiesta shortly after "opposite week," but we found we didn't have much in common (besides competing in chili cook-offs) and fell out of touch soon afterward. Afer that dim sum lunch, I would hang out with Keith many more times and still do—but just as friends. I still have yet to invite someone over for dinner as a first date (which I didn't think would be too nerve-wracking until a friend brought up the point that it eliminates the question "Your place or mine?"). There hasn't been another enactment of the SOS supper club to date, even though I and most of its founding members are still very much single. I still haven't launched that food newsletter start-up with Saha, but in the planning process we created a mini-supper-club series with homemade vegetarian food and about eight carefully invited guests at a time.

In the winter of 2008 and 2009, Michael Cirino and the A Razor, A Shiny Knife supper-club crew executed a nine-part dinner series spanning three cities inspired by the notorious $1,500 a plate, twenty-four-course menu created by chefs Thomas Keller and Grant Achatz that same winter (our version cost only $300 a plate, however). I joined the team in New York and San Francisco to help pull off the feat. There are at least five new supper clubs that I've visited, met the members of, or cooked with since the writing of this book. Overwhelming numbers of amateur cook-offs have been held in front of shoulder-to-shoulder crowds in bars in New York City since, too, inspiring *The New York Times* to publish a story on the trend in its dining section in the summer of 2009, for which I was interviewed.

In the spring of 2009, Karol and I hosted our second annual Risotto Challenge. We made it a fund-raiser for the local, sustainable, and food-justice-promoting nonprofit Just Food, and raised more than $1,800 for the organization through everyone's risotto efforts. Also that spring, I started a supper club and cooking community with my friend Akiko, called the Hapa Kitchen. For each dinner, we source the night's meal from local farmers and food purveyors and often bring them to the event to dine with the guests. Founded on the idea that people who are half Asian share a unique take on food from their multicultural households, our signature is innovative dishes peppered with Asian references.

Also in 2009, I decided to tap into other people's thoughts on dating without going to restaurants by hosting a podcast radio talk show called *Cheap Date*. The weekly program on Heritage Radio Network features different in-studio guests, like food or dating experts, as we tackle the subject.

Then of course, I wrote this book. Thanks so much for reading.

Acknowledgments

I might not have thought to write this book without the instigation of Libby O'Neill, my former agent. Her patient encouragement in conceptualizing it, and convincing me that enough people would want to read about "not eating out in New York" to print a book was truly a gift. And when she left for law school, she couldn't have trusted my project to a more thorough, professional, and food-loving successor than Ethan Bashoff at Inkwell Management, who completed the job seamlessly.

Hats off to my hardworking editor, Jessica Sindler, whose insights were always right on, and everyone at Gotham/Penguin for believing in this book. I'm so glad to have worked with the talented illustrator Evah Fan, who put such imagination and whimsy into drawing my likeness, and who was a joy to get to know along the way. And uberthanks to Robert Sietsema, who is just about the coolest guy, ever.

Writing a book solely based on real experiences involves trusting people around you to have an iron tolerance for humility. Which, of course, few people do. So my deepest thanks to Karol, Matt, Jordan, my family, and all the folks who walk through this book, as they did in my life. Thanks, in the first place, for touching my life.

Most of all, I want to thank anyone who's read my blog, attended a food event I hosted, or anyone I cooked beside. It's such an exciting and warm surprise to know that I've made so many friends through cooking. And knowing how awesome these people (who love food and cooking) are, it's been such a blessing. Let's keep cookin', and keepin' it real, fun, fresh, and delicious.

About the Author

Cathy Erway writes the tremendously popular blog "Not Eating Out in New York" (www.noteatingoutinny.com), featuring recipes, ruminations, and rants about all things home cooked. She also writes about food, agriculture, and green living for *Saveur* and *The Huffington Post*. Her work has appeared in such publications as *Edible Brooklyn*, *Time Out NY*, *The L Magazine*, and *Serious Eats*. She lives in Brooklyn.